23,-

MORMON SPIRITUALITY

LATTER DAY SAINTS
IN
WALES AND ZION

by

Douglas James Davies

UNIVERSITY OF NOTTINGHAM

Nottingham Series in Theology

Distributed by
Utah State University Press,
Logan, Utah 84322, U.S.A.
And in Great Britain by
The Department of Theology,
University of Nottingham, NG7 2RD.

Hardback edition   ISBN 0 951225 11 1
Soft cover edition ISBN 0 951225 10 3

© University of Nottingham and Douglas James Davies.

For John Heywood Thomas

Printed in England by the University of Nottingham,
Library Photographic and Printing Unit

Mormon Spirituality
Latter Day Saints in Wales and Zion

Preface   i

Part One   The Nineteenth Century

1. A Vision Born 1830 – 1855.   1
2. The Language of Zion 1856 – 1860.   19
3. Tithes, Sects and Prophecy 1860 – 1869.   26
4. The Sacred Space of Temples 1870 – 1879.   32
5. Anti-Mormonism in America and Wales 1880 – 1889.   43
6. Church Order and Salvation History 1890 – 1899.   53

Part Two   The Twentieth Century

7. Decline in Wales.   65
8. Religious Revivalism.   69
9. God and Kingdom.   74
10. Evan Stephens and Mormon Hymnody.   81
11. Comparative Theology of Sacraments.   86
12. Wales Reorganized.   95
13. Active Salvation.   101
14. Coming into their Own.   108
15. Cumulative Confidence and Identity.   111
16. Institutions of Salvation.   115
17. Individual and Corporate Religiosity.   121
18. Mormon Homo Religiosus.   131
19. A New Era, The Decade of 1960.   137
20. Other Restoration Groups.   143
21. Reflections on the Decades of 1970 and 1980.   148
22. Restoring Transcendence   151

Notes   158
Bibliography   168
Index   174

PREFACE

The Mormon religion is a distinctive and fascinating world of its own with interests for members and non-members alike.

In the following pages I have used a historical framework constructed from the Mormon Journal called *The Millennial Star*, which was published in Britain for some hundred and forty years, as the basis for analysing numerous features of Mormon doctrine and ritual. Details of local developments have been extended into wide themes of universal concern. Mormons should find that a degree of depth is added to their understanding as a result of the historical material made available here, and I hope that some might find the concluding discussion of some use in reflecting upon Latter Day Saint theology.

Many studies of Mormonism stress a sociological or historical perspective or else argue fervently against the religion. My concern is to provide a far more descriptive form of analysis which expresses my own experience of Mormonism over a period of seventeen or so years. The reader ought to know that I am not myself a Latter Day Saint. I am, in fact, a clergyman of the Church of England who has studied Mormonism as an anthropologist. In this book I have also engaged in some comparative theology to show even more clearly how Mormon thought is related to life and to ultimate values.

Friendship and acquaintance have been a constant feature of my research, and without the welcome given by many little would have been possible. I would most especially single out Mr. Arnold Jones and Mr. Ralph Pulman of Merthyr Tydfil in South Wales who supported my initial venture into Mormon studies. Many others there and elsewhere in Britain and Utah have tolerated my inquisitive presence.

I must acknowledge the research studentship granted me by the Social Science Research Council at the Oxford Institute of Social Anthropology, and Dr. B. R. Wilson of All Souls College who then supervised my initial work. At the Brigham Young University in Utah Professor Merlin Myers was a gentle host. More recently I have been much encouraged by Mrs. Maureen Ursenbach Beecher of the Mormon History Association. I must also thank Linda Speth of the Utah State University Press for support and assistance in the American distribution of this book. One of my students, Mr. Andrew Stocks, has assisted in some archival work on material concerning the Reorganized Church for which I thank him. Thanks are also due to Mr. Keith Harris and Mrs. Gwyneth Harris at Nottingham University's Library Print Unit for much help and patience in producing this volume. Much of this book was written in manuscript during my last years at Hugh Stewart Hall at Nottingham University. I appreciated the gentle good humour of my fellow Senior Common Room members as they asked after the state of my pen and of the advancing text. Their friendship over the years in a common concern for research and scholarship is no mean thing.

Finally I am most grateful to Professor John Heywood Thomas and colleagues in the Theology Department for agreeing to place this book as first in the new Nottingham Series in Theology.

D.J.D.

Derby Hall,
University of Nottingham,
Spring Term 1987.

PART ONE THE NINETEENTH CENTURY

Chapter One

A Vision Born: 1830 — 1855.

The life of faith is a life of inspired imagination. It brings to the ordinary world a sense of profound significance as passing moments are set within an immense sweep of divine purpose.

In the following pages I have sought to do justice to this highly personal dimension of religion by setting it within a particular view of history generated by the Church of Jesus Christ of Latter Day Saints. Our subject is none other than the Mormon Church, as the group is more widely known throughout the world, and our special emphasis is upon the relationship between members in America and Wales.

Two distinctive features lie behind our study and need to be mentioned at the outset. The first concerns the vision of history and divine action which Mormons came to see as pertaining to themselves as instruments helping to attain God's will for the universe. We have drawn a large amount of material from the journal called the *Millennial Star* to depict the Latter Day Saint sense of history as a process of divine dispensation. Such heavy emphasis on this source is intended to illustrate the point that new religious movements often construct distinctive theories of time which differ from those of the world at large. Indeed the very word 'history' is potentially deceptive inasmuch as to the religious mind the outworking of events is sometimes deemed to be a revelation rather than a series of neutral events. Part of our task is to explore the nature of Mormon history in this religiously endowed sense of the word.

The second major preoccupation is with comparative theology. I have used Mormon doctrines and practices in relation to wider Christian traditions to show the distinctive nature of Latter Day Saint theology. This means that various readers should find areas of interest throughout the book. Those curious about Mormon doctrine will find a fairly full account of central beliefs and ritual. Latter Day Saints will discover aspects of their faith illuminated by the historical material which is not otherwise conveniently available, especially as far as Wales is concerned. Historians, anthropologists, and phenomenologists of religion will benefit from the Mormon material as exemplifying aspects of human symbolic behaviour. Christian theologians should also find the discussion beneficial since it presents a form of systematic theology in a comparative way which throws sharper light back upon more traditional forms of theological reflection.

The Millennial Star was first published in May 1840 at Manchester though it soon moved to Liverpool. From the outset it was a committed voice of the church leadership in Britain as R. L. Evans has shown in his well known history of Mormonism in Britain, (1937:139ff.). It saw itself as a journal which would hand to posterity an account of world and church events which would elicit admiration from succeeding generations. It would be no common record of political or commercial news, indeed it would stand aloof from such material so as to devote itself to documenting the revolutionary events of Christ's second coming and the establishment of God's kingdom of truth.

From the very beginning the detailed records of baptisms, ordinations and other rites, served to emphasize the success of the gospel preaching of that message which, according to Mormon reckoning, had now been restored to mankind after some eighteen hundred years absence. When it later became apparent that a dramatic return of Christ had not taken place the self-same statistics came to be used for the purpose of incorporating past generations into the all-embracing community of Saints through a variety of rituals and in relation to extensive genealogical research. As data on long-dead non-Mormon ancestors were marshalled so a new religious phenomenon emerged within Christendom; as factual material was sacralized Mormons were able to capitalize upon the early documenting zeal of their earliest forebears in the movement.

Initially the *Millennial Star* dealt with immediate concerns of faith and the faithful, with apologetic arguments and news of church breakthroughs in winning new members. The Church of Jesus Christ of Latter Day Saints had been formed in 1830 and so was already a decade old before it touched the British Isles. It arrived with several running arguments already underway, not least the accusation of its necessary immorality grounded in the belief that its members were practising polygamists. A major theme running through the polemic between Mormons and their antagonists in Wales and the rest of Britain was that of morality. Orthodox churchmen played on the deviance of the Mormon faith, often seeing its perversity as arising from its devilish source. In the realm of mainstream churches and denominations Mormonism was the enemy within the gate. Accusations made against it are typical of those negative inversions which anthropology has identified as the regular motif of witchcraft accusations or the accusation of cannibalism levelled against neighbouring peoples.[1] Whatever else they were Mormons were unnatural. One theologian writing in 1853 even traced, or rather conjectured, an etymology of the name Mormon, connecting it with the Greek mormō which, he assures us, signifies, 'a bugbear, rawhead, hobgoblin' and from which he concludes in an apparently watertight logic that 'a Mormonite is a frightener, something terrific especially to children,' (J. Haynes, 1853:5).

The vexed issue of polygamy, or plural marriage as the Mormons preferred to call it, was so important in the course of introducing the faith to Britain that the first edition of the *Star* formally and officially denied the practice, stating quite clearly that 'one man should have one wife and one woman one husband, except in the case of death when either party is at liberty to marry again' (1840:187). The reproach of fornication and immorality was often to be raised in attacks upon the Mormon movement over the next fifty years. Even after plural marriage was officially banned in the church in 1889 the rumour of it lingered in the popular mind as characterizing the Mormon way of life. The denial in the 1840 *Star* (and we will often use this abbreviated reference to the *Millennial Star* for simplicity's sake) contrasts with subsequent practice and shows something of the heterogeneity of opinion and doctrine in the church during its early decades. What is clear is the desire to present a message which does not come adrift on the issue of morality.[2]

The same year, 1840, witnessed the founding of the first Mormon branch in Wales, at the picturesque rural village of Overton in Flintshire. Henry Royle reported a membership there of thirty two in October and by the end of the year he announced a total of fifty six converts baptized. All was not as easy as these numbers might suggest for just before Christmas James Burnham let it be known that some leaders had been stoned twice by local antagonists. None daunted he went on to open groups at Oswestry and Whittington. By the end of 1841 these groups along with others on the Isle of Man were organized into the Liverpool Conference boasting one hundred and seventy members. Of these two were elders, five priests, three teachers and three deacons, so that thirteen of the total membership of one hundred and seventy were regarded as worthy of active leadership roles.

This profile of members is worthy of further comment at the very outset of our study since it can be easily overlooked when quoting statistics of membership. The point is that the hierarchical structure of Mormonism is quite unlike most other religious groups, and that it itself underwent change as the church developed. Those admitted to the listed offices may be viewed as the core membership of high commitment to the central tenets of faith. The larger number of the total membership includes the more peripheral clientele. When talking about Mormon church membership it is important to know whether one or both of the categories are involved, and to be alert to the relation between office bearers and others for it is this very interaction which forwards the work of the movement.

The earliest leaders in Wales were much concerned that those ordained to the priesthood be characters of the highest standing. By 1844 the Liverpool Conference felt the time had come to allow elder Joseph Martin to decide who these local worthies might be and to ordain them. He was to do this to the extent that he feel led by the spirit and also see a need for the offices, (1843:194). This marks a slight shift of power from the American elders to local leadership and certainly emphasizes the growth of commitment locally. At this conference the Abergavenny group, which had been linked to the Liverpool Conference, was relocated so as to join the Merthyr Tydfil Conference under the guidance of Henshaw. He was an Englishman who wrote in the *Star* that he had gone to Merthyr in 1842 and had met with much opposition. But some believed so that by 1845 there were four hundred and ninety three members there comprising eleven elders, fifteen priests, fourteen teachers and seven deacons.

This South Wales growth heralded a turning point in the Welsh work since Saints in North Wales had fewer than one hundred members by the same time. The 1845 conference was important for another reason. It hosted Captain Dan Jones. This maritime title was entirely appropriate for this Welshman, a native of Flintshire, who was to supervise the transatlantic emigration of many of his countrymen. He himself had been converted in America and had been with Mormonism's founder, the prophet Joseph Smith, on the night before Smith's death when the prison where they were being held was stormed by a mob. The tradition holds that Joseph told Dan that he would live to see his native Wales and to preach the gospel there. After Smith's death his words were to assume greater significance for Jones and became a charter for his mission.

The Millennial Star faithfully presented the call to emigrate to America as an intrinsic part of response to the Mormon message on the part of British converts. In May 1843 the term Babylon is used to describe that sinful world from which the devout should flee to avoid the plagues which would inevitably come. 'It is the voice of God inviting us to the assembly of the Saints of the Most High, that we may receive instruction in the House of the Lord, partake of the blessing of his spirit and be prepared for the Coming of the Son of Man', (1843:14).

The Prophet Joseph Smith's death on 27 June 1844 was announced formally in Britain in a special supplement to the *Star* published in August. It was an editorial which, necessarily, had to deal with two particularly vital issues. The leadership of the movement and the call to emigrate.

For some Saints in Nauvoo, the site of the mob killing, the whole question of the future of the Mormon cause was very much at stake. There was no shortage of candidates for the prophetic mantle. Wales was itself to witness the growth of one of the emergent schismatic groups, albeit one which has subsequently gained legal title to the primacy of status over the original church property held by Joseph Smith. We will look later at this Reorganized Church of Jesus Christ of Latter Day Saints and its twentieth century presence in Wales. Suffice it to say that the *Millennial Star* remained under the control of those who supported Brigham Young who was then President of the Twelve Apostles and who argued that power should be administered by that group after Smith's death. Leonard Arrington's magisterial biography of Brigham Young affords valuable accounts of the way in which the majority of church members came to accept Young's leadership, even to the point of seeing visual resemblance between the dead prophet and Brigham at public appearances soon after Joseph's death. That same biography shows how Brigham Young was instrumental in encouraging the birth of the *Millennial Star* as an organ of church life, (1986:84,114).

The *Star* intimated that this tragic event had been in some measure anticipated and that Smith had told the Twelve in the spring of 1844 that they should have the same effective power as he held, should any catastrophe befall him. British readers were, accordingly, called to support the Twelve and were assured that, as a letter from a key American figure — Orson Hyde — put it, 'our principles still live though our prophet is dead', (1844:12). Some suggestion was made that the half-hearted would now withdraw, the dead-wood be pruned away, and the honest hearted reorient themselves towards God more firmly than ever. As though Joseph's leadership had involved too many non-spiritual attractions for some members, who now had a chance of purifying their motivations.

Those principles which still lived on included the necessity to move to America where the Saints could gather as a nation and find protection in large numbers. A large enough group with a sufficiently heavy impetus had formed around the prophet to ensure that his prophecy did not fail at his death. Not only so, but those social, political and economic factors that had initially made Joseph's millennial message appealing were still powerful. It was not the case that Joseph Smith's message was so intrinsically tied to his person that it would vanish or shatter at his decease.

As far as Wales was concerned the very fact that Dan Jones came to preside over the area in 1846 was testimony enough to anticipate a sound and hopeful future. For had he not lived through that mob attack on the prophet with a growing certainty that the work started by the prophet would progress and flourish? Here we see exemplified a process which often repeated itself in Mormon circles as the teachings of the gospel came to be focussed upon, or expressed through, the life of particular emissaries from America. These missionaries were, as they continue to be, witnesses to the fact of the church's strength in the New World. Dan Jones, of course, was also more than this. Not only was he a convert and eyewitness of what had constituted the prophetic core of the movement in America, but he was above all a Welshman. He was a symbol of the transformation preached in the Mormon gospel. He was a type case of the new man, of the desired goal of the religious call. This fact may have been crucial for the success of Mormonism in Wales, an additional and catalytic factor which should be placed alongside all the usual economic, social and democratic forces regularly adduced as reasons encouraging emigration in the mid-nineteenth century.

Dan Jones presided at the Welsh Conference at Merthyr in March 1846. The Welsh membership stood at six hundred distributed through twenty four branches and the prospect was said to be flattering. The church was not without its growing pains. It was necessary to restrain headstrong individuals and to return, or as the Saints put it, to restore these aspiring spirits to full fellowship. At this same Conference four elders, eight priests, nine teachers and four deacons were ordained. The July Conference recorded further expansion into twenty nine branches and a membership of seven hundred and eighty. Interestingly the occasion is marked as one at which 'not a whisper of an apostate's rumour' was heard. This hints at the problem of mixed opinion which attended, perhaps almost inevitably, this expansionist phase. It was at this Conference that a Missionary Society was formed to raise funds for the aid of travelling missionaries. One large tea-party, attended by about a thousand people, dedicated £22 to the cause. Such a reference to tea-parties is interesting in the light of the Mormon disapproval of tea drinking, it also touches on the question of Mormon identity.

Mormonism had inherited the idea of teetotalism from its native environment of New York State, but had incorporated it into its ideology as a revelation from God and not as a judicious opinion on healthy living. The section of the book called *Doctrine and Covenants* concerning this and other prescriptions on diet came to be called the Word of Wisdom, originally produced in 1833. As far as Wales was concerned these early Saints seemed very little troubled over the consumption of tea. Indeed it seemed to play a normal part in their communal gatherings. It was only about thirty years later that any specific and systematic attention was given to the habit. We learn from Merthyr in August 1867 that all the missionaries observe the Word of Wisdom to a great degree, at least as far as tobacco and alcohol were concerned. Only some did not drink tea and coffee. The implication is that only some ordinary members follow suit. A report of January 1868 says that tea drinking was quite a problem of conscience for many members 'though some are leaving it off'. A similar picture emerges in 1886 when some are said to abstain wholly from the use of tea, coffee, and tobacco, while others 'are observing more moderation'. The overall impression on the tea element in the Word of Wisdom is that it seldom emerges as an important concern in the nineteenth century. Occasional references are but passing reminders of an aspect of Mormon practice which impinged very little on Welsh Mormons. And this is quite intelligible as far as the process of identity formation is concerned since we are here dealing with a period in which mere abstention from alcohol and tobacco would not serve as a strong and distinctive enough demarcator between Mormon and many non-Mormon religious groups. For a considerable number of churches opposed the drinking of alcohol and stressed self-control and moderation. By sharp contrast the distinctive nature of Mormon doctrine and the call to emigrate were powerful marks of differentiation between Mormon and Gentile. It is instructive to note that Mormons used the name Gentile as a way of describing those who were not within the Latter Day Saint fold. So tea abstention was not as useful an identity marker as was the pattern of church organization, the possession of the *Book of Mormon*, and the call to Zion with its American geographical focus.

Later, in the twentieth century the whole of the Word of Wisdom edict became increasingly encumbent upon members as they realized they would have to remain in Wales without any hope of emigration. In the post nineteen forties period, as religious life decreased in significance amongst the general population in Wales, the role of behavioural factors like abstention from tea and coffee and alcohol did come to assume increasing significance as what might be called domestic rites which expressed distinctive Mormon identity. It was the active presence of American missionaries in the nineteenth century which kept the Word of Wisdom issue alive and, as we will see in a later discussion, these model persons perpetually presented local members with Mormon ideals. When they were withdrawn from Wales for a short period at a later date a vital mode of pragmatic instruction was lost.

But returning to earlier days we find Dan Jones a man who 'delighted in the trophies of war' as he set about his missionary work. The particular war of words to which he referred in 1847 was one fought against local ministers of religion at Merthyr. It was believed that they held secret meetings to organize themselves to oppose Mormonism. Their last plan at Dowlais was to bribe thirty daring and shameless men to interrupt and harangue the preaching. Dan Jones well understood this response since the Mormon cause was, in his own estimation, making havoc amongst the flocks of the regular churches. In August and September 1847 Merthyr was a very active centre with a Conference of Saints and hearers numbering about a thousand. Writing to inform Orson Spencer, the British President, of all this Jones speaks of 'having retreated for a few hours from the battleground while my guns are cooling for another broadside'. This kind of Frontier spirit applied to evangelistic endeavours gives some insight into the way this remarkable man approached his work. His own reading of the local situation echoed his earlier experience in New York State at the time of Joseph Smith's death, for not only were the sixty thousand inhabitants of Merthyr said to be 'drunken with infatuation and rage for or against the Mormons', but Jones said that he would not be surprised if the former tragedies of Carthage and Smith's shooting were repeated in Wales. Some ministers of religion were believed to have declared that Mormons should indeed be treated after the fashion of their founder. One other faction was apparently trying out a different approach in accusing Mormons of political, Chartist, intentions so as to bring upon them the not inconsiderable wrath of the local iron-masters.

This strife and challenge was the element in which Jones flourished. His fellow Saints were not slow to appreciate his worth. R. L. Evans has written about the Captain's native gifts of fluency in Welsh and of the Prophet's intimating to Jones that he would serve in Wales before he died. Evans shows how these facts were stressed by Wilford Woodruff when he called for the appointment of Jones as the president over the Saints in Wales, and Evans cites the *Millennial Star* on this material, (Evans 1937:189). More locally his compatriots produced an acrostic published in the January *Star* of 1848 and which originated in Rhymney, an industrial mountain town to the east of Merthyr:

>Did you hear of our brave Welsh captain

> A spirited man without deception
> Noble in battle as a Nation's champion
>
> Jesus-like he loves his nation
> O yes he does beyond expression
> No matter what his trials are
> Everything proves he is sincere
> So God bless his future career.

And Dan Jones was indeed concerned with his 'nation', but now that word carried two senses as far as he was concerned. His nation of birth, Wales, had come to be the object of his proselytizing zeal in the hope that many Welsh people would convert to the new nation which was nothing less than the Mormon cause, the nation of God. In January 1848 we read of continuing success at Merthyr with its six hundred members. Jones encouraged many of these to separate so as to spread the word of Restoration to as many as possible. The North Wales area, for example, possessed only one hundred and three members by the close of 1847, while the total Welsh membership, largely in the South, totalled nearly two thousand.

Glamorgan continued as a major source of recruits, there being approximately nine hundred new members made over 1846 and four new branches established. Jones was writing and publishing much religious literature, some one thousand five hundred tracts per month and one thousand two hundred copies of the *Star*. 'Never were the affairs of the kingdom more prosperous'. In March 1848 he was stricken with some illness akin to pleurisy and was unable to carry out his exhausting programme, especially the writing to which he attributed his weakness. He took this as a hint that he had written enough for the present. His consolation lay in the ten or so people a week being baptized at Merthyr. Hence his fond name for Merthyr as the 'mother branch of Britain'. This growth increased as the months passed with about a hundred a month reported from May of 1848. Employment was generally poor and the hope of a bright future in Zion, as the Mormons called America at this time, was quickly increasing. Jones observed that quite a few Saints were keen to emigrate and he himself was very keen to return to America since his lungs were in a bad condition. But the question 'When shall we go to Zion?' was glossed by him with the further question of which ship would be large enough to take them all?

Religious zeal currently flowed at a high level and speaking in tongues was reported from Rhymney, with healings at Merthyr and Newport. One Mormon funeral at Merthyr attracted a crowd of nigh on a thousand mourners. The General Conference held in Manchester in August reports a Welsh membership of two thousand seven hundred and forty seven along with a significantly large group of leaders: fifty elders, one hundred and ninety five priests, one hundred and thirty teachers and fifty nine deacons. This burgeoning number was soon to be reduced in a symbolically climactic manner as Captain Jones led the first group of Welsh migrants from their homeland to the new land of promise. This was in February 1849.

A month before leaving he had opened a chapel at Llanelli and the general excitement of that occasion was still abroad months later as Dan's praise was still sung in Wales. He was succeeded by William S. Phillips in Wales and at Merthyr, a man said to be full of the same spirit as Jones whose identity as an Elijah was not totally inept.

One factor aiding the continued success of the Mormon message was the cholera, an illness which was almost personified by the Saints. It was certainly perceived as a biblical plague. The strong eschatological perspective of Mormons tended to invest passing events with a profound religious significance. Reporting from Merthyr in June 1849 John Davis refers to the cholera epidemic as assisting him greatly since many were now seeking baptism in an active way. The implicit assumption being that the rite would protect them from the sickness. He is quite explicit on the fact that while many have died in the general population only three or four Saints had succumbed. And of these some died because they were lacking in faith, while others could not gain access to the anointing with oil which the elders practised. Yet it seems that such ministrations were themselves fraught with danger lest an anointed person die and the church be blamed for his death. So families were encouraged to call for the doctor as well as for the elders. It looks as though various people in Aberdare and Cardiff were seeking to accuse the Saints of manslaughter in several such cases.

A further entry for July directly links the announced deaths of four hundred and sixty eight at Merthyr due to cholera with the fulfilment of prophecies for the last days. It is 'observed that this plague is more dreadful in places where the gospel has been most preached'. So clearly was the cholera identified with the plague that it was rumoured to have been seen with the naked eye in Cardiff, 'like a cloud of rather dark colour', so reports the *Star* for July 1849. In a similar way a colliery explosion at Cwmbach near Aberdare which killed fifty five men was seen as a divine sign, since the dead were reckoned to have been sad persecutors of the Mormons who had remained unharmed by the catastrophe.

That God was blessing his people was evident from the 1849 membership figures of four thousand five hundred and twenty nine spread through ninety two Welsh branches. There were three hundred and twenty five elders, two hundred and eighteen priests, one hundred and eighty nine teachers and one hundred and seven deacons. Approximately three hundred had emigrated. This is the first record of an emigration and refers to Dan Jones and his party. An entry for November tells of the success of his company as they reached Sandy Bluffs, two hundred and eighty miles from Winter Quarters. Their camp resounds with the songs of Zion each night while their prosperity and rejoicing should, it is argued, stimulate their brethren to imitate their example and cross 'the mighty deep', (1849:346).

The contemporary Mormon evaluation of other denominations saw them as having little benefit: 'their interest was not with truth, for they resemble prize-fighters in a fair who shake hands before they box, then give themselves playful knocks with all the love of a brother'. The Saints, by contrast, were dedicated to the truth not only in word but in action, especially in the act of emigration which held its own goal. A goal with two closely related dimensions, one which might be called materialistic and the other spiritual. It is, in fact, quite important to grasp the interconnectedness of these elements since they are ever present features of Mormon thought during the mid-nineteenth century. At its simplest it is the linking of secular wishes for independent existence with the religious hope of Christ's second coming. Two songs of the New Year of 1850 express these two strands of Mormon hope. The first is shorter, as befits its sharp advent message, while the longer, second, song gives vent to that optimism over a better future. Somewhat ironically the suggested tune for it is 'a life on the ocean wave': as though the medium was the message, emigration for settlement, sea first and land later.

1. Ye L.D.S. to Zion flee away
   For there shall be safety for all who will pray.
   For this is God's promise through Joseph the Seer
   Flee then ye righteous in the present New Year.

2. A life on my own free soil,
   A home on the Salt Lake sod,
   I'll never at labour recoil.
   But thankfully worship my God:
   For Babylon has not a charm
   With its turmoil noise and strife
   Oh give me a flourishing farm
   With a kind and endearing wife.

   Chorus

   A life on my own free soil
   A home in a farmer's cot,
   Among Mormons I'll labour and toil
   And ask for no happier lot.

The early months of 1850 encouraged the Saints with some seven hundred and thirty one baptisms falling between January and June. A considerable change in leadership followed Dan Jones' departure and also a shift in organization with the Newport branch being embraced by the Hereford Conference. A letter from Aberdare speaks of such a concentration of power taking place in Wales that one might anticipate the Principality soon becoming 'a general Zion of the pure in heart'. Dan Jones was much missed despite the fact that the young William Phillips, who succeeded him, was deemed a worthy leader. The figure of Phillips does not however fully replace that of Jones and there is a hint of factionalism with members being warned of the dangers of speaking evil against each other. On a different note the use of the expression 'general Zion of the pure in heart' in the March Star of 1850 is worthy of comment since it was not until the turn of the century that places beyond America were thought of in terms of being a form of Zion. This early use of Zion language in connection with purity of heart outside Utah should probably be seen as signifying high levels of religious response in conversion linked in part with the American Zion through the ideal of emigration.

The overall style of religious language employed in Mormon hymns, sermons, and other church correspondence tended to be rather exaggerated and loaded with biblical metaphor and allusion. It was, in a double sense, a language of Zion, both because it shared in the religious language of the day which varied from purely mundane parlance, and because its prime focus was on the New Jerusalem. The call to emigrate was said to be as binding upon the Saint as was the call to repentance and baptism upon the Gentile. By the June of 1850, seventy one had emigrated from Wales which at that stage boasted a membership of four thousand three hundred and forty two with about 10% being elders and a further 10% in the lower order of the Aaronic priesthood.[3] As is indicated, or at least implied by these figures there was a large group of non office holding members even if it is recalled that women do not hold office themselves within the hierarchical structure of the church.[4] This large group of about three thousand four hundred and twenty seven was a problem for a movement dedicated to purity of intention and sincerity of purpose as well as to the typical attitude of exclusivism which often features prominently in sectarian movements. The maintenance of purity is attested in a statistic which now makes an appearance in the records, it is the number of those who have been excommunicated.

The first half-year of 1850 lists two hundred and twenty two excommunications. In terms of general policy this severing of membership must not be read as it would in the Catholic and sacramental traditions since the excommunicate is not a heretic but, usually at least, one who has lapsed in active church participation. Some would have been put out for a moral misdemeanour only to be admitted after a period of repentance. This practice is not unlike penance within some mainstream Christian traditions, it certainly served to hold people steady within a degree of commitment which more established churches failed to do.

For Mormons, commitment and ideals of faith were seldom represented as abstract phenomena. They were physically represented in a variety of persons and institutions. The most obvious of these was the prophet himself as the first president of the church along with the central group of twelve apostles, but at the local level it was the emissaries from America who stood for all that Mormonism represented. The constant presence of missionaries, and especially the dynamic presence of Dan Jones who, in his day, was both missionary and actual friend of Joseph Smith, was a direct statement about the power of the message. In June of 1850, as though to reinforce the American connection, a special guest attended a general conference at Merthyr. This was John Taylor. Not only was he English by birth, from Westmoreland in fact, and now living in America, but he had been ordained an Apostle in 1838. As the first Apostle to visit Britain he was much feted at Merthyr. A welcome hymn was sung for him which had been composed for the occasion. The large crowds attending the event necessitated an outdoor meeting in Merthyr's market-place. The part of his address emphasized in the *Star* is not without interest for our own analysis of emigration to the American Zion which will follow shortly. For Taylor dealt with the issue of language, having Welsh obviously in mind, and argued that language was 'nothing to boast of since the best of them was only the remains of Babel', (1850:214). His talk had to be translated into Welsh since so few would otherwise have understood it. But we should not think that only Welsh speakers were attracted to the Mormon message since enough monoglot English had been converted to necessitate one specifically English speaking branch at Merthyr. Not only so, but many English tracts were much in demand to explain the faith to prospective converts.

With growth in numbers there was a drive to organize lists of members in 1850 and records were now kept in each branch, with certificates of membership provided for the faithful. There seems to have been a fair amount of confusion in Wales over matters of membership since, in the rush of millennial zeal, records had not been kept as carefully as they might have been. Not only did the drive for accuracy of records gain in vigour, a feature which was to typify Mormon bureaucracy and statistical carefulness in subsequent periods when the computerization of records and genealogical material took place, but more care was also taken lest indiscriminate baptism brought unworthy members into the church.

Not only were the Saints keen to preserve their purity and integrity of membership within the movement, they also felt a need to defend themselves against certain outsiders. Some persecution originating with the Methodists and Anglicans is reported in 1850. The former are accused of having members in North Wales who pulled knives and threatened Mormon preachers, while at Neath in South Wales the Anglicans publically destroyed Mormon tracts in the pulpit. But the Saints were far from discomfitted by these events since other things were taking place which heartened them very much. This applied with particular force to events deemed miraculous. In September, for example, one David Richards of Abercanaid was crushed by an immense stone while working in the colliery. Though a doctor declared his back broken elder Phillips laid hands on him and, with the sound of crushing an old wicker basket, the bones came together again in the name of Jesus. In June 1852 an earthquake was reported in Merthyr and this was interpreted as a sign of the last days. Even so this supernaturalist perspective is balanced by a pragmatism which typifies Mormonism in each phase of its development.

A clear example of this practical commitment is that of the Perpetual Emigration Fund. This had been established in 1849 under the impetus of Brigham Young, himself an archetypal pragmatic prophet, as a means of assisting Saints in Iowa to complete their vocation by moving to the Salt Lake Valley. It soon expanded its scope and by October 1850 this cooperative economic venture was advertised in the *Star*. Initially the call was to the economically able members asking them to contribute money to facilitate the migration of the less well-off: 'Come on ye rich with all your gifted store, Give to the poor and God will give you more'. And it seems as though the poor were the very Saints who did wish to move. William Phillips writes from Merthyr that the rich are rather quiet. When he prompts them in asking when they intend emigrating they reply by posing further questions concerning the political and economic stability of the Mormon regime in the Valley of Utah. They seem to balance this against the likelihood of the cholera striking again in Wales. So it is that as president of the Welsh church Phillips expostulates; 'Oh what faith some have in their God! I teach the Saints that they must bring their hearts and their gold into this kingdom and not be members in the banks, for if their treasures are in the banks there will their hearts be also', or so it seemed in June 1852.

What might be seen as the secular strain in Mormon religiosity can be identified in this cry from the heart. There is no exhortation to poverty or the abandonment of wealth, rather it should be relocated in the Latter Day movement. And but little time remained for the transfer. The coming of Christ to America to initiate the millennium demanded human preparation. There was 'no more time for the Saints to hesitate', if they wanted to meet their Saviour they ought to gather in Utah, since, 'all this must take place in this century', (1852:11).

Brigham Young, Heber Kimball, and Willard Richards, all key church leaders, signed this declaration which warned of hesitation. 'Arise and come home', they said, for 'if any man will not gather when he has the chance he will be afflicted with the Devil'. Such authoritative words devalued the world lying beyond Utah just as they extolled the benefit of that Zion in the hills. Yet the picture was not quite as simple as this might suggest. More interesting, perhaps, is the observation that the *Millennial Star* published material which can be read as differing from the straight contrast between Zion and Babylon. We have already referred to the thought that Wales possessed a power which united its church members and which might yield a general Zion of the pure in heart. It is a vision which shows how church leaders at the local level may well see circumstances in a different perspective from the more distant authorities. Another case will exemplify this situation. When William Howells left for America in 1851 he cast a farewell glance at Wales. Writing on St. David's Day, though without any reference to that fact, he observed with due pride the astonishing unity of faith prevailing in Wales, especially bearing in mind the great diversity of denominational origin of converts. Their corporate dedication seemed to surprise him, and obviously to please him. In 1850 the noted American church leader, Orson Pratt, had spoken from Manchester at a general conference and stressed the need for unity amongst members in the widely dispersed branches of the church. He believed that active pressure needed to be applied by leaders to ensure unity. Unity was strength and it also 'prevailed with the heavens', an outlook which in terms of religious causation put another perspective on Howells' view where unity was the outcome of divine activity.

This variation over the point of unity, a variation which embraces the pragmatic and the supernatural dimension of religiosity, raises again the relation between sacred and secular streams within Mormonism. The dichotomy of sacred and secular may not be the best way of handling the complexity of religious motivation and thought but at least it allows us to come to grips with an important set of processes operating in the religion during the mid-nineteenth century and beyond.[5]

In Wales the coming millennium had been grasped in the light of a pre-existing piety possessed of a strong other-worldly colour. The land of promise in its geographical concreteness was apprehended in the light of biblical geography and the spirituality gained from pre-Mormon days of religious teaching. In Utah, by contrast, the coming millennial kingdom and the earthly kingdom, which human endeavour would do much to foster, were more closely entwined; this is not to say that Utahns did not hold to a supernaturalist hope of a millennial transformation by God. They did, and so did the theological understanding of the church, indeed it was a doctrine which was to change slowly only over the turn of the century. But the human task, the place of men and women in preparing for that millennium, was more to the forefront of church attention in America. In Wales the very task of attaining to the actual land of America was an ideal on top of which the idea of the coming Kingdom of God was a further idealization. Dr. Willard Richards, a well known early Mormon, expressed something of the practical view of the Kingdom when he called upon the editors of the *Star* to publish far and wide the fact that the elements of truth and liberty enshrined in the American Constitution would be best practised and enforced when citizens adopted 'political Mormonism'. In this and similar addresses, both in Wales and Utah, Mormon leaders presented aspects of what can, in retrospect, be seen as a valuable variation in outlook. There developed what might be called a pool of potential orientations from which later Saints were able to draw as they sought to explore the possible meanings of their faith.[6] While the central message of Mormonism was that of the 'restoration' of truth, of priesthoods, of temples and their rites, and of an imminent millennium, the way that message was perceived, held, and developed, was not uniform. Especially after the death of Joseph Smith doctrinal elaboration was influenced by numerous factors, not least by the cultural distance from the centre of Mormon religious organization. These varied orientations were to be of great value as time went on, for it seems to be true that those religious movements with variety of interpretation are better able to survive and flourish across a wider spectrum of society than groups with very narrow interests and explanations of life. This is to be expected as ever changing social, religious and historical circumstances make new demands upon believers. The wider the base on which to build the more possible is creative response to problems which might otherwise prove intractable. As our study proceeds we will see several examples of this process emerge in Wales.

We have already cited cases of colliery accidents and death in which Mormons survived and which were interpreted in terms of God's wrath vented upon the Gentiles. But even this interpretation had to change fairly rapidly since it did not take long before Saints were themselves killed in the not infrequent industrial accidents of the time. The death of church members made such religious and eschatological glosses less valid. In 1852, for example, there was a serious accident at Cwmbach near Merthyr when nineteen of the sixty nine dead proved to be Latter Day Saints, including elder Ebenezer Morris the president of the Cwmbach branch of the church. His two sons died with him. Four further elders, two priests, three deacons, and two teachers were also listed. The one comment which the *Star* includes on this incident hints at the blame due to those working there on account of the fact that it was a place of known danger where earnings were significantly higher than elsewhere.

The social life of church members came under scrutiny from their leaders on such occasions of disaster precisely because Mormons were thought to be God's elect and privileged people. The larger part of the nineteenth century was an experimental period for them as their religious ideas were reflected upon and tested through experience. Not only so, but there was a constant production of new ideas and interpretations of doctrine in what was proving to be a period of intense production of literature. For semi-literate people, or literate people with a limited education the degree of exposure to a restricted kind of material was very influential in forming their religious identity. The fact that Mormon religious literature was an extension of other Protestant modes of thought should not be overlooked. *The Book of Mormon*, which by 1852 was available in Welsh, French, and German as well as English, shared in the status of the bible with its assured place guaranteed by Protestant tradition. Concurrently a new hymnbook of some five hundred and seventy five items testified to the continuing power of hymnody. Also in 1852 there was published a Welsh translation of the *Pearl of Great Price*, a doctrinal volume of revelations and encouragement. Along with the weekly paper, *Udgorn Seion*, or Zion's Trumpet, these works brought a continuous pressure to bear upon the general membership. It is easy to see that church leaders not only told the poor and oppressed that they needed revelations from God, but they also provided access to them in a saturation of Mormon literature. In 1854 some fifty thousand Welsh tracts were distributed, (1854:766).

Some of the Mormon teaching struck notes that were quite unfamiliar to Welsh ears. This is noteworthy in the overall theme of continuity-discontinuity between the message of the Restoration and the well-known forms of Protestantism, Anglicanism and Catholicism, which had been the prevailing background to Mormon conversion. The doctrine of the Virgin Birth of Christ is but one example. In the September *Star* of 1853 readers were told that when the truth on this doctrine was announced then 'blasphemy would be nothing to it'. It was obviously expected that the Mormon perspective over the mode of the conception of Jesus would surprise those brought up on more traditional fare. Having prepared the ground the *Star* now sketched the Mormon theological picture:

> 'Jesus our elder brother was begotten in the flesh by the same character that was in the garden of Eden and who is our Father in Heaven ... Adam ... Michael the Archangel, the Ancient of Days. He our Father and our God and the only God with whom we have to do', (1853:770).

This kind of theological novelty obviously caused a stir. For Protestant critics it was deemed an obvious perversion and heresy, but for the faithful its distinctiveness was seen to be evidence of a Restored truth with which the anaemic theology of other churches could not compare. Doctrinal distinctions helped create boundary distinctions between Saint and Gentile, and conversions could be understood as proof of the truthfulness of what initially appeared an odd message from Zion. Cases of conversion like that of a Merthyr Baptist minister, and the young Unitarian who prayed for no less than forty nine hours after his baptism, were quoted with pleasure, (1854:269).

Church leaders remained constantly alert to what they saw as non-religious factors influencing members' piety. The cholera was a regular candidate and they noted how 'that most popular of preachers' served to strengthen the hearts of the faithful or at least of the fainthearted, (1854:766). In an 1854 epidemic no Saint died at Merthyr though a few did elsewhere. In 1866 an interesting qualification on Mormon safety during epidemics is added. Some members had died after having used 'other means to their cases' than the official healing rite of anointing with oil which others had used to their cure.

Social pressures of a hostile nature continued to foster internal solidarity in 1855 and the goal of emigration is again stressed. The 'word of the Lord is to gather', and the Saints know, 'by the testimony of the spirit within that America is the land where the Kingdom of God is first to be established ... where the physical, social, and political influence of His Kingdom is to be first developed', (1855:9). Some are said to want to reach that land to obtain more than one wife, so the polygamy issue is now publically known and acknowledged in Britain, (1855:19). To these and to all, the necessity of sincerity is stressed. It must be with a pure heart and clean hands that the Perpetual Emigration Fund should be approached since 'this fund is sacred'. Not only was it sacred as a means of bringing converts into Zion in a literal way, it also expressed the material base of the new religious movement itself.

The otherworldliness of a heavenly reward was an impressive theme of religion in Wales at this time and much of its piety was directed towards a passive, almost Stoic, view of life's hardship. There was a great stress upon basic ethics as a religious outworking of faith, and while domestic religion with its bible reading and prayer was the practice of the more pious, the chapel was the dominant focus of and for religious life. This was what we might call a centripetal religion with a pull towards the chapel, to its hymnody, preaching, corporate sentiment and fellowship. The ultimate anticipated exit and final direction of human life lay through death into a supernatural heaven. By contrast the Mormon message contained a centrifugal dynamic as far as Saints in Wales were concerned. Though the word 'contained' is slightly misleading since it was the entire organization of the religion which comprised a system serving to project or catapult members from their home base to the American arena where Zion would be built. So most meetings of Merthyr Saints, as with other British and European members, would have been suffused with a message of another place. But, unlike the Protestant and Catholic case, that place was attainable in this life and even within a relatively short space of time.

Furthermore, that place was a locale which united within itself the actual land that some had already reached through emigration, and a far more abstract idea of a sacred place which, hitherto, would only have been apprehended symbolically through hymns, sermons and the institutions of faith. So the concept and doctrine of Zion was one dominant symbol which integrated purely supernatural and pragmatic Mormon concerns. Many converts would have been well prepared to accept religious ideas of a promised land through their prior religious membership of other groups.[7] With the Mormon message there suddenly appeared a material possibility, a real opportunity of experiencing a physical and geographical promised land. Such preadaptation was of considerable use to the Mormon cause and helps us see the way in which the Perpetual Emigration Fund expressed the outward and institutional form of Mormon commitment to a land of Zion here and now. We will see later how these ideas and hopes were reflected in Mormon hymnody which itself was able to build upon doctrinal foundations drawn from the bible and long enshrined in the hymns of other churches.

So it was that an energetic impetus to emigrate was accompanied by constant reminders of the uniqueness of Mormonism. Frequent mention of polygamy throughout 1855 was glossed with a clear message to members not to be offended or astonished by the introduction of new doctrine by the church authorities, (1855:738). Mormon success lay to a certain extent in its capacity to unite familiar items of Christian history and doctrine with the quite new disclosures of the restored message. Part of the success also arose from the active manner in which doctrine was held and developed. The presence of Dan Jones in Wales throughout 1855, for his second mission to Wales lasted from 1852-1856, itself provided a concrete example of an outward directed, non-parochial, religion. Change rather than custom emerged as the keynote of the Restoration. This was precisely the right note for those local inhabitants who were unhappy with the status quo. But here we need to be careful not to slip too easily into that position of deprivation theory which places excessive stress on the poverty and on the pitiable aspects of life from which converts sought release.[8] Doubtless many poor people did see America as a secular land of economic promise. This is a well known feature of nineteenth century emigration. But to it must be added the further, and perhaps more significant, element of religious longing for salvation. The critical scholar can find it too easy to reduce the wish to be in Zion to nothing more than an economic desire. That kind of reductionism strips away too quickly the very human yearning for a quality of experience and fulfilment which is best described as spiritual.

Chapter Two

The Language of Zion: 1856-1860

For many Welsh converts this religious quest soon came to be perceived in terms of the threefold biblical model of exodus, wilderness journey and promised rest. As part of the total transformation inherent in this journey and metamorphosed identity was the question of language. The English language lay across the Welsh convert's path. It was seen as more than a mere utilitarian necessity.

In March 1856 it is reported from Swansea that a renewed interest in English was emerging as a consequence of the desire on the part of the Saints 'to avail themselves of the advantages of direct communication with the Spirit from Zion'. At this stage in the history of Mormon theology the revelations to the prophet along with the *Book of Mormon* were not believed to be in English simply because Joseph Smith had been an English speaker. On the contrary, English was taken to be that language through which the restored kingdom would be established. It was nothing less than a divine intention to use English as the medium of the Restoration. It was no arbitrary social accident since 'the Lord saw fit to reveal his Gospel in these last days in the English language'. And because 'all the ordinances are administered in that language', converts were the more pressed to learn it, (1859:79).

So it was that Latter Day work was said to be breaking down old nationalities among those who received it. That work included English revelations even though they might be translated into Welsh for purposes of primary evangelism. The call to America was a call to a new form of life. One which was organized under divine control through the prophet, for the assumption was that 'the basis of social regeneration is theocratic government', (1856:784).

The progression to this ideal may itself have been a continuation of a convert's life before joining the church. There is little by way of statistical evidence to clarify the picture but it seems likely that many who accepted the message in South Wales would already have engaged in a degree of migration, albeit from England to Wales or else from rural Wales to its industrialized southern counties. The call to 'arise and come home' to an unknown place needs special consideration since it is easy to draw on overly romantic notions of patriotic sentiment. Any assessment of temperament and sentiment in the past can quickly turn into a poetic rather than a critical endeavour. One hymn in particular captures several of these points.

Hiraethu wyf yn Mhabilon
Am fynd i Seion wiw
Yn disgwyl am y newydd llon
Yn amser da fy Nhuw

Dywedair prophwyd Brigham Young
In English tongue so grand
A welcome you shall have among
The saints in Zion's land.

(Millennial Star 1865:640).[9]

To begin, we can stress the way in which that 'hiraeth' of the first line, which in Welsh hymnody had conventionally referred to a longing or homesickness for heaven, and which was normally used in the patriotic sense, was employed to denote the Mormon world of a promised Zion. An active process of world reclassification accompanies conversion into membership of the Latter Day Saint movement. The native land of birth comes to be devalued as it is denoted as Babylon (Mhabilon), that wicked city of the biblical apocalypse. Zion (Seion) is where the convert wants to be and he looks forward excitedly to going there in God's good time.

The two energies which hitherto had been directed elsewhere, one towards the worldly association of national identity, and the other to an otherworldly piety, now combine in a commitment to a geographical sacred place attainable in this life and through the effort of faith. One of the creative moves of the early Mormon religion lay in this form of spiritual materialism, expressed in a "hiraeth" or longing for a sacred space. As a further part of the total change aspects of political and family life also came to be viewed pragmatically yet as a spiritual process. Yet all this lay within the embrace of the English language which the hymn sees as being the vehicle for the prophetic welcome to Zion. While the linguistic switch was made comparatively easy for the actual migrant, those remaining in Wales needed repeated exhortation, as witnessed by the Merthyr leader Elias Morris writing nearly a decade later of his duty to 'impress the Saints in Wales with the importance of speaking and reading English', (1866:29).

While it is obviously natural that a resident population should continue to use the prevailing local language and would need some persuasion to adopt another it should not be forgotten that Mormonism had used Welsh fairly extensively in its initial missionary period. The fact that Dan Jones had throughout the 1840s and 1850s produced a considerable number of Welsh tracts, and had managed the translation of the standard works of the church, may well have fostered a certain ambivalence in the popular mind over the status of Welsh. This would probably have been especially problematic to the many who experienced conversion through the medium of Welsh. Attachment to aspects of the medium of conversion is often deep seated and not easily eliminated, yet in this cultural context such a transition was required.

Despite the novelty of some doctrine Mormonism was much helped in fostering a change of language because many other aspects of its teachings were already familiar to converts from their former religious experience. In fact Mormon religion seems at its strongest when extending and applying religious culture beyond those boundaries already familiar to people. It offered the benefit of well-trodden paths with the challenge to step out in faith into new territories.[10]

Fasting and prayer were two such established religious practices with strong biblical warranty. Daniel Davies tells how his Saints at Swansea found these to be favourite patterns of religious life. But at that same time, 1856, many other Welsh branches seem to contain a considerable number of half-hearted members. E. T. Benson, writing himself from Swansea in 1857, doubts whether half of the church membership would stand up to a great shaking. There is talk of a much needed reformation of the church and in particular that those thousands who believe in Mormonism but who remain unbaptized should take the plunge into a full and active commitment. This mixed nature of reports from branches during the later 1850s and at some later periods ought to be read less as a sign of rapid fluctuation in ethos than as marking the true sectarian spirit of the movement involving a high expectation of individual commitment freely given. It is forever self-critical with a stress on the ideal of sincerity. Aberrations from the prized, lofty, goals are noted with sadness. But, at the same time, leaders praise any move in the desired directions and take pains to chart each significant advance. The status of local leaders is heightened the more they scrutinize the faults of their people than when they acquiesce in tacitly approving laxity.

The same stringency ensured that potentially damning news items were not hidden. One article on Mormon society argued directly that monogamy was a 'cruel and vicious system' of family life and of social organization when compared with the divinely instituted laws of God enshrined in plural marriage, (1857:580). The world might slander the church for its seemingly perverse practice of polygamy but that very antagonism was turned to positive advantage since it was seen as a divine command. But it was also true that Mormons did not want to convey the impression that they were religious extremists of an unthinking and bigoted kind arguing, for example, that in Salt Lake City children did not have 'premature attendance at church inflicted upon them', (1857:628). A keynote of increasing clarity is heard in the *Millennial Star* as it develops the theme that the Restoration movement is also a cultural movement. It perceives itself as an emergent society and not as a sectarian group. 'Sectarianism is the opposite of true religion', (1858:59). Mormon religion is a restoration of divine truth enshrined in a 'strictly theocratic society', (1859:3). Its goal is not to thrust a religious message down the throats of people living in Britain or America, but to construct a society grounded in the message. Unlike other denominations the Restoration seeks converted and transformed lives which will be fulfilled within an essentially Mormon society. Other groups wish to convert people who will then live their own distinctive form of ethics but within ordinary social worlds.

In sociological terms Mormonism, even in this early period of its history, is not a conversionist type of sect. It is not a sin-ridden heart within each individual which needs cleansing through the substitutionary atonement of Christ. It is the entire social framework of life which demands transformation. The need for repentance and faith, for forgiveness and grace does have a part within Mormon spirituality as we will see later, but it is not the centre of Mormon theology.[11] The Restoration movement is concerned fundamentally with a new and divinely sanctioned social order. So when Saints in America come under pressure from the secular authorities because of the polygamy issue and matters of Mormon political power it was natural that British Saints would respond sympathetically. Any attack on one part of the Mormon world is, inevitably, an attack upon the entire community.

In 1858 the *Star* editor underlined the difficulties of the American membership, and he also noted the fact that the British Saints felt out of touch with America since 'nearly all communication has been suspended between us and the Presidency in Zion'. During that year there was considerable reorganization of the Welsh branches. The Brecknockshire Conference was dissolved with its remaining members added to the Monmouthshire Conference; Duffryn Conway and Anglesey constituted the Carnarvonshire Conference to which was also added the branches of Harlech and Ffestiniog. The Cardigan Conference was extended by the addition of Machynlleth, Dinas Mawddy, Brechfa, Pencader, and Llansawel branches. The Carmarthen Conference was also 'disorganized', a technical term for a bureaucratic change in structure rather than the usual sense of a state of chaos. So Carmarthen and St. Clears branches were added to that of Llanelli, (1858:27).

As all this change took place there was an increase in concern over the utilization of organizational and administrative talent amongst the members. Many of the structural changes in the church were due to personal factors, to the migration or death of elders and to the increased level of membership in new areas. The ease with which changes now occurred is testimony to Mormonism's capacity for adaptation to changing circumstances. Indeed we might regard this adaptability as a distinctive feature of Mormon organization and of the efficient way in which manpower and plant were used. Unlike Welsh Nonconformity with its particular attachment of members to their specific chapel with its family and regional loyalties and favour towards individual ministers, Mormonism kept interest from stagnating and forbad preoccupation with purely local issues. Unlike Anglicanism and Roman Catholicism the Mormons were oriented to the newness rather than to the traditional nature of religious truth. For the concept of Restoration presented what it reckoned to be traditional doctrine in a new and freshly discovered manner.

Since the prophetic restoration of truth lay at the heart of the new movement ordinary members were called to speed the passage of that divine communication. The mass of activity of 1858 sought order and efficiency in so doing. 'We now look for administrative ability, economy, productiveness, and internal growth', the call was for 'efficient administrators', (1858:378). The priesthood was described as possessing a double character. Its 'abstract and primitive' element covered the notions of authority and perfection which, to the readers of the day, implied more recognizable religious functions, while its 'governmental and progressive' element dealt with ways in which the abstract message could be implemented, (1858:617). Benjamin Evans writes from Swansea so that the missionaries who had served there might know his members had been convinced of the 'indispensable duty to be always practical in business and accounts'. This strengthening of institutional bureaucracy seems to have marked a novel dimension in Wales, though church leaders also remind people that they also 'set a high value on religious fervour'. There is little doubt that the interweaving of emotional religiosity and organizational efficiency required a degree of sustained pressure on the part of the leadership before it was widely and deeply accepted in Wales.

Popular Definitions of Religion

This raises the question of defining religion itself. Not in the specifically academic sense, but at the popular level of religiosity where Mormons afford an interesting case. This particular issue is often overlooked in the study of religion even when scholars are caught up in the analysis of how the great traditions of religions relate to popular religiosity.[12] The point is this. The Restoration movement demands an alteration in the very framework of understanding Christian religion. The radical nature of this shift makes conversion to the Latter Day movement unlike a conversion from one form of Christianity to another within the traditional streams of denominations and churches. Baptist to Methodist to Anglican to Catholic, to Presbyterian, to Salvationist, to Quaker; these moves represent changes within groups bearing strong family resemblance to each other. The emergent Mormon religion, or the Restored Gospel as the believer would call it, possessed doctrines and practices lying beyond the customary bounds of broad Christendom.

If it is possible to generalize we might suppose that the average man and woman in Wales in the 1850s could well understand a religion involving doctrines of God and of His dispensational activity amongst an elect people within a stream of history and with a millennial goal. Religious enthusiasm, experience, and piety also comprised the grammar of faith, even to those outside the faith-community of the chapel or church. In asking converts to orientate their lives to America, and to commit themselves to a deeply pragmatic and even utilitarian outlook towards their religion, Mormonism was demanding a new dimension within an enthusiastic form of religiosity, despite the possible precedents of eighteenth century emigrant Welsh Dissenters discussed in chapter six. In terms of folk-definition or indigenous classification of religion something of a revolution was taking place. Something of a similar revolution would occur nearly a century later when the first Mormon temple was built in Britain. A reorientation of life was being called for which did not mean that a person now attended a different place of worship on Sunday and lived a more rigorous ethical life, they certainly did that, but in addition there was to be a transformation of world-view which demanded a relocating of intellectual stance which few could have grasped in its fullness at the outset. The *Millennial Star* editors were conducting a major operation of re-education. It was a restored truth and not simply another new church which they preached, and this Restoration would itself engender a new culture and civilization. The whole language of discourse employed is one of development and progress grounded in corporate action and focussed on the priesthood. Its unified character would be guaranteed as all members came to speak English and grew into an appreciation of the consequences of priesthood which the English based revelations to Joseph Smith had disclosed.

Priesthood

The concept of priesthood in Mormon thought is distinctive as far as Christianity is concerned and will repeatedly emerge in subsequent pages in connection with a variety of Mormon activities. An 1858 entry deals with it under two perspectives which are informative both as to the doctrine itself and to the way in which it was presented to new members. This double character embraces on the one hand the 'abstract principle of authority and perfection', and on the other its 'governmental and progressive' nature. Church officers were unlike any minister or priest a convert might have known in their former church life prior to Mormon membership. These elders bore the power of the eternal priesthood which afforded the link between time and eternity, between the proximate and ultimate aspects of reality. Priesthood doctrines personify abstract notions in the sense that theological ideals come to be expressed in and through actual individuals. One consequence of this was that it became less easy to see truth in non-Mormon movements, though it must be said that the Mormon ideology as a total explanation of life did account for other religious movements and events. The Protestant Reformation, for example, was likened to John the Baptist and, just as he heralded the Christ, so the Reformation prepared the way for 'the dispensation of the fulness of times', (1859:36). This is a good example of Mormon hermeneutics.[13] Its method follows its intrinsic view of reality and is none other than a model of progressive development. It neither negates, condemns, nor attempts to destroy variant or opposing views. Instead it identifies those alternative perspectives as being partially true in their time and place. But now that the Restoration message is known they can be fulfilled and their partial truth developed away from its adhering error.[14]

The practical and perhaps psychological importance of this scheme of transcending development is that converts did not need to totally reject their prior beliefs. They were called to a developed extension of them in new directions. The fact that such a new path often went on to involve a radical revaluation of ideas and an investing of them with new significance may not have been totally clear to converts at the outset. Yet it became part of their new found life in Mormon fellowship. Even today converts speak of the change inherent in their intellectual and emotional growth as Mormons with their prior religious knowledge undergoing a moulding transformation.

The decade of the 1850s ended with a further emphasis on the need to emigrate and gather as one form of progressive development. The individual Saint should become a repository of 'mental culture, self-improvement, and the necessity of acquiring useful information', (1859:28). Whilst advocating these idealisms the *Millennial Star* also reported failures among members. Even a former president of the Edinburgh Conference, William Jarvis, had been excommunicated for adultery, (1859:206). Failure and moral lapses among members were not confused with failure of the Mormon system of religion, and precisely because the system was morally pure and intrinsically true, given its divine and recent origination, it was vital that poor performance among members be pointed out as a lesson to others and as a means of upholding the ideal path in life. Finally we should bear in mind that the *Star* was not a completely serious journal. As befitted a family magazine it printed jokes and stories. One such may fittingly end this chapter and the decade of the 1850s, it was the case of the reverend divine, and therefore a non-Mormon, who was not noted for his partiality to the fair sex and who cited part of the first verse of the Apocalypse chapter twelve, and cited it selectively and with special stress: 'and there appeared in heaven a great wonder, a Woman'.

Chapter Three

Tithes, Sects, and Prophecy: 1860-1869

In the last report from Wales for 1859 we are told that at Merthyr Tydfil much effort had recently been put into revitalizing church members, in fact no work at all had been done in connection with "the world". Backsliders were returning to the fold and the wish to emigrate seemed to be growing, especially among "small farmers and shopkeepers". A similar picture of pastoral concern with lapsed members comes from Benjamin Evans at Swansea where public preaching had been kept up and where he now sought to hold meetings in the homes of hitherto inactive Saints as the new decade began.

The theme of emigration becomes rapidly more insistent and is closely linked to the poverty of those wanting to leave Britain as is explicitly mentioned for Saints at the Cheltenham end of the Cardiff district as well as in Llanelli and Swansea. Writing from Tredegar in January 1861 elders Lyman and Rich tell of a visit to the Crawshay Iron Works in Merthyr where they saw women carrying out heavy manual labour fit only for men. Thomas Jeremy, now the Welsh President, also reports from Carmarthen touching the relative poverty of members, though he is glad to have got the *Carmarthen Weekly Reporter*, a secular newspaper, to publish some of the revelations of Joseph Smith: (thought to deal with the American Civil War and in particular the rebellion of South Carolina. The war was indirectly seen as contributing to Welsh poverty because of a reduction in trade). Cardiff is said to be furnishing large crowds listening to the preaching. At Swansea the Market Square is freely allowed as a meeting place while Thomas W. Rees, who now replaces John Davies as leader of Merthyr Saints, writes of large congregations gathering to hear the word. At Cardiff an Anti-Mormon Society is active while the Anglican parson at Lampeter is doing all he can to prevent people hearing the elders speak (1861:653). The contrasts between actual life in Wales and the anticipated future in Utah's Zion were not only drawn in a religious way, for secular notions of freedom and captivity were also utilized as a means of evaluating hope and experience. Amos Lyman could write in February 1862 of Aberdare Saints as having an "increasing anxiety to be free from their enthralment to join the gathered Saints in Zion".

Between July 1860 and June 1862 some three hundred and nine Mormons had emigrated from Wales, this compares well with the two hundred and fifty one Scots, though the Irish furnished only nineteen, while English numbers reached two thousand six hundred and twelve.

1863 continued in a similar vein with two hundred and ten having departed by July. There was a general increase in tithing and in paying into the Individual Emigration Fund, for since 1856 the famous Perpetual

Emigration Fund had been suspended. The stress on personal effort by church members was now high and explicit mention is made of the fact that preaching is not used to stir-up over optimistic expectations. Even when gifts of healing occur in various parts of Wales they are not interpreted apocalyptically.

Editorials in 1864 warn leaders to "studiously avoid using persuasion to induce any of the people to emigrate" lest they go under pressure and be subsequently dissatisfied (1864:58). By now there are one thousand eight hundred and twenty eight Saints in Wales spread throughout nine conferences. During this year two hundred and sixty four were baptized and one hundred and fifty one emigrated. Most members are said to be miners and the emigration of many such was even reported as affecting the mining industry through loss of labour, at least it drew attention to the fact of emigration as a Mormon event. If spiritual sincerity rather than a mere profit motive was to be sought in emigration the same was also true in the cognate Mormon practice of Tithing.

Tithing

This particular form of church activity lay open to several kinds of interpretation precisely because of its centrality as an indicator of commitment to the movement. At its best tithing showed an open-hearted thankfulness to God for the restored gospel message: at its worst it was, ironically, a mechanical means of selfish gain. Mormon teaching was itself in a potential dilemma here, for it argued that if individuals did pay tithes then God would bless them both spiritually and materially. A priesthood meeting in Cardiff in 1864 yielded a unanimous agreement that when tithes were paid and duties done "they were blessed and lost nothing by doing so". Not only so but "means would come into their hands in a manner that proved to them that God was blessing them". The authorities noted the idea of reciprocity behind this widespread theory of balance and could instruct members "not to do it in order to get rich, because their motives would then be selfish". A similar statement from the Flintshire Conference held at Abergele in May tells of a flourishing condition of prosperity "which, no doubt" is caused by their liberal tithing. The practical and materialistic ideology of Mormonism could cope with the notion of a divine reciprocity between giving to and receiving from God, but at the same time appreciated that many members probably held an immature Mormon conception of this exchange, and might seek to manipulate wealth by this intrinsically sound means. This issue is mentioned as early as 1853 in the *Star* and is still dealt with in church circles to the present day, (1953:437, 1854:767). Its continued appeal is grounded in the pragmatic expression of commitment to the movement. To pay a tithe is an unquestionable mark of seriousness, it becomes part of the identity of the Saint in good standing with the official leadership and does this simply because the domestic economy of a household has to be organized in a way that takes account of the church commitment. So one more aspect of life, namely family expenditure, is brought into direct relation with the entire Mormon institution. We shall see a further aspect of this much later when discussing the role of the temple in L.D.S. life, for being a tithe-payer is one precondition for gaining access to temple rites.

Mormon leaders not only had the task of trying to teach a novel pattern of religion to a largely Christian population, but occasionally came up against the somewhat more awkward problem of handling schismatics of a Mormon conviction. In 1864 "Strangites" are mentioned as having made an appearance in Britain from America. These followers of James Strang represent an early disagreement in Mormon affairs and seem to have had limited success in gathering some L.D.S. excommunicates into their membership. Strang led his dissident faction to Michigan where, on Beaver Island of Lake Superior, he established a colony having been crowned "King in Zion". He was shot in 1856. Despite initial headway in Britain the church died out as it also did in Michigan shortly after Strang's death (O'Dea 1957:70). Just two years later in August 1866 elder Wride writes from Tredegar about "apostates" called "Josephites" who were also making some headway there amongst excommunicated people. This persuasion disapproves of Brigham Young and the revelation on plural marriage and came to be called the Reorganized Church of Jesus Christ of Latter Day Saints having a lineal descendant of Joseph Smith as a prophet in continual reception of divine revelations.

Although we consider this and other Restoration groups more fully in chapter twenty we will rapidly sketch this one group here since mention of it will occur several times in intervening chapters. The Reorganized Church, which gained its name from those who gathered round the dead prophet's son and who have maintained a leadership consisting of descendants of Joseph Smith ever since, was brought to Britain in the person of one Charles Derry. In 1863 a Conference was held at Penydaren near Merthyr Tydfil and the following year at Llanelli. A branch was organized at Birmingham in 1864 with some seventeen members. The following year a fund was set up to assist emigration, while in 1866 a conference was held at Merthyr. In the same year this movement began publication of a journal called the *Restorer* which continued until April 1870.[15] Some emigrations took place in 1869 but this was no major element in the rather small numbered church of the Reorganization. In 1872 one J. T. Davies was appointed President for Wales and reports a fair amount of mission endeavour and some conflict with "Brighamite" opposition, as the Utah Mormons were called. In 1873 Davies tells of baptizing two elders, one deacon and a woman who had been "Utah" Mormons living in Aberaman. Davies left Wales later in the same year, being asked to retain the presidency until his return. The President of the English Mission, M. H. Forscutt, ventured into Wales, preaching at New Tredegar, before returning to America in 1873. In October of this same year the European Conference of the Church was held at Aberaman.

The one continuing area of success in Wales lay in branches at Penllergaer and Skewen near Swansea which have continued as marginally surviving groups to the present day.

One fairly repetitive feature of the *Star* and therefore of its readership's awareness, is controversy. The 1865 edition carried the testimony of Oliver Cowdery to the fact that he had himself written down the text of the Book of Mormon "as it fell from the lips of the Prophet", (1865:58). Sidney Rigdon had not written it, nor yet did Mr Spalding; this latter-mentioned clergyman had, according to widespread belief, composed a fantasy depicting pre-Christian life in the New World, a manuscript which had provided the basis for the *Book of Mormon*, or at least this is what was said by accusers of the L.D.S. Church.[16] They also made the charge that Cowdery had defected from the church, thereby calling its claims into question. This charge is plainly rejected by the *Star*, for while it admits that Cowdery had once left, it argues that he was finally received back and died in full confession of the Restoration's truthfulness. As we will see in a later consideration of apologetic and of anti-Mormon literature in the nineteenth century, the church thrived on abusive attacks, claims and counterclaims. Its leaders could take nothing for granted as common ground shared with opponents. Even belief in God was dubious because of the concept of God they held. The strength of nineteenth century Mormonism amidst this debate lay in the actual action of emigration and state-building in America. People, especially the large number of relatively uneducated folk involved in its mission, might be confused by abstruse debate, but the key message of restoration in preparation for a millennial advent was clear, precisely because it was enshrined in the practical endeavour of migration and construction of a place where the Messiah would appear.

Whilst the opposition of the world might become fierce or at least extremely bitter its days were numbered. "Know ye not, ye great, proud ones of the earth, that governments as they now exist, must yield to the fate of annihilation? A theocracy has been decreed and will surely transpire", (1865:358). The future offered to the many poor people adhering to L.D.S. tenets was deeply shot through with political themes of power. It was not only spiritual longings which Christ would satisfy. America was already a name speaking of economic promise and opportunity for personal betterment, the L.D.S. message magnified this, while British social conditions underlined the need to be elsewhere.

Some Merthyr Saints had been struck again by cholera in 1867, as were some in North Wales, this made for an increased hope of emigration among their fellows. By March 1867, two hundred and seventy seven had emigrated from the Welsh District over the preceding twelve months. Many were so poor that even emigration was not a viable option, reports John Parry from Merthyr in August 1867. He was the new successor to Abel Evans who had died on 30th November 1866 of consumption. Even so of the one hundred and thirty to one hundred and fifty thousand people in

Utah, some eight to ten thousand of them were claimed to be Welsh Saints by 1867. This kind of statistic was quite impressive and yet another sign of the coming of Christ. Readers were told that the day of His advent was very near at hand. Just what this meant for those unable to emigrate we cannot say. Nephi Pratt writes from Merthyr just before Christmas 1867 telling that many, indeed most, local members are of long standing. Their membership of fifteen to twenty years in the church has borne witness to their trust in the Lord despite their lack of even the commonest comforts let alone the ability to emigrate. Some children are destitute, without clothes or shoes. A glimpse of the attitude engendered by this tension between the call to Zion and the impossibility to comply is presented in Barry Wride's report of the gifts of tongues, prophecy and interpretation at Merthyr in January 1868. So too, just three weeks before, John Parry notes that Aberdare Saints have the gift of prophecy, to the extent that one sister produced a portion of the *Millennial Star* Editorial word for word, presumably before it was published. Its message being the longing for an elder to baptize converts in a forthcoming period when such a blessing will be unavailable. It would be wrong to draw a complete correlation between ecstatic phenomena and periods of marked deprivation or external aggressive hostility, but there is a link between them in the *Star* reports.

Prophecy

What is intrinsically telling is the reference to this "spirit of Prophecy". For prophecy was central to the Restoration in the person of Joseph Smith and later in his successors to office as prophet, seer and revelator of the church. Rapidly during Joseph's lifetime the ability to receive prophetic messages from God was restricted to the Prophet himself. In this sense there was a routinization of charisma, as the sociologist Max Weber expressed the process by which supernatural power was constricted and channelled in institutions, (M. Weber, 1968). But, and it is an important qualification for Mormonism of the Utah type, the individual member was believed to have open access to God and might claim revelation of a kind which pertained to the office and calling of that single individual. Here the assent to divine communication as a dynamic ideal of Mormon life was qualified and complemented by a constraint resulting from the duties given by church authorities. Revelation for one's own inspiration and direction was possible, but not to cover any other member's office in the church. This avoided conflicting revelations on church matters.

The contents of the Aberdare and Merthyr prophecies were exhortatory rather than directive. In this they resemble the substance of glossolalic "translation" of other religious movements.[17] What is most instructive in the *Star* entries is, firstly, the statement that this prophecy came "while the Spirit of the Lord was mightily in the meeting" and secondly, that the message closely resembled the official editorial. In other words, the prophetic message demonstrates the unanimity of the various segments of the church and therefore demonstrates God's working throughout the full extent of it.

As this decade drew to a close there was a general sense of success in Wales expressed most clearly in the *Star* of 1869. In January and April Elias Morris writes from Wales about Merthyr and Llanelli Saints. Many have received hopeful letters from friends and relatives who have already emigrated. Not only so, but many non-Mormons have had flattering accounts of Utah sent to them from emigrated neighbours. Interest in the church is running high and Gentiles attend some services and various celebrations and Mormon parties over Christmas. By July Elias Morris is writing from the 15th Ward or area of Salt Lake City informing Welsh readers that Mary Humphreys of Cwmbach had died at Cheyenne City. Here Welsh geography and American counterparts combine to give a picture of realistic emigration. Morris had led a party to America earlier in the year. Nephi Pratt commented in June on the way that particular departure had made a hole in the Mormon ranks. Five branch presidents had been party to the journey and most members of some branches had been with them. Initially it looked as though some remaining groups might have to close, but in the event they survived. Never, says Pratt, had the Welsh Saints been in better heart. News from Utah is carefully scrutinized by Mormon and Gentile alike. Many accept L.D.S. tenets but under social pressure do not commit themselves to membership.

Members are themselves more deeply committed to the Word of Wisdom in alcohol avoidance and tithe paying. Savings schemes aimed at emigration are active and in general there is a sense of Mormonism as growing in respect amongst the population at large. The 1869 Conference records one thousand five hundred and ninety Saints remaining in Wales as active members. These and other British readers are provided with a poem or hymn on the Word of Wisdom.

> Amidst a world of speculation
> Men have sought to live by craft.
> And have made adulteration
> Of their merchandise the shaft.
>
> Nearly all we eat or drink is
> Sold for real tho' tis not.
> And is mixed with untold oddments
> Gain is seldom fairly got.
>
> Drugs and all unwholesome compounds
> Are employed which poison man.
> The weak and short lived generations
> Bespeak life dwindled to a span.
>
> Where is truth and where is wisdom
> To lead Saints right while such is done?
> The truly precious Word of Wisdom
> Shows what to eat, to drink, to shun.
>
> Forewarned of drinks both strong and hot
> Tobacco (snuffs) pernicious are
> Flesh meats in summer should scarce be eaten
> In famine times and winter spare.

Chapter Four

The Sacred Space of Temples: 1870-1879

The concept of time often varies between religious groups. Its precise nature is extremely informative in gaining an accurate sense of a movement's sense of duration. The great world religions have generated a patient outlook on processes which endure through millennia, whether or not their philosophical approach to time is more linear or cyclical. Even so there emerge sectarian groups from time to time which bring to these long-standing traditions a sense of urgency in mission and immediacy of the divine presence. To this intensity of purpose the devotees ascribe a sacred quality and a heightened awareness of supernatural involvement in current events perceived as wonders.

So it was with Mormonism. Though, as our unfolding description shows, the quality of perceived time at the outset is not maintained uniformly for the entirety of its history to date. We will have more to say on the issue of eschatology later, after the entire scheme has been plotted, but for the moment another process needs to be identified. No name exists for this, but perhaps this variation in perceived intensity of divine acts might be called the qualitative variability of religious response. The burden of this concept lies in the rapidity of alternation in the perception of events as religiously good or religiously bad. The reports presented in the *Star* hardly ever maintain a judgement of a fixed trend for long. From year to year the situation changes with the world appearing as civil and then as hostile, as cooperative and then as belligerent. This is perhaps to be understood as the inevitable outcome of a group living with the expectation of the end of the immediately present world. In Greek terms Mormonism was functioning not with a sense of chronological time but with an awareness of *kairos*, of that highly potent and auspicious period in which momentous events are to take place.[18]

Furthermore the *kairos* in Wales differed from that in America. In Utah preparations for the Lord's return anticipated positive eras of fulfilment, while in Wales as in the rest of Europe only judgement and wrath could be anticipated. Not that Utah was viewed from afar as devoid of difficulty; the political strife which actually was grounded in the growth of power in Mormon hands and which non-Mormon politicians feared, but which was expressed in terms of hostility to polygamy, this was given pride of place in the 1870 *Star*. The Cullom Bill, which enshrined this antagonism towards plural marriage and which nearly twenty years later in another form was to bring about submission of the church to the United States Government, was explicitly debated.

Nevertheless Utah's attractiveness remained high especially as social and economic conditions in Wales dropped yet further below the level of acceptability. In 1875 and even more so in 1878 the "fearful distress in South Wales" is much in the forefront of attention. Lack of bread and destitution are common descriptions of the situation, as in J. H. Parry's report from Ebbw Vale in August 1878. Even so a few still try to save a little money towards their emigration, and actual numbers of those emigrating are high throughout this decade. It appears that Welsh Saints in Utah were providing some money for the relief of Saints in Wales, and comment is made on the lack of support for English members by their emigrant countrymen (1878:155). That all assistance possible was needed is shown by the positive mention of the Anglican Rector of Merthyr Tydfil who had established a soup kitchen and was providing food for some five to six thousand children every day. Many are coming to Merthyr on foot across the mountains to seek help. Many young men are preparing to emigrate to Australia, a fact which places the concept of journeying to Utah in a shared and publically available category of possible response to hardship, (1878:60). Not only so but there is movement within the country itself as Samuel Leigh writes from Merthyr to explain that some branches have broken up simply because of this enforced mobility, whilst others are depleted to the point of non-viability through emigration, as in Swansea in 1870, where elder Horace Eldridge sees his work after the 1869 emigration as more like that of a teacher starting from nothing and having to go from house to house. This rapid turnover in staff or church personnel itself enhances the belief in the seriousness of times of change which now were upon the overall movement. Even relatively slight changes in local popular opinion are read as signs of the times and of an eternal significance. It seems that from one year to the next quite different attitudes prevail both in and outside the Welsh church. While in 1869 Nephi Pratt reports from Merthyr that foolish prejudice has given way to interest amongst the scores now attending meetings, the outlook a year later in Wales talks of "phlegmatic times of stolid indifference".

There is a particularity in evidence which makes small events into religious signs, as with the widow of former Anglican persuasion who is baptized and whose son is persecuted at work through a reduced wage as a result of his mother's conversion. But a significant theme rises in the middle of the decade and marks out Mormon ideology from the Gentile world-view, and perhaps more importantly from preceding Latter Day Saint thinking as publically portrayed in the *Millennial Star*. This concerns the theology of the temple which is associated with other doctrines, like that of the Mother God, in a complex and unique ideological configuration.

Temples

Although mention of the intended Salt Lake City temple is made in the *Star* of 1874 telling how a baptismal font is to be placed in its basement, it is the 1877 volume which stresses so emphatically the place of temples in Mormonism. It does so in the form of historical recapitulation such that a reader can set himself within a flow of events and feel personally involved in the life of the great leaders of the movement.

The chronology of temples began its modern phase on 6 June 1831 when the Melchizedek priesthood was given to Joseph Smith and was thereby restored to mankind. This qualitatively distinct form of priesthood increasingly came to employ temples as the sacred space within which it came to its own full expression. Temples and the remains of temples stood both as markers of the westward progress of the Mormon faith in all its purity and of the mounting opposition of Gentiles. Initially 2 August 1831 saw the dedication of a site for the Land of Zion in Jackson County Missouri, June 1833 produced a vision calling for a temple in Kirtland which was completed by 27 March 1836. On the occasion of Kirtland's dedication not only did people speak in tongues as visions of angels occurred but the Saviour himself was manifested in open vision to Joseph Smith and others. Again a cornerstone was laid in Far West in July 1837 but opposition hindered building.

The famous temple of Nauvoo had its cornerstone laid on 6 April 1841 and "with increased revelation" came to differ from its predecessors. It is worth pondering the symbolic significance of this Nauvoo temple for it itself was but short-lived even though the ideal it helped generate was finally established as perhaps the central tenet of the new religion. Baptism for the dead had been revealed and thus was the church now said to be fully organized in the sense that human personnel in the form of the Melchizedek priesthood were coupled with the function of vicarious baptism. This linkage will be explored later to demonstrate the internal logic of the Mormon cosmology. In the immediate Nauvoo setting of 1841 it necessitated a font for baptism. This was dedicated on 8 November 1841. Work on the complete temple continued despite growing secular hostility. A major exodus from Nauvoo in February 1845 heralded the next phase of community migration, but some Saints remained to complete the temple and saw its completion and dedication in April and May 1846. On 19 November 1848 it was burned to the ground.

To Mormon eyes that temple, shortlived as it was in an architectural sense, stood as an expression of the new faith with its belief in vicarious priestly work through which time and eternity were united.

The westward move continued until new ground was broken and consecrated for a temple site in Salt Lake City on 14 February 1853. It would be many years before that temple was completed as we shall see later, but the very process of its construction spoke of the expectant and progressive nature of the new faith. Temples were now beginning to supply a focus of Mormon creativity in a theological sense. In 1892 the *Star* contrasted Mormons and the first Christians in terms of temple building. Those Christians neither built temples nor gathered to live about them, and thus demonstrate a lack of perfection in organization and life, (1892:348). The Saints of the Restoration are more advanced, they interpret the laying of the cornerstone at the Nauvoo temple as a representation of the First Presidency of the Church, (1892:364). The prophet Joseph laid the stone and a basis for theological reflection is established. The First Presidency and not Peter the Apostle is the rock base for this new institution. But it is no mere arid bureaucracy. On the contrary, Brigham Young spoke in tongues at the consecration of the Kirtland temple and thus marks the dynamic power of the might of God in the Restoration, (1892:350). Temples are further interpreted as major forces in the decision of converts to emigrate and gather to Zion, (1884:361). Not only are they concrete manifestations of the idea of a fully restored gospel, but they are effective means of facilitating its expansion. Physical temples are the arena of ritual action for material bodies as they process to the eternal dimension. The sacredness of temples embraced human intelligence as much as the soul. In one sense it is said that the pursuit of intelligence is the worship of God to the extent that temples should possess libraries and lecture-rooms as part of their status as seats of learning, (1888:77).

The temples are pivotal institutions which unite apparently diverse strands of Mormon religion. Earthly concerns of family become eternal themes of corporate salvation, earth and heaven are united in the sacred space of temples. Once having assumed their role in Mormon thought they increasingly proliferated an apt imagery of the faith. Because of this there will be many occasions in the following pages when temple ideology will recur as the framework for describing and interpreting Mormon thought. In the nineteenth century scheme temples and emigration furnish transition points in the flow of Mormon spirituality. Emigration mobilizes people to shift spatially. Geographical mobility is the necessary first-step on which is built the threshold of the temple as the meeting place of time and eternity. Population growth in temple localities speeds up ritual performance and the consequent potential for salvation among the living and the dead. The fact of sacred space being localized in a temple and serving as a ritual zone assisted anthropomorphic perspectives.

Mormon theology fostered a spiritualizing of human behaviour and relationships rather than a metaphorical view of faith. The idea of a Mother God is linked to temples in such a way, for the growth of temple ritual increasingly idealized family relationships. Indeed it may even be that the idealization emerging from human analogy caused a degree of confusion in some quarters.

Two 1899 entries hint at this. One commends the Mormon hymn writer and poetess Eliza Snow whose well known hymn "O My Father" contained a reference to heavenly parents:

> "In the heavens are parents single?
> No the thought makes reason stare!
> Truth is reason, truth eternal
> Tells me I've a mother there".

In this hymn all other reference to "Father" seems to denote God, so the association of Father with Mother could naturally be viewed as investing the mother figure with the highest status. So the editor appears to suggest for, as he puts it, "before Theodore Parker preached his father and mother God a Mormon poetess had sung the above words", (1899:481). Parker had been a mid-nineteenth century New England Unitarian minister, an advocate of temperance and women's education. But the second entry is more explicit and yet potentially more confusing. It is an error to believe that the Trinity contains a woman; the Trinity is one of Father, Son and Spirit. But there is another institution or reality besides the Trinity and this is a kind of sacred eternal union in which the Father has a relationship beyond the Trinity with a mother figure. At least this is the way in which the Genesis creation reference is made to explain "God created man in his own image ... male and female created he them", (1899:550).

Normal reflection in Christian theology is so far removed from this view that many early converts must have found the Mormon discussion hard to follow.[19] It is quite intelligible once it is realized that Mormon ideas of the Trinity are quite unlike anything else in Christian history, but it took some time for a genuine appreciation of Mormon cosmology to get established. The Trinity in Mormon thought is not the only arena within which the Father functions. The "family relation" in which He is caught up with a "mother god" is a second and additional sphere of operation. The status of family is thus made very high indeed and does not pertain only to the human and earthly sphere of existence. Earthly longings are not projected into heavenly realms, nor are human moods anthropomorphised, but Mormon theology sees the "soul's instinctive sigh for a Divine Mother" as awaiting a real fulfilment when we ultimately "draw nearer to Divine Man and find the Divine Woman smiling upon us. In the Father's many mansions we shall find her and be satisfied", (1872:140).

Following from the maternal vision arose the obvious thought that children were a continuation of the eternal stream of life, flowing and increasing to occupy immensity. Like heavenly mothers, children were not restricted to mundane life, but intrinsically possessed a cosmic dimension. Mormon identity is broad and extensive beyond all normal apprehension. Conversion is no simple acceptance of one creed amongst others, but inevitably involves a profound reorientation of thought. Just how much of this esoteric doctrine was taught at the local level in Wales we have no means of assessing. The *Star* tended more to allusion than to detailed coverage. And in any case it seems that as temples grew in significance some such distinctive teachings were restricted to them as far as instruction was concerned.

Pragmatically the political situation in America and the plight of Saints in Wales took precedence over detailed doctrine of abstruse kinds. Merthyr reports for 1871 covered one thousand and three members in twenty four branches; eighteen baptized, six dead and fifty five emigrated.

Federal opposition to American Mormonism took the usual repercussion of a rallying round the standard in Wales and a continued pressure for emigration. In June 1872 elder John Lewis succeeded David John at Merthyr as the former president prepared to emigrate. The *Star* statistics on the growth of Utah's population thus ever exemplifying the ideal in actual lives:

1850	—	11,380	3rd among the territories
1860	—	40,273	3rd among the territories
1870	—	86,786	2nd among the territories
1872	—	106,000	1st among the territories

Through 1873 and 1874 many references to emigration give a sense of a dynamic church. Branches are encouraged to prune dead members to encourage in turn those keen to fulfil their duty and move to Zion. A constant feature of reporting publishes good and bad news together. L. J. Herrick and others are ready to leave Merthyr for Liverpool and thence the U.S.A. but at the same time the death of a Merthyr man, Richard A. Thomas, in Salt Lake City, is announced: and he but 25 years old, (1873:720). Towards the close of 1874 a district meeting records eighty emigrants from that Welsh area of a total of about six hundred and seventy Saints. Some sixty further members had been baptized between January and December of that year. The social context with many rumours of further strikes was as unsure as the Utah setting. From its outset the Mormon religion was fringed with hardship, political, social and economic. Religious opposition complemented this to yield a state which could not fairly be identified as peaceful. An active, dynamic and future oriented optimism was a more obvious feature of the faith. This is one clear reason why the Old Testament spoke very directly to Mormons and was read as a description of their own life context. As God's nineteenth century people they relived and echoed the paths trodden by the covenant people of the old dispensation.

The following year of 1875 continued as a hard time with hunger and privation striking workers in Merthyr. Even so most Mormons are said to be in jobs. Out of door preaching continues and extends to West Wales. Thomas C. Martell writes from Kidwelly in November and informs readers of his work in Llandyssil, Newcastle Emlyn and Llanybyther. Most of the Saints there have already gone to America, so his work is a new one once more. William J. Lewis writes from 24 Mary Street, Merthyr in July marking the return of brother Daniel Jones from visiting friends in Cardiff. Such an innocuous entry is important in showing the links of friendship and religion flowing across the area and extending to America.

The Mormon religion of this period was nothing if not a network of faith, a brotherhood of actual contacts which turned ideal notions of a divine kingdom into a limited but actual reality. With the last few years of this decade we see more clearly than ever that feature of Mormonism expressed in self-conscious self-analysis. From its birth the movement was certain of its distinctiveness and with time became increasingly aware of its unique place as a Restoration movement. Unhappy with the designation of "sect", they preferred the grander title of "religious empire founders", with Brigham Young as one in the character of a "Modern Moses", and a "fulfiller of the prophet". Continuity of authority is complemented by novelty. Although committed to the historical past Mormonism was actively looking to future fulfilment, not only in a millennial kingdom under Christ's rule, but also in more immediate moments of human endeavour. Mormonism's cosmology aligned, and continues to associate, great and little things. Its avowed materialist ideology can glory in the hope that the "almighty will so order events that the great Temple in the centre Stake of Zion in Jackson County Missouri shall stand in its glory and receive its King", but can also descend to the particular and include a dedicatory prayer to bless the putty in the building of the St. George Temple: "that no unclean thing be permitted to enter". This was at the Southern Utah site of St. George on 9 November 1871. Temples had vital ritual power to give the Saints but the *Star* also sees in them a prospective significance. Temples are signs of the gathered community. At least that is their value to the Saints in Babylon, telling them they must gather, (1877:120).

It is quite likely that temples functioned one way for those still to emigrate and in quite another for those having gathered to Zion. Part of the power of the temple as a theological idea lies in this early variation of the meaning held for people. Temples served as "root metaphors" for Mormons and continue to do so.[20] They were at once concrete locations and abstract ideals, and as such reflected that fact of Mormon life best expressed as a pilgrim journey. They stood as outposts of a supernatural world amidst a geographical reality, but because they were arenas of ritual action performed by Melchizedek priests they also marked the peculiar identity of Mormonism as a quite distinctive movement. Increasingly temples afforded the distinctive feature of this church amongst all other churches and did so because of a two dimensional thrust. On the one hand they claimed a link with the Old Testament people of God and the various tabernacles and the Jerusalem temple of the bible, and on the other they looked towards a new Jerusalem in a future kingdom of God. The present ritual performed in them thus gained a certain authenticity from perceived links with the Old Testament, whilst actively working towards the salvation of human lives in the kingdom yet to come. Temples provided a pragmatic source of self-identity transcending that available in many other religious groups. Architecturally they matched the conceptual separateness of the idea of restoration in the sense that this new movement focussed upon a novel building.

But the benefit of a fixed sacred space was only a generalized ideal for Welsh Saints in the 1870s. Temples served as a symbolic expression of Utah as a geographical zone. Though it would be fair to say that geographical and religious ideas fruitfully interlinked in the concept of Zion. Whether spatial or spiritual the Zion appeal was in marked contrast to Mormon life in the Merthyr of, for example, 1877. Depression in the iron trade compelled many men to move away in search of work and this, as Samuel Leigh reported at the time, caused many lively branches to be broken up. Of the six hundred and thirty four members in Wales, thirty emigrated by July of that year. In August Brigham Young died.

Young had been to Britain in 1840 and had been a major influence in establishing the *Millennial Star* as the major organ for Mormon communication in this country. His death did not significantly influence the British Church. For some three years the Twelve Apostles assumed their role as temporary leaders and in October 1880 its president, John Taylor, was chosen as president of the church, this office he held until his death in 1887. Taylor was English, born in Westmoreland in 1808. His family had emigrated and he followed them to Toronto in 1829 and there he met Parley Pratt through whom he was converted. He had been sent on a Mission to Britain in 1840 and took the Restoration message to Ireland, Scotland and the Isle of Man. He was known in Wales and even once wrote an article on Mesmerism from Merthyr Tydfil (15 February 1847). His influence in Wales was small because of the more extensive work of Dan Jones. But at least the new prophet was one more firm link between Utah and Britain, the personal nature of Zion being increasingly accentuated.

The message of a restored gospel and the insistent call to gather to Zion in Utah did not come to a neutral world. The year 1878 may, for example, have been excessively trying, but like many others it saw Welsh Saints in a state of great distress which the *Star* described in some detail. Looking back to 1877 the Saints could triumph in the fact that of some five hundred and eighty three Welsh members, eighty eight had emigrated. Here was a small but dynamic church where the message yielded results practically visible in emigrants. But the dynamism is also evident in the twenty one excommunicated members, whilst the twelve dead Saints proved that miracles could not be summoned to protect Saints in any millennially magical way.

Leaders in Wales continued to travel in the knowledge that fixed bases in Babylon were undesirable. At Merthyr the "Conference House" was sold in 1878 as premises used infrequently and deemed a luxury. From Utah clear messages proclaimed Babylon to be doomed: "Come out of her, O my people that ye partake not of her sins and receive not of her plagues", (1878:176). Meanwhile Welsh Saints in Utah were trying hard to assist the emigration of others still in Wales. At the Welsh Conference held in a Baptist Chapel in Swansea on 10 March 1878 elder T. F. Howells from Utah reminded members of their duty to emigrate and set a very positive mark on Mormonism since its gospel benefits man "socially, morally, temporally and religiously, here as well as hereafter". It was this pragmatic optimism which had Utah as a goal that afforded an attractive curiosity among outsiders.

But it was the intrinsic non-sectarian ethos of the religion in Wales which made it possible for those interested to attend meetings to discover more.

It should not seem odd that a movement which at first glance should be deemed sectarian can also be open to non-members. The attribute of exclusivism so often used as a partial characterization of the sect needs careful evaluation. In nineteenth century Mormonism in Europe the local meetings were nearly always public, the exclusive feature lay in the demand for emigration. Local inclusivism was transformed into the exclusivism of commitment to emigrate. In Utah other criteria applied.

Even so there was charity shown to those Saints who did not, or had not yet migrated. The non-migrating nineteenth century Mormon is not totally unlike the non tongue-speaking Pentecostal in the twentieth century, in that ordinary duties well performed assure status even if other acclaimed acts are missing. So it is that the death through pleurisy of Edmund Harmon at Merthyr on 11 April 1878 aged 50 was proudly noted. He had been an elder well regarded and energetic. William Morgan, another elder from Blaen Garth, Merthyr, died on 20 March in the dramatically beautiful area of Spanish Fork in Utah. Morgan had been born in Brecon in 1788, baptized in Dowlais 1840 and emigrated in 1853. Not only was he an old man in the church but his father Morgan Morgan had lived to be 103. In 1878 yet another Merthyr member, Sarah Jane Anderson, died of fever in Utah. All this is reported, the good news and the bad, giving the impression of a realistic enthusiasm. Saints die in Merthyr and in Spanish Fork, Zion does not confer immortality, but it does afford joy in preparing for the day when the millennial kingdom will be established

The close integration of ideal and practical issues was ever to be a characteristic feature of Mormon life. Women were told of the high temperatures awaiting them in Utah in the summer months and of the necessity of dress which, when saturated with sweat, did not display the minutest detail of their bodies, (1878:534). So too over the emigration of those who scratched together enough to leave Wales, for with every departure there was an alteration within the resources of the church. Wales was weakened both financially and in the number of committed members while Utah was strengthened.

By and large Mormon endeavour had been concentrated in South Wales and especially its industrial areas. The North was seen as offering bitter and persistent opposition because of the deep rooted religiosity there. W. N. Williams reports from Holywell in September 1878 in a way which balances this inherent prejudice with the fact that meetings have still been held with quiet and attentive congregations. But by the close of this year by far the largest grouping of Mormons was in the valleys area of South Wales, many in the Rhondda Valley itself. Wales boasted sixteen branches with five hundred and sixty five members. But around the active Mormons lay an interested circle of "outsiders" many of whom apparently subscribed to the *Star* according to J. G. Jones at Merthyr, (August 1879).

The end of 1879 saw the resumption of work at the Cyfartha works under the management of the late "Iron King", Richard Crawshay's sons. Work was, however, paid for at a reduced and compromised level so that branches of the church were not flooded in any sense with new cash. It is interesting to observe how Mormons are said to be poor, but that by comparison with their Gentile neighbours are relatively well off.

An insight into the situation comes in the report of the 1879 Welsh Conference held at the Welsh Harp in Pontypridd and at which Orson Pratt was present. Looking back on the preceding year it recorded four hundred and eighty two members, eighty baptisms and one hundred and thirteen emigrants. For the same period the number of emigrants from other British areas was: London one hundred and seventy seven, Nottingham seventy one, Glasgow one hundred and thirty one, Leeds fifty one, Manchester seventy six, Birmingham seventy nine, Liverpool forty five, Bristol fourteen and Norwich thirty four.

On the statistics a distinction is made between those initiated into actual offices of the church, as with deacons, teachers, priests and elders and the broader body of members who were baptized. This latter group includes the women, and numbers about three hundred and twenty in relation to the roughly one hundred and fifty church office holders. Very approximately, then, there were two general members to every one office holder. Since gender is not recorded it is only speculation to suggest that men and women existed in the ratio of 1:2. At least as far as *Star* figures go.

For this same year in Wales £155 had been tithed, with over two hundred and ten people paying more than fourteen shillings. One person had given £30 whilst the lowest tithe was three pence. From the tithe income of £155, £107 went to pay for the renting of meeting places while £48 was given to the Liverpool office and headquarters. Here was a rapid turnover economy which did not employ itself in local investment. The whole timescale of the movement was geared to millennial ideals and investment ideals were not especially appropriate at the periphery of the movement.

In addition to baptized members a further three hundred people, identified as strangers, had been in attendance. This number means that in very general terms the Mormon religious gathering was likely to possess a profile in which for every office holder there were two other baptized members and a further two unbaptized but presumably interested parties. This speaks of an unusual breadth for what is easily called a sectarian movement. Openness to the general public was, inevitably, a great necessity or else converts would not have been made. But the accessibility of Mormonism lay in the gathering for worship and instruction as well as in the public programme of evangelism. No distinction between member and non-member was made at the level of religious gathering. This was possible because of the call to America and since exclusivism lay more in that direction than in group membership at the peripheries of the church.

Outsiders might go elsewhere, too, and the Saints were happy that they should be kept where the Mormon message was most likely to be influential. Among other options reported in 1879 was that of the Salvation Army whose presence in Cardiff and message of "Come to Jesus" was apparently being very successful. It was thought odd that so many women were in evidence in preaching the Army call to repentance, and what is of interest is the suggestion that in some towns nearly all inhabitants had been converted while, William Williams continues, some converts had engaged in devotion to such an extent that they had prayed themselves to death (April 1879).

Chapter Five

Anti-Mormonism in America and Wales: 1880-1889

This case of the Salvation Army will be reflected again some twenty or so years later when the Welsh revival brought with it dramatic examples of intense religiosity. What it shows so clearly is the Mormon acknowledgement of religious enthusiasm along with its general disapproval of such emotional excess. It is especially easy to presume that a millennial movement like Mormonism must have exhibited dramatic sectarian behaviour, yet that would be a misapprehension even though very occasional and sporadic outbursts of unusual phenomena did take place. In Nottingham Charles W. Stayner tells of one brother Newbold who spoke in tongues in September 1880. Interpreted as being, "the pure Lamanite language", it was accompanied by one sister in the congregation seeing a bright light over the platform where the tongue speaker stood. Stayner adds the note that it had been two years since any glossolalia had been heard at Nottingham.

Most Mormon gatherings were more this-worldly and pragmatic in outlook. Supernatural incursions served the purpose of validating Mormon theology and especially in stamping with approval the work in America along with emigration endeavours. Mormon spirituality is primarily pragmatic, but because it is also in part biblical it did not ignore the potential of the isolated miraculous event. God was thought to use moments like those of tongues or lights to support his chosen people. Sometimes it was misfortune in an opponent that gave rise to supernatural interpretation as when David Morgan wrote from Llantrisant of a man who reviled the Saints for their doctrine of marriage and took his revenge on a Mormon pamphlet at which moment he fell to the ground with a gurgling noise and duly expired and died, (March 1880).

But death also came to Mormons who had emigrated to Utah as we have already seen. John D. Rees from Merthyr had emigrated in 1852 and died aged 65 on 19 March 1880. So too with one Sarah Lewis. To note their decease alongside statistics of emigration is to show how Mormons had to be realistic over eschatological doctrine.[21] The ideal of an American Zion was only attained in a geographical sense by hardship, and once gained was itself a physical and this-worldly venture in which pain and death still had their part. The American Saint community was certainly an eschatological community, one which saw itself as intermediary between the purely secular world and the anticipated rule of Christ. It was an eschatological group experiencing the dynamic creativity of social growth. As a self-confessed Restoration movement it also was quite aware of a future open to divine intervention.

The church society as a theocracy was an earthly institution preparing for the millennial rule of Christ. The 1880 *Star* is quite clear on this. The community of Saints prepares itself to be the bride of Christ, and when the bride is ready the heavenly bridegroom would appear. And in 1880 this event and this appearance was deemed to be near at hand. The consequences of preparation were not only evident in Utah, for the *Star* considered the Mormon construction in the Western hemisphere to be matched by a renewal of the actual Jerusalem of the holy land. The Restoration message to the American frontier was the light to lighten the Gentiles and anticipated Jewish renewal. The Jewish link was further accentuated in the Mormon support for the theory of the lost tribes of Israel. When the Lord deemed it right the ten lost tribes would in fact be found again. The language used of these lost old world tribes echoes that used for Mormon emigration. These tribes were to be "inspired with the gathering spirit and will commence their journey from their present location to the lands of their fathers", (1880:443). To parallel the gathering of Mormons to the American Zion and that of Jews to the Zion of Jerusalem was to further validate the self-image of the Saints as a chosen people; it was also to find a place for the historical chosen race within Mormonism's recently constructed theology and society. This anticipated blessing of both Mormons and Jews contrasts with the death and judgement foretold for the wicked and ungodly beyond these folds. J. R. Matthews at Merthyr ends 1880 by seeing the Lord's manifest approval of the Saints in prophecy, tongues and interpretations by which the Spirit of God encouraged the Saints and set them apart from the sinners. Similarly J. G. Goold at Merthyr some three years later is convinced that the Second Coming is drawing near because on the tenth of January there appeared in the sky what he took to be "a fiery serpent of exceeding brilliancy which remained visible until about twenty minutes to seven the following morning", (1883:88). At about the same time there was an earthquake of some sort. By 1889 glossolalia and prophecy were very frequent at Merthyr and spoke of great trials close at hand. The shift in ethos over the decade from one of blessing to one of trial may be explained in several ways, the undoubted fact is that Welsh Mormonism was undergoing a change in the dynamics of its membership and relation to the broader society. In part it reflected difficulties in the Utah Church.

The American Senate had passed the Edmunds-Tucker Act in February 1887. It was directed against Mormon polygamy and sought to abolish the practice or else destroy the church by stripping its assets and arresting the leadership (K. J. Hansen, 1981:144). The general American membership read this political move as an act of persecution but was keen to see in it the possibility of uniting and invigorating the church in its defence. The *Star* quotes the *New York Evening Express* to the effect that Mormonism is one of the "best wearing political corpses", so often apparently killed yet seeming to thrive on fatal blows. In 1885 the *Star* publishes an article taken from the *South Wales Daily News* of 2 June: "Mormonism in Wales", which refers to the Utah Church Presidents John

Taylor and George Q. Cannon being virtually in hiding because of State hostility to their polygamous institution. In 1886 the London *Times* of 11 January is cited to let British Saints know that a Mormon Suppression Bill had been passed by the Senate placing the "entire property of the Church in the hands of trustees" nominated by the American President. Not only did it forbid polygamy but it also took away the right to vote from women in Utah. It was this last element that caused a few Senators to vote against the Bill. The church leadership finally responded by accepting that polygamy should cease to be practised and the October *Star* for 1890 carried the official declaration of Wilford Woodruff, the current President and Prophet of Mormonism, that he intended to obey the law and advised all Saints to do likewise. The tone and content of this declaration hint at major differences of opinion within the church. One case of plural marriage being performed in the Endowment House in Salt Lake City is raised and Woodruff says not only that he could not find out who performed this act in the Spring of 1889 but that this ritual building was dismantled on his authority because of that dissident episode. He is also keen to specify that it was during the immediately preceding period of legal directives that the church had made no official teaching about or encouragement of plural marriage. As an ideal practice it was to retain an important place in Mormon theology. Its temporary suspension served the "temporal salvation" of the church in keeping it alive as a religious institution. Not only was political and broader Christian pressure believed to be responsible for United States' antagonism, but in the November editorial of 1890 the Woodruff manifesto or official declaration is regarded as the "direct interpolation of the wisdom of Almighty God expressly given to subvert the cunning of the devil".

Divine power and the social forces of American and British life were not conceived as totally distinct entities. This entire period of the 1880s and 1890s is but one, albeit a rather clear, example of Mormonism's conviction of itself as a chosen people under God whose various victories and apparent defeats were but an expression of divine will. The political antagonisms of Utah Mormonism and the State were obviously clearly reported in Britain, and they were made the more intelligible because of changing circumstances on this side of the Atlantic. Indifference to the message by many and active opposition on the part of very few summarize the Welsh situation.

As J. R. Matthews set about organizing the "winter campaign" for 1880 in Cardiff, which basically involved visiting with tracts, he was well aware of the indifference shown towards the church. Throughout 1880 a total of one thousand four hundred and seventy nine converts had emigrated across the Atlantic, of these one hundred and eight were Swiss and German, seven hundred and fifty eight Scandinavian and six hundred and seven were British. A steady trickle of Welsh Saints continued to seek emancipation through their journey to America, some fifty five in 1882 from a total Welsh membership of only three hundred and ninety one; sixty in 1883; twenty three in 1884 out of a declining membership now standing at two hundred and twenty eight; nineteen in 1885; a similar number of about twenty emigrated in 1886 and 1887, while it rose to forty six for 1888 only to drop to fourteen for 1889. The total number of European emigrants for this last year of the decade stood at one thousand three hundred and ninety one. The *Star* for 1890 provides one useful table of the age and sex distributions of emigrants towards the end of the decade.

YEAR	MALES	16-20 FEMALES	20-25	25-30	30-35	35-40	40-50	50-60	TOTAL
1887	607	14	15	2	11	1	9	20	679
1888	674	15	15	8	1	2	1	31	747
1889	651	22	13	6	1	0	5	15	713
	1932	51	43	16	13	3	15	66	2139

This ratio of practically nine men to one woman belies the claim that polygamy was widespread and, if the pattern of emigration had held roughly this profile in earlier days, would support the Mormon claim that only very few men, perhaps only two percent, were ever polygamously united. But the claims and counter-claims on polygamy were by now well-known in Wales and in general caused very little response. W. G. Reese reflects on the Welsh Conference at Merthyr in 1883 and compares the minimal response and attention with the great interest evident some thirty four years before when John Taylor had preached to large open-air groups. So too W. B. Williams and L. J. Mantle who are able to gather some crowds in Pembrokeshire but to very little benefit. The position in 1885 is one of marked indifference and elders comfort themselves with the knowledge that effort counts more than results which themselves must be left to God. But in 1886 there is some disturbance in Bristol, Sheffield, Nottingham and Leicester where an apostate caused much trouble. The Saints were advised to license their chapels or meeting houses so that they might claim the protection of the law against disturbances. Similarly in September 1887 President Teasdale addressed a gathering at Swansea which after a basically polite reception turned into a free fight which looks as if it had been staged by a rougher element according to a *Western Mail* report for 14 September. A certain Adolphus D. Bolitho had recently caused trouble at a Christadelphian debate so the whole issue of apparent heresy and orthodoxy was significant in the area.

If the elders had to make for the door in a retreat,"as consistent with apostolic dignity as circumstances would permit", at the Swansea fracas it was worse the following year when some elders were both attacked and injured by mobs incited by the rather violent anti-Mormon, Jarman; while at Swansea, 4 Grove Place, an elder's house was stoned. President David Williams thanked the general fair mindedness of the press in allowing church leaders to defend and express their position. Jarman was, in fact, bound over to keep the peace at Swansea and charged £100. Despite that Jarman went on to cause trouble in Merthyr and in an anti-Mormon riot in London in October 1887 while another man, Barnfield, agitated at Cardiff. The

Swansea area was especially keen to oppose Mormons, and the *Star* reports in July 1888 that an Anti-Mormon Association had existed there for some time: it had utilized the rhetoric of the apostate Jarman, and its secretary was Bolitho. At least one public disputation was held, in which elder B. H. Roberts took part and this event, in the town's Albert Hall, also ended with much shouting. Similarly T. B. Davies and A. C. Davies wrote from Narberth, Pembrokeshire, in January of 1889, recounting the hostility of mobs at open-air preaching. Though they felt their ministry had reduced the prejudice somewhat the local people remained inhospitable. S. R. Brough at Merthyr saw Glamorgan with parts of Cardigan, Carmarthen and Monmouthshire as having been extensively covered by Mormon teaching. Though the language he uses is that of warning and re-warning, as though to emphasize the negative and hostile ethos growing between church and wider society. Pockets of success occurred and could trigger slightly exaggerated language as when John Thomas describes a revival in Llanegwad Carmarthenshire on the conversion and baptism of four people in June 1887. But further North opposition was conspicuous according to R. T. Owens at Aberystwyth and Machynlleth in July 1886. To preach in public could easily result in the crowd fleeing once the Mormon identity of the preacher was made known. So from his own experience, as from that of others, R. T. Owens can be sympathetically understood as he reports that a great harvest had been gathered in Wales and that the mid 1880s, as indeed later years of the century, was a period of sparse gleaning. To warn the people of the coming Kingdom was as much as elders could expect to do.

Owens is an interesting figure for he is an early example of a missionary son of emigrant parents. They had left Merthyr Tydfil for Utah some thirty two years before and Owens had now come as a travelling elder in 1886. His message to those eager to emigrate is simply that of tithe paying, observing the Word of Wisdom in its entirety and abandoning all luxuries. God's blessing follows all who do so. It seems that in the Welsh Conference only some actually abstained though others are said to be more moderate than they had been. But the outside people of the world were unconcerned with religion even in its denominational "easy ways of popular Christianity". The phrase "spiritual lethargy" is used to describe the Gentile world at large in which elders meet only with "frigid indifference, calumny and persecution".

The call to Zion is now as strong as ever, delays are seen as dangerous in many ways, (1886:201), while the social evils, natural calamities and spiritual phenomena all conduce to the conviction that the end is increasingly close. The *Star* can even report that the fig tree in the Utah garden of one Godfrey Lienhardt is producing three crops a year, (1886:654). Such apparently transient information speaks both of dramatic signs and of a land reminiscent of the biblical promise of milk and honey and of the fig trees under which the divinely blessed man sits at ease. In Europe unconcern with religious dedication is often compared with the days of Noah when materialism captivated life. Sparse success is noted as with the baptism of a former member of the Salvation Army in Pontypridd in 1887. But Sunday Schools have largely closed in the South Wales area, a fact bemoaned by D. R. Gill and T. B. Davies for had they been able to support them the many children could have been kept from going to other churches.

In the conferences of the Welsh Mission both in 1888 and 1889 the President, Apostle Teasdale, speaks of the radical change affecting Wales. Some fifteen thousand to twenty thousand Welsh people were now making a living, hard though it was, in Utah. In 1887 the total population in Utah was one hundred and fifteen thousand six hundred and ninety nine with some forty six thousand six hundred and eighty four children, (1888:163). This would give a Welsh population of say seventeen thousand to one hundred and sixteen thousand or approximately fifteen per cent.

Total Immigration to U.S.A. between 1847-1890:

Irish	2,541,148
English	1,178,157
Welsh	60,033
Scottish	277,766
German	3,425,208

This list includes people of all religions or none, but when linked to *Star* statistics it suggests that approximately one-third of Welsh migrants were Latter Day Saints, (1890:295). Teasdale does not exaggerate the plenty or idealize Utah life: the church is an organization which possesses what can even be called a beautiful structure and it is preparing for the coming kingdom, but it still involves and even embraces hardship. The time was drawing near when the Welsh would no longer have the privilege of the visiting elder; the gospel would be taken from the Gentiles. Welsh people as a whole were now seen to be rejecting the message and the testimonies of the elders.

If indifference and opposition were the twin attitudes of the world a forthright testimony was the stance of the elders. The Mormon concept of testimony itself had a long tradition in America and the Welsh context of antipathy gave a new dimension to it, in the sense that Saints believed a new phase to have come over the people. In this period of hard-heartedness testimony was to ensure a clear conscience on the part of missionaries. As Alma M. Matthews expressed it, preaching to those indifferent souls was the elders' mission, but once done "we rid our shirts of their blood", (February 1890). The allusion to the Old Testament prophet and to Jesus' disciples of the New Testament is obvious: leave a man with the truth and his conscience and you are guiltless of the outcome; his responsibility is to do as he will whilst the messenger is freed from the hearers' blood and can shake from his feet the dust of irresponsive streets. Matthews mentions some four thousand tracts distributed over the winter period which attest to the elders' labours.

A continued theme was that of instruction and rational education. Tracts sought to dispute by clearly putting the Mormon case before the people. B. H. Roberts had written to the press in 1888 to stress the position held in the church that Mormonism, and he was prepared to use that name, did not thrive best where ignorance was most profound. Arguing that in one sense the pursuit of intelligence is a worship of God he wanted such reason to be used to scrutinize the ideas and principles of Mormon faith. Superstition and mere tradition were enemies of Mormon religion, for the intrinsic reasonableness of the scheme was enough to commend it, if only inquirers gave it a fair opportunity. Clarity not mystery in religion was a key force, so much so that the *Star* advocated religious buildings as places where libraries, classes and lecture rooms should be provided, (1888:77).

Along with clarity should exist a basic uniformity of status among members as far as wordly statuses were concerned. Censure awaits any who through conspicuous alms-giving seek pride of place, or who would "create, claim, or maintain class distinctions in the community of the Saints". Here is a community of thinking persons guided by restored and intrinsically reasonable religious principles. It is a community which is internally differentiated into offices or functions believed to originate in a divinely revealed hierarchy but despite which regards all as intrinsically equal before God. As far as these Mormons were concerned status difference was, and remains to this day, acceptable insofar as it reflected the divine plan of church and social organization. Once derived from wordly ideas of class and the like all such hierarchy immediately became unacceptable.

Its unacceptability also lay in the corporate ideal of religion which denied that any person could "be saved alone, unassisted by or unassisting others", (1886:716). Despite heavy stress on individual accountability, responsibility and achievement, Mormon theology dissociated itself from the protestant conviction that salvation pertained to the radical act of individuals in response to the radical self-offering of Christ as we have already seen. The same corporate convictions obtained or perhaps it is better to say were most clearly manifested in the values of family life. Divorce is an evil of great proportion especially if it touched the lives of those who had undergone the temple ritual of "sealing". Only the authority of the Mormon Church could separate those united previously under the same power. It is only in the occasional statement that doctrines like that of sealing come to be discussed at the general level rather than in the more restricted circles focussed on temple ritual.

The linking of total groups such as the church with specific and exemplary individuals shows the dynamic framework within which the Latter Day Saints grasped their doctrines of salvation. The reference to several Harmons at the end of this decade is but one short example of a family group emigrating and thereby exploring the possibilities of the church. In 1885 Mary Harmon of 1 Windsor Terrace Merthyr died just after Christmas Day (27 December), she is remembered for having kept an open house for fellow Saints and their conferences. April 1888 witnessed the death of Ann Harmon born in South Wales in 1838 leaving five sons and two daughters.

In 1889 one Robert Harmon, an elder, is expressing thanks for the fact that both his parents had adopted the Mormon faith. The best known Mormon concern with family membership and with corporate salvation is in the process of vicarious ritual and with the family trees required for the information underlying the rites. And it was to drawing up appropriate genealogies that the *Star* called its readers early in 1888. An interesting theme, for but little attention had hitherto been placed on it for the obvious reason that emigration itself had prime of place in Latter Day Saint interest. It was with the firm establishing of a Mormon sub-culture in Utah that vicarious rites came into their own as a form of religious group reflection.

But it was that same distinctive culture which also challenged orthodox Christians to respond to Mormonism and its religious claims. As a result there emerged a large body of material in the shape of booklets and tracts which sought to argue the false nature of the Mormon case. This literature is valuable as an indicator of how orthodox Christians viewed the emerging movement and in particular of the distinctive doctrines and practices singled out for refutation. Two major areas stand out and we will look at each in turn. Firstly, that concerning theological matters and secondly, that which focusses on church organization embracing methods of proselytizing and emigration.

Theological Topics

The authorship and content of the *Book of Mormon* received the most detailed consideration and criticism. Some thought that Sidney Rigdon, an early associate of Joseph Smith, had dictated the subject matter to the prophet,[22] others thought that the book was based on an historical novel entitled *The Manuscript Found*, written by the Reverend Solomon Spalding.[23] An even more remarkable suggestion was that the model for the book was the fiction, *The Everlasting Gospel*, by the thirteenth century monk named Cyril.[24] Yet others did believe that Smith had produced the *Book of Mormon* but went on to show how its contents were fundamentally heretical.

The Mormon doctrine of priesthoods was opposed on the grounds that it permitted the ordination of men from the tribe of Joseph while the biblical books of Numbers and Deuteronomy limited ordination to the tribe of Levi. The doctrine of God was also hotly contested with Conybeare arguing that the Mormon anthropomorphic idea of God had hitherto been matched only by fifteenth century monks anathematized by Theophilus.[25] For Mormonism had developed the doctrine of Adam-God in which Adam was regarded as having attained deity whilst retaining his man-like and material nature. On another front the developing polytheism of Mormonism was frequently noted and its resemblance to Mohammedanism in its political organization was stressed. Parallels were also drawn with the historical heresies of Montanism and the Anabaptist Movement as far as ideas of eschatology and revelation were concerned.[26] Each comparison was intended to liken the

Latter Day Saints to some historical and previously discredited movement.

The many grammatical errors of the *Book of Mormon* were singled out and seen as evidence of an untutored author and therefore of possible theological error.[27] Much of this kind of criticism could be summarized in the poignantly directed words of Mark Twain. 'The book is a curiosity to me, it is such a pretentious affair, and yet so slow, so sleepy, such an insipid mess of inspiration. It is chloroform in print. If Smith composed the book the act was a miracle — keeping awake while he did it was, at any rate'.[28]

The prophet was often described as an epileptic and therefore not fit as a source of revelation,[29] while his supposed drunkenness and the lack of overt piety in Mormon missionaries was regarded by many British churchmen from the major denominations as sure signs of false religion. [30] Though many opponents concentrated on these doctrines and attitudes many more stressed practical aspects of Mormon church organization as worthy of condemnation. It is to these factors we now turn.

Organizational Factors

The opinion was often voiced that the motive force behind proselytizing in Britain was the need for women in Utah. Indeed, the very name of Mormon became synonymous with that of woman catcher, and all young women were warned to flee from missionaries who were deemed to possess strange powers over females. This power was said to lie in a form of hypnosis associated with animal magnetism, an idea which itself was becoming popular towards the end of the nineteenth century. So much was this the case that the Mormon church warned its missionaries not to learn hypnotism lest the wrong impression be conveyed to outsiders, (*Star*, 1903:90).

Numerous articles and novels appeared in which the evils of Mormonism were 'disclosed'. As one set of disclosures graphically depicted the situation: 'What lives these low grade Mormons lead. By continued excesses in the satisfying of carnal passions many of them have ruined their constitutions and are little better than confirmed invalids. My marriage was a mere farce...a contract to which I was an unwilling and protesting party'. [31] Books carried titles such as, *Female Life among the Mormons*,[32] *Aweful Disclosures of Mormonism*, and *Mormonism Unveiled*.[33] All contributed to a popular image of Mormonism as an evil to be avoided at all costs, best exemplified perhaps in the derivation we have mentioned earlier where the etymology of the name Mormon is said to signify, 'bugbear, rawhead, hobgoblin', so that, 'a Mormonite is a frightener, something terrific especially to children'.[34]

The fact that the Latter Day Church was recruiting mostly from the working classes was also considered a reason for suspicion. The success of the message was reckoned to lie in the promise of benefits in Utah, in the claim to absolute truth, and in an organization which deployed its manpower efficiently. Though some saw the nature of this organization as guaranteeing a successful future, others thought that such high levels of zeal could not possibly be maintained.[35]

Many pamphlets ended by exhorting the reader to escape from Mormon associations: 'Beware of idle curiosity, do not read Mormonite books or attend meetings, or talk with Mormons. The system is false and wicked. If by the preventing grace of God the Holy Ghost you have been kept from this terrible delusion, thank and bless the name of the Lord'.[36]

This nineteenth century literature which exposed secret rituals and societies in Utah was, to a large extent, reinforced by men like Jarman who were former Mormons returned to Britain for the purposes of exposing hidden elements of the church organization. Others, like Adolphus Bolitho, were of fixed Protestant conviction and conducted public debate on that biblical platform. All such encounters and accounts served only to increase the social visibility of the Latter Day Saints.

For the larger part of the twentieth century anti-Mormon literature has dramatically decreased. Only very occasional interest is shown by the main line churches, as for example in 1971 when some local groups in Manchester sought to dispute doctrinal issues on the occasion of the very large Conference of Mormons then held in that city.[37] Of a slightly different nature was the account of incidents involving bombing of private individuals who were connected with documents purporting to explain the origin of the *Book of Mormon* and which would possibly undermine the received explanation of its source. This story was carried by the *Sunday Times Magazine* in March 1986, but what was especially remarkable about it is the neutral and descriptive nature of the account. No longer is general comment of a negative kind and it would seem that anti-Mormon propaganda was strongest when emigration was at its fullest. As emigration declined and was replaced by residential congregations so the nature of the wider public's attitude altered. Various pamphlets now written by non-Mormon churches do stress the doctrinal stance which differs radically from received tradition but they do not engage in moral accusation.[38] Indeed it is not unusual for the organizational rigour of the Mormon Church to be commended, as is its missionary system. Even so at the level of passing conversation the old favourite topic of polygamy still commands mention.

So hostility of orthodoxy to Mormonism was most intense when the movement was most in the public eye through emigration. That opposition was encouraged by the fact that, to leaders of other churches, Mormonism was the first plainly unorthodox group to gain a large following in Britain and to draw many converts away in a geographical sense. Even so by the close of the nineteenth century the more vituperative form of apologetic was in decline.

Chapter Six

Church Order and Salvation History: 1890-1899

By the close of 1890 Wales could lay claim to fewer than two hundred members. Only forty four elders manned the church along with nine bishops, three high priests, five seventies, in the high Melchizedek priesthood; and with two teachers, four priests and four deacons in the Aaronic priesthood. There were some hundred ordinary members balancing this relatively heavy body of officers. The Saints saw themselves as unpopular with the world as is indirectly reflected in the three hundred and seventy two meetings held by Saints for Saints in 1890 in contrast with the low number, twenty four, outdoor meetings for Gentiles. The belief that Christ's advent was near at hand is strong, (1890:102) and the obligation to warn the people intense as the forty nine thousand seven hundred and eighty three tracts dispensed in this period indicate. Giving out tracts rather than holding meetings for evangelism hints at the shift of emphasis in Mormon attitudes.

The 1892 *Star* editorial in expressing the hope that its pages might help direct benighted travellers westward to a land of promise is but echoing the lingering wishes of the elders in this movement as it stood on the brink of change and a new century. In its pages a wide variety of thoughts is expressed, some very practical, some personal, while yet others air points of doctrine. The distinctive features of Mormonism as a definite and different religion are not all immediately visible; historically speaking they took time to emerge, just as today they take time to be assimilated by new converts.

Order and Organization

Sometimes the character of these ideas differed quite markedly from the theology of the historical Christian churches. The idea of blood atonement was one such, even though as a phrase it seems to reflect Old Testament motifs. As an idea it applied to murderers arguing that the only atonement which they could make was one involving the shedding of their own blood, quid pro quo, for the blood that had been shed in the act of murder, (1891:148). Here the responsibility ultimately lay with the condemned man who could, for example, choose to be shot by a duly appointed executioner. Personal volition remained the key Mormon idea, but as in all church thinking that private will needed executing by an official and in accord with a church principle.

Mormons claimed special authority for their religion which they believed made it stand out from the many competing religions of the day. This sense of special validation made the increasing heedlessness of the world all the more significant. But it is important as a key value underlying much Mormon thought and practice, so that when George Q. Cannon, speaking in the *Star* Preface for 1892 and as one amidst the Utah hierarchy, says that many Saints were "more pleased to hear the manifesto" ending plural marriage than to hear the original revelation initiating it, he gives an insight into basic Mormon spirituality. Authority is the nature of the relationship between God and the Restoration movement as well as between those within it. Cannon's reflection on the plural marriage issue is an intriguing example of Mormon logic which might have been baffling to Britons raised on more biblically rooted ideas of absolute truths. He admits that few Saints had obeyed the initial law, perhaps nineteen out of twenty had not honoured it. Of the few who had adopted the prescribed practice some had behaved improperly in it. These reasons, he adduced, might have been enough for God to have altered the custom, but more than this, the loss of temples and their attendant rites which would have ensued had the church not capitulated to the State, was an evil which presumably God would not allow. President Woodruff waited until God gave the authoritative command to change the system before any action was taken. For those who believed that God's command of plural marriage was an inevitable first step to final exaltation Cannon suggests they think again, for God was more concerned with motive and opportunity than with mere ritual event. And Cannon adds as a powerful rider that the initial doctrine had in fact been revealed to him before he ever heard that Joseph Smith had received it, (1892:19). If *he* could trust authority once, and now follow it in a change of direction, then others should have little difficulty in so doing.

Among the more concrete instances of authority which became increasingly apparent in the 1890s is a formal publication of ritual formulae to be used in church services. Before immersing baptismal candidates the officiant is instructed to say: "Having been commissioned of Jesus Christ I baptize you in the name of the Father, and of the Son, and of the Holy Ghost. Amen". Immediately following this, and as a necessary part of that "birth" which initiates into the kingdom of heaven, the elders are to lay hands on the candidates' head and confirm them as members of the church by the conferral of the Holy Ghost. In the same year readers are rehearsed in the fact that the Prophet Joseph Smith had first administered the "emblems" of bread and water on 21 May 1843, (1892:365). So both baptism and Lord's Supper, as well as the confirmation rite, are stressed as church rites. The sense of a growing institutionalization increases at this very time when proselytizing is at its lowest ebb and, for example, in 1895 the *Star* publishes the Sacramental Prayers to be used at the Communion Service. The prayer over the bread itself affords sufficient evidence of the strongly memorialist doctrinal position of the Restoration movement. All possible allusions to bread being sacramental-body are discounted as the acts of human will and remembering are brought to the fore:

> "O God, the eternal Father, we ask thee in the name of thy Son, Jesus Christ, to bless and sanctify this bread to the souls of all who partake of it, that they may eat in remembrance of the body of thy Son, and witness unto thee, O God the Eternal Father, that they are willing to take upon them the

name of thy Son, and always to remember him and keep his commandments which he has given them, that they may always have his Spirit to be with them, Amen", (1895:70).

The authority perceived to be inherent in the church, which was now slowly beginning to regain its stability in legal peace with the State following the polygamy issue's demise and the restoration of former seized property, is now increasingly set within a framework of world religious history. So the reforming transformations of Luther are viewed as among the most important events in history, and for the Latter Day Saints as a preparatory step to the Restoration movement and its consummation in the kingdom which the God of heaven is establishing, (1895:351). As with history so in church organization which is in a sense one outworking of divine plans within history albeit at the level of bureaucracy. To preserve good church order against the potential threat of disorganization which is a phenomenon high on the Mormon list of evils, the church regards the Twelve Apostles as possessing equal authority with the Prophet; and by extension the Seventy also have an equal authority in the event of the Prophet's death: "this provision of a multiplicity of quorums of equal authority is a specially designed safeguard to the perpetuation of the work in spite of all emergencies that could arise", (1899:568). Not only so, for if these three groups of First Presidency, Twelve, and Seventy were somehow removed, there would remain a large number of authoritative High Councils of the regional stakes of Zion said to number some six hundred members in 1897.

The scene portrayed in such an account is one of impregnable organization with authority subsisting in all its many parts. The holding of regular conferences for the regions of the church as well as for the central areas and dignitaries provided a visible arena within which those holding authority could be seen and their teaching heard, (1899:648). Authority thus possessed visible agents extending throughout the many levels of church life.

What has obviously occurred by the close of the century is a firm distinction between secular and religious authority. President Lorenzo Snow is unequivocal in describing the Mormon Church and American State as "entirely distinct and separate", (1899:33). Many issues of loyalty and commitment lay behind this clear assertion but they were all enshrined within the polygamy debate. Snow emphatically argued that plural marriage had ceased entirely in Utah, that no new unions had been solemnized since 1890 and that any existing family groups of this kind were but vestiges of the previous years doomed to inevitable demise with time.

Just how British readers interpreted the ground swell change implicit in this capitulation to secular authority it is hard to assess; what is of interest is the fact that emigration to and interest in a forthcoming and imminent kingdom of God, where political power was as much under prophetic leadership as church power, was now a minority interest.

At this very time attention is diverted from the change in earlier projected ideals to the theme of change as such. Mormons were not allowed to become lax in old expectation. They are reminded that in the age of the railway none should be content with slow-going stage coaches, or with candles when electricity is at hand, (1899:1). Further reminders are given that Mormons are self-motivated individuals. Heber J. Grant stresses this as he answers the question of how to be saved. Speaking in Salt Lake City's Tabernacle in October 1895 he reiterates the importance of the Commandments of God and that all believers are architects of their own lives both in this life and in the world beyond. Further Mormon teaching extended this capacity to embrace others in the rationale of vicarious ritual. The discarnate or disembodied soul has capacities of its own, including a will and the ability to choose between moral options. That same spirit of man can also exercise faith and repentance, but the ritual acts remain necessary before such decisions can be implemented. Rites on earth performed by proxy can enable discarnate souls to reap the rewards of faith and repentance, hence the power of living earthly Mormons in helping the earthly dead to sculpt their continuing destinies, (1896:296).

In commitment to change there remains the firm sense of corporate responsibility. The individualism of decision-making is anchored to the entire church membership in this world and the realms beyond. It is of some interest that Saints from Wales retained their ethnic associations in Utah. The drive to ensure uniformity of language among earlier emigrants had been successful but had not extinguished all original cultural values. Indeed there soon emerged in Utah and among Mormon leaders the sense that an ethnic identity was a good and useful dimension within the total and overarching Mormon identity. Not least because it provided a context against which Welsh or Scandinavian or other national groups could tell the story of their salvation to even greater effect. To have a national identity is a fine and worthy base in life just as it provides a framework for particular values. But when another set of beliefs then arises it can throw the former into a very negative light. In the Mormon case this did not happen in the long run even though it had nearly done so in the mid-century period.

Earlier we described that more negative age when converts abandoned Wales and were encouraged to abandon Welsh all under the view that the homeland was part and parcel of evil Babylon which had no part in the new dawning age of Zion. This did take place. But as time went on and as that conversion to a new Mormon identity came about there was less need to maintain boundaries of religion against boundaries of race. More than that, those older ethnic ties came to serve purposes of motivating missionary zeal towards those former fatherlands as well as affording the starting point in a history of salvation. At the close of the century the need for more Welsh speaking missionaries was expressed (January 1899).

History, Narrative and Salvation

Mormon salvation history did resemble parts of the history of ancient Israel in possessing shifting contexts. History with a geography is more powerful, and certainly more intelligible than any idealized and abstract history. Most church and sect groups tell a story of salvation originating in God, touching the earth in the Incarnation of God's Son and announced by various timely prophets and leaders. Persecution and forced migration or else battle without movement then afford another phase in that faith. Mormons knew all these elements for their restored message and rituals in the early nineteenth century had rapidly caused immense geographical shifts to occur with a whole religious history emerging as a result. The Welsh Latter Day Saints had been a major part of this history.

Still, by the close of the century, this history of but one ethnic group was very much alive. It was focussed in Utah through cultural gatherings. In 1895 the Salt Lake City Tabernacle itself was the location for a great eisteddfod of the Cambrian Association of Utah. More interesting still is the visit of Dr. Joseph Parry to be the chief adjudicator at the Utah Eisteddfod of 1898. This was the third eisteddfod held in Utah and Dr. Parry thought it quite up to the standard of the National Eisteddfod in Wales. Whilst there this eminent Welsh composer met some Merthyr people who had attended the same nonconformist chapel as himself when young. He tells that the Welsh in Utah are well regarded and that polygamy is "absolutely a thing of the past", (1898:719). The very fact that the *Star* publishes material centred on a famous Gentile reflects that acceptance of coexistence of Mormon and Non-Mormon which the invitation of Parry to be an adjudicator also expressed.

This example enables us to confront one of the fundamental theoretical problems running through this book, a problem which some have also taken to be of critical significance for Mormons of the following twentieth century: it is the issue of history itself.

Joseph Parry and the many individuals we have already mentioned in connection with emigration provided a personal link between America and Wales. This personal dimension had also been powerful in the first forty or so years in the history of the church through the memories of those who could recall the earliest leaders and the hardships of establishing a Mormon community in Utah. By the inevitable process of time those persons were reduced in number and finally died out entirely. It was also the case that the church increasingly became bureaucratic and may have lost the original vision of personal freedom in a changing world. This has been argued forcefully by Mark P. Leone who makes a further assertion which cannot be ignored in our present consideration of history and salvation. Leone argues that a major feature linking nineteenth century Mormonism with the present day church is what he calls 'memorylessness', (1979:212). He sees nineteenth century Mormons in America as lacking a memory, as not enjoying precedents. In their stead he places 'sanctity', or the attribute of unquestionned truthfulness, as a means of justifying action. I will explore this notion of sanctity in chapter eighteen where we consider the idea of Homo religiosus in Mormonism and I will show it to be deficient in certain respects. For the moment I will remain with the argument on memory and memorylessness to suggest that it may be more useful than the idea of sanctity in understanding the nature of Mormon identity.

Leone speaks of 'the historical puzzle of Mormonism', (1979:209). By this he refers to his observation that many Mormons 'who conscientiously do genealogical work cannot talk coherently about the past that they themselves have lived through', (idem). It is as though their preoccupation with aspects of their own family's past has so caused them to build that past into their own present life that they have developed a blind spot as far as the contextual events of the past are concerned.

In other words the past is only an aspect of their present experience and, more than that, their present religious outlook completely colours their historical vision. This leads Leone to argue that professional and academic historians have a hard time within the church as do other professional thinkers. If they are applauded it is because they have already gained fame in the wider world. History for the multitude of Saints is a popular and non-professional activity. Leone writes as one who seeks to explore some of the difficulties which serious thinkers may experience within their church membership. This is a valuable exercise but it differs from our task which is to place this problem of history within the study of religions. As we do this it becomes clear that Leone's problem is certainly not an isolated one, though it is a slightly extreme example of a widely prevailing tendency in Christian forms of religiosity.

For at least the last century Christian theologians have given extensive attention to what has been called salvation-history, or *heilsgeschichte* as the Germans framed the theme.[39] Alerted to the fact that ultimate values and beliefs were inextricably bound to past events like the birth and death of Jesus, they sought the precise nature of the bond. How, for example, were the Jesus of history and the Christ of faith to be related? How did God affect events in the world through prophets and wonders in the Old Testament? In what way is the Incarnation, or the Resurrection, an historical and material phenomenon?

One obvious feature emerging from this debate is that faith, the personal and collective sense of divine action, is intimately related to the way events are perceived. Any strict, neutral, view of events soon vanishes once mere description passes into interpretation, since the significance of events seldom lies open for all to see in an unquestionnable explanation.

Religions interpret past events. Values are brought to bear upon them. Meaning is attributed to things. One of the significant differences between religions is the extent to which scholars provide fixed interpretations or ordinary members are left free to make their own sense of the past. Mark Leone's conviction is that Mormons have their own, rather personalized, form of history which is at variance with more scholarly and detailed analyses of the past. In strictly factual terms and over material events he may well be correct, but the point he ignores and which must be added is of more fundamental importance. It is that all religious groups construct their own history of the world, and since faith in an unprovable God is usually part of the religious outlook it is necessarily the case that a religious history and a secular history will differ. This is patently obvious though it is often veiled in cultures where Christianity is generally supported. It is only when atheistic philosophies encounter theistic positions that fundamental presuppositions clash and history and the very processes of history become matters of debate.

The Mormon situation is complex in this context. On the one hand it is part of the general Christian and Jewish tradition which acclaims creation and redemption as effected through mighty acts of God, but on the other hand it then asserts unique acts of God in establishing the Restoration of truth through priesthoods and ordinances. Mormons would not be Mormon if they did not think that God had intervened in the history of America. That intervention created the person of the first prophet, Joseph Smith, and through that person a focus emerged which enables contemporary Mormons to see their own identity in a clear way. In other words the distinctive feature of Mormon history is that of a personalized revelation.

But an individual's sense of revelation is a quite subjective experience. Authenticity is subjective despite the communal and church-based framework within which that sense of truth arises. The initial commitment to Mormon truth is at the same time the moment when an historical perspective is born. In different terms this means that personal conviction of truth is also a belief in Joseph Smith as a prophet of God. Belief weds present and past in a personal way. And personal convictions are highly idiosyncratic which is why views of the past, of history, are varied. We will explore the question of testimonies when we consider Mormon spirituality later.

One reason why Mormonism is a church highly committed to history, even though the precise meaning of that word is vague, is because it formally links present experience with the life of Joseph Smith. Because the actual duration of the religion is relatively short, with the church established in 1830, some people may expect present members to have an accurate picture of the movement between then and now. Leone is surprised to find that relation blurred. But, I would expect to find a blurring within this field of faith. Many Christians would argue a sense of relatedness to Jesus of Nazareth, to Paul the Apostle, and to other first century figures, but the relation is one of imaginative faith and does not express factual images of those persons.

Faith as an experience is intrinsically hard to describe, there is usually a vagueness associated with words and concepts related to experience. I have discussed the nature of what I call 'straddling terms' elsewhere in connection with Rodney Needham's philosophical and anthropological study of belief, language and experience.[40] The hypothesis I would make here is that history as a concept is a straddling term in Mormonism. It embraces the dimension of personal religiosity, the medium of church evangelism, and the period of Joseph Smith's reception of Restored principles and practices.

The fact that scholars in the academic world have developed historical methods of analysis, and that history is a branch of investigation, should not blind us to a religious phenomenon in the lives of ordinary church members. Problems over 'actual' events as opposed to mythical 'events' are found in the intellectual life of the major Christian movements, it is the shortness of duration of the Latter Day Saint movement which makes for a specially acute version of the general problem of belief and interpretation.

So we might suggest that Leone's 'historical puzzle' is caused, to a certain extent at least, by the confusion over the use of the very word 'history'. Once we draw a distinction between history as an academic endeavour, and history as a straddling term uniting personal faith with the past and present structure of the church, we are in a better position to understand the problem of the historian in Mormonism.

In several respects the historian in Mormonism is also the theologian. This is not often the case in most other major Christian traditions except perhaps in the complex liturgical faith of Eastern Orthodoxy. But the theological duty of the Mormon historian leads to an inevitable conflict of commitments between church and academic world precisely because there is no firm class of theologians with whom to share responsibility. But the nature of conflict should not be assumed as overwhelming. All intellectual life involves conflicts of interpretation and within religious traditions these simply become more complex because of psychological issues of identity and commitment, and not least because ideas of divine action are involved. And this is where the problem of theology itself usually begins.

Our task is not to argue whether Mormon thinkers should seek to develop systematic theology or whether to focus on history as a means of engaging in theological analysis, it is to depict what occurs in the church. With that in mind it is instructive to see how, for example, Edwin S. Gaustad, in the 1984 Tanner Lectures on Mormon History, devoted himself to the title, 'Historical Theology and Theological History: Mormon Possibilities'.[41] More particularly it is worth noting how he sees Mormon historians as occupying a place within their church which no other group of historians do in theirs. Historians constitute *the* professional group within the Mormon church, he tells them. And for most practical purposes the word history could be replaced by the word theology without any loss of meaning. Gaustad does not say that, but it is one very real way of interpreting his argument which goes on to encourage Mormons to develop historical theology as a means of engaging in comparative theology. For he thinks that Mormons would gain much if their own theological ideas were reflected upon in the light of the many debates on similar theological issues conducted by other groups. The Mormon historian Richard L. Bushman similarly ends his own study of Joseph Smith with the reflection that Mormons have found themselves 'unable to take much interest in formal theology or systematizing treatises', and that, 'Mormonism was history, not philosophy', (1984:188).

There would seem to be real justification in employing the term salvation history in Mormon studies as long as it was extended to include the present-day life of believers and not simply used on the large scale canvass depicting God's mighty acts in the history of his elected peoples. This is a critical point and merits one further comment occasioned by Maureen Ursenbach Beecher's Presidential Address of 1984 to the Mormon History Association.

In her task of tracing personal elements within the development of the Mormon History Association she shows how certain past presidents and others came into a sense of open discussion of matters which deeply touched issues of faith and church commitment. One participant is quoted as saying that through these informal meetings of church historians it was always the issue of historical evidence and personal testimony which came to the fore.[42] Another participant felt no tension in these areas. Whatever the individual stress, the significant fact I wish to note is this dual factor of historical evidence and personal testimony. We will explore the idea of the testimony later when discussing Mormon spirituality, for the moment I want to suggest that history in Mormonism is precisely a conjunction of historical evidence and personal testimony. Leone has a methodological problem because he sees many ordinary Mormons as stressing the present testimony to the point that they are oblivious to historical evidence. It would be equally unfortunate to stress an academic history devoid of personal testimony. All religious traditions actually engage in a degree of confessional interpretation of the past but where complementary disciplines of theology exist the issue of fact and faith is less obvious and acute than it is in Mormonism.

Many of the world religions have been studied in ways which have thrown up distinctions between the formal theologies of the educated, and usually, of the priestly castes on the one hand, and the relatively uneducated masses of the laity on the other. This distinction of great and little traditions, between official and unofficial religion, or between priestly and folk religiosity, has an extensive literature devoted to it.[43] What I wish to point out here is that history seems to serve a function in Mormonism which doctrine or theology does in some other religions. So that there is both an official form of history and folk-histories, the folk-histories taking the form of family and genealogical history. But precisely because the extended family is a major arena of salvation for Mormons it is quite proper to speak of family history as a central focus of salvation history.

The official history of Mormonism is the account of Joseph Smith's dealings with God. To any non-Mormon this will not count as actual history, as real events which took place, for they are, in fact, matters of belief. And this is the crux for Mormon thought, namely that events which are reckoned to have occurred only a century and a half or so ago can, in fact, be disputed since they are matters of belief.

But Mormons do believe them, and they believe them as part of their testimony. It is the realm of religious experience which generates a sense of those events having occurred, just as it is the account of those events which triggers faith in the first place. Mormon spirituality is thus grounded in the dual framework of official history and personal testimony. The fact that some academic historians may find the official history wanting is because the nature of that history is intrinsically religious. It depends upon faith for its authenticity. The Mormon historian is, almost inevitably, set within the same situation as the theologian in other churches. Such theologians may find the attitude of the ordinary believer to be naive, but it is often the case that believers at the uninstructed level have more in common with the scholars than may at first sight appear. They share commitment to certain religious beliefs which to the non-believer are unacceptable whether proposed in their sophisticated or unsophisticated forms.

In recent decades it has become much more fashionable in western theology to talk about narrative theology rather than about salvation history. Narrative theology, including the theology of story, has been widely employed in the two major though rather different domains of South American Liberation Theology, and the charismatic field of suburban Christians concerned about their personal fulfilment.[44]

In essence narrative theology uses the stories of the bible to show how people have understood God and human dealings with God, often in situations of injustice and hardship, so as to understand their present life contexts and to do something active about their problems.

A close identification of the present with the biblical past serves to give groups a sense of identity and purpose. Indeed the whole question of the authority of scripture, which preoccupied Protestant thought so long, tends to give way, or is simply an irrelevance, as individuals take and use scriptures as triggers for their own thoughts about God. Theology in these contexts is said to be done by ordinary people. They make their theology as they go along. Theology is popularized and wrested from the hands of the professional theologian.

In many ways it appears that Mormon history, or rather, history as it is used in Mormonism, is a type of narrative theology.

With the growth of interest in history in Mormonism in more recent decades it might be tempting for Mormons to employ the salvation-history theme, but it might also be interesting to explore the whole area in terms of narrative theology. In chapter two we spoke of the threefold biblical model of exodus, wilderness wandering and a journey to the promised land of rest, as a major way in which nineteenth century Mormons had pictured their own lives. In the terms of social science it is a pattern which fits well the anthropological scheme of rites of passage. Of those processes which take people from one identity and social status to another. Rites of separation from existing states and identities through a period of new experience and re-learning to a new identity. Having been separated through conversion and early congregational life in Britain many converts underwent the marginal period of transition in the act of emigration, before being incorporated into the new society of Saints in America.[45] Underlying this extensive cultural rite of passage, a movement from one culture to another and not simply from one social state to another within the same culture, was the theology of world change at Christ's second coming. In terms of the history of religions there was a millennial myth undergirding the popular response to the Restoration message. Personal existence and the end of time coalesced. Doctrines of creation and redemption often enshrine a sense of value. Qualities of present experience are expressed in the way time is conceived.

So it was with eschatological ideas in the early and mid-nineteenth century period of Mormonism not only in America but perhaps more especially in Europe. And in terms of narrative theology we can see that period as a time of intense theological creativity. Not in the technical and academic sense of theological scholarship, but in the popular use of biblical motifs along with Joseph Smith's visionary account of world history in Israel and earlier America. For many Welsh men and women, boys and girls, along with their other European fellows their involvement in the Restoration movement was a form of liberation theology. The poverty of life experienced in the great industrial areas of Britain, so carefully observed and influential upon Engles in his emergent sociology, was not at all far removed from the political hardship more recently experienced in parts of South America and elsewhere. Mormon missionaries served functions not unlike those of Catholic priests in contemporary areas of constraint. They brought a message enabling people to understand and respond to their world situation.

As we end our reflection upon the nineteenth century phase of church life, and as we see the power of theological ideas to motivate people, we should recall the earlier eighteenth century vision which had attracted some Welsh settlers to America. It is hauntingly instructive to recall that in the 1790s there were emigrant non-conformist Welshmen seeking to build the idealistic city of Beula in Pennsylvania. Not only so but there emerged an entire mythology of the Welsh Prince Madoc who supposedly discovered America in 1170 and whose followers begat a tribe of Welsh Red Indians. This ethnic elaboration of the lost tribes of Israel was not insignificant, so much so that Gwyn A. Williams could speak of the last years of the eighteenth century as producing a Madoc fever in the United States of America when 'belief in Welsh Indians became universal'.[46]

One important difference may be made between the Dissenting eighteenth century Welsh with their ideas of Beula and Madoc, and nineteenth century Mormon emigrants with their hopes of Zion and the revelations of Joseph Smith. Gwyn Williams stressed the fact that the Madoc myth had been 'connective' rather than 'constitutive', (1980:42). It had been a story which might have helped forge ideas which already had powerful motives behind them. The desire and wish to emigrate and found a new homeland, *Gwladfa*, in America, was already present. The myth helped connect these ideals with other forms of the wish. The case of nineteenth century Mormons was different. For them the account of the New Zion and the coming of Christ to a community God had restored was constitutive. It was the very basis and justification of their faith and their hope to emigrate.

The entry into the twentieth century involved a much fuller rethinking of emigration and of the nature of the Mormon Zion than even the latter years of the nineteenth century had occasioned. As far as British Mormons were concerned the great changes in emphasis which were now emerging would themselves become part of the narrative theology of Mormon life in Britain.

PART TWO   THE TWENTIETH CENTURY

While all dates are inevitable, some are viewed as special and some actually become significant. The turn of the century was just such an important moment for Mormonism in Wales. In January 1900 the Welsh Conference was held in Cardiff. It recorded a total membership of three hundred including nineteen missionaries and ten local elders. There were five priests, thirty two teachers and eleven deacons. In July 1904 the Welsh Conference was closed. The first four years of the twentieth century thus witnessed a major change in Welsh Mormonism, and the fact of this close of an era demands careful attention.

Chapter Seven

Decline in Wales

Two prime factors combined to produce a situation compelling the Mormon authorities to draw their work in Wales to a halt. First, the large number of emigrants whose departure had depleted membership to the point at which a large religious institution could no longer be sustained. Second, the meteoric rise of religious revivalism in South Wales which suddenly diverted the flow of converts elsewhere. Both factors involve numerous complex elements.

The year 1900 began without any special emphasis. A public meeting in Penarth witnessed a slight interruption by some odd and enthusiastic Baptist but apart from that meetings are said to be well attended by Saints and strangers. Some thirteen Theological Classes were being held and the Mutual Improvement Association was active in five branches in Wales. Numbers declined by two hundred and sixty three by the close of 1900, some eleven emigrated.

At Salt Lake City on 23 September George Q. Cannon issued a firm reminder to the people that they ought to do everything possible to prepare for the coming of the Lord.

On 7 October President Cannon again drew attention to this oldest and most basic of Latter Day Saint doctrines. "Many", he said, "who are now within the sound of my voice have been promised that they shall live, if they have faith, to behold the second coming of the Lord", (1901:17). Even so the Mormon Church in Britain no longer placed emigration as the most important form of preparing for this advent. In fact the church and its message found the first few years of 1900s an ambivalent and paradoxical period.

In the early millennial message emigration and second advent were inextricably linked. Now the theme of Christ's second coming is stressed but without that link with emigration. The 1903 editorial is perhaps the first clear sign of a change within the leadership in response to the situation the church now found around it. The Saints are told to be in no hurry to emigrate. The need is to stay and build strong branches with local priests. This local deployment will then enable the missionary elders to be free to move further afield. Saints should accept the laws of the land and use whatever influence they have for helping to mould good government, (1903:8,9). The editorial for 1904 is even more explicit in this matter and helps us grasp one dynamic of Mormon life that had hitherto been implicit. The elders no longer preach emigration; more than that, they positively advise converts not to seek emigration. Despite such official counsel "many imagine that they are possessed of the true spirit of gathering...they refuse to believe that the emissaries of evil, vice and crisis...and a host of other sins are to be found in Salt Lake just as much as anywhere else on the face of the earth." This January editorial adds that the temptations of Satan reach their climax almost under the shadow of the temple. Later in the year it is stated yet again that emigration is uniformly discouraged but that once "the gospel takes possession of a man he seems moved upon to get to Zion as soon as possible", (1904:484). The same report notes for Britain that if emigration continues those departing will exceed those being baptized into the church.

This is clear testimony of the difficulty in preaching Mormon truth without implicating participation in the community of a geographical Zion. Both the doctrinal centrality of a site for the millennial reign and the socio-economic attractiveness of an American relocation which had once combined were now dissociated. The pattern and content of the message had to undergo a radical transformation. This was not easily accomplished and it is quite possible to interpret official utterances as containing basic contradictions. A dissonance exists between the restoration adventist gospel and the call to remain away from Utah. The stress on the imminent advent is strong; indeed President Cannon strengthens it further, but at the furthest peripheries of the movement that emphasis is now used to justify continuing residence and not emigration. This was a fundamental change.

Though not used as a justification the British are told that many a zealous emigrant convert has lapsed, once settled in America. The journey is no guarantee of fidelity. There is even a suggestion that the "spirit of Temple work should be born here" with records gathered and genealogies compiled. Perhaps this answered the question of rituals as key LDS practices. To stay was to miss the benefit of temple ordinances which had been strongly advocated hitherto. It would, in fact, be another fifty years before a British temple was consecrated and that local spirit of temple work could blossom. For the moment the question of efficiency of organization took predecence over harmonizing conflicting ideas.[47] At the same time as the Latter Day movement in Wales came virtually to a standstill, and in England to a much reduced level of life, the American base was increasingly preoccupied with ritual and doctrinal refinement.

President Joseph F. Smith writes in 1903 on the inadvisability of repeating sacred ordinances. It seems that the custom of re-baptism had been followed by Mormons in the sense of a repeated rite within the movement as such. It had been self-evident to Saints that any baptism undergone in Gentile churches was invalid so that the power of the Restored Melchizedek elder was demanded in a baptism prior to admittance into the Mormon fold. But that was not the point at stake here. Assuming a Mormon baptism on first joining the church a second and further Mormon baptism had then come to be accepted as customary. Such "re-baptism" seems to have been interpreted as essentially different from the original rite of membership, coming to be administered prior to entering a temple and performing its rites. Joseph F. Smith attacked the implicit assumption that had grown alongside this practice, namely that these subsequent baptisms secured forgiveness of sins. He was worried on ethical grounds that people might think of sin in less drastic ways and come to believe they could sin with impunity because frequent re-baptism would make all well again. The convention which now came to formal recognition was available only for those who, after being formally excommunicated, had repented and were being re-admitted to the fellowship of church membership. Smith added the further point of clarification that this rule did not apply to the many vicarious baptisms people might undergo in the temple. They constituted a different class of ritual.

Anointing with oil must also have fallen into some abuse for that too is made less generally available. Some firm guidelines are laid down on the service at which babies of church members are named and blessed. The setting is the monthly fast meeting and at it the bishop asks the father of the child to bless it and name it, (1903:50). If anyone wanted or needed the blessing in the home rather than at the appropriate service then special permission had to be obtained, (1903:90). At baptism there should be a ceremony of laying on of hands as soon as possible after the immersion. This is needed prior to any reception of the Lord's Supper. The general public ought not to witness the baptism and laying on of hands, (1903:744).

One of the clearest examples of this process of formalizing rites and practices as a general institutionalizing of theology was the Book of Mormon Convention at Provo in Utah where a committee was appointed to agree a standard pronunciation of names in the Book. It was in 1920 that the new format in double-column pages and given pronunciation was published, it having been divided into chapter and verse by Orson Pratt in 1879. Though these details were all worked out by contemporary leaders, others were rehearsed by them having been taken from Joseph Smith's own sayings. As with the dictum that all come from the grave in resurrection as they died whether young or old, tall or short and so on, (1903:56).

Mormonism was said to flourish precisely because it possessed a clear theology bringing people from blind belief within other churches to absolute knowledge in the restored gospel, because it possessed a divinely directed organization, and because it dealt clearly with temporal affairs in moral training as well as physical and intellectual preparation, (1903:403).

Chapter Eight

Religious Revivalism

If Mormonism flourished for these reasons in Utah the main reason, after emigration, why it declined in Wales lay in the upsurge of Nonconformist revivalism. Revivalism was no strange thing to Mormon history. The Latter Day Saint movement had come to birth in that area of New York State which had been called the burnt-over district precisely because the Spirit of God had been so much in evidence there in zealous, enthusiastic revivals that it was a kind of scorched zone of holy power.[48] But, be that as it may, all revivals are not the same. Much depends on context, culture, and the mood of a people. In particular they depend on social and economic elements as factors influencing human outlook, motivation, fears and hopes. Prior history of religion in an area adds yet a further dimension.

The interpretation of revivals is a particularly clear example of sociological analyses of religion in general. From what has briefly been said in the last paragraph there is a clear social key to the religious excitement of revival. But all such keys are questionable. Mormon theology has a different explanation just as mainline churches in Wales had several different suggestions as to why revivalism occurred.

Two modern writers on South Welsh culture-history saw the 1904-05 revivals as partly an expression of the kind of anguish which they think is experienced, or was experienced on that occasion, by a first generation industrialist population which sensed a denial of a previous pattern of life, presumably an agricultural one (Francis and Smith, 1980:7). If there is any truth in their suggestion then it might be argued that the decrease in Mormon membership and in Mormon emigration over the turn of the century reflected a need of the local populace to come to terms with changing circumstances not by adopting the earlier radical alternative of a different religion and another land, but by the equally radical alternative of revivalism within a known religious tradition and in the social world which needed to be validated and sanctified. The 1904 revival thus becomes a sanctification of industrialized society.

There may be much truth in that, but the same authors provide the information that because of subsequent secular emigration as the century continued "the industrial population hardly increased at all between 1935 and 1965", (ibid. p.38). This might hint at some other cause of the revival, or else it could mean that the generations following immediately upon the revival felt freer to act as industrial migrants having had their parental generation legitimated as industrial beings through the revival itself. All such speculation has a low level of validity to it. What we do know is how Mormons interpreted these revivals.

Generally the *Star* only touched on other religious groups and seldom dwelt on them for long. The Mormon certainty of its own distinctive identity grounded in the restored gospel made comparisons and evaluation between it and other churches redundant. In 1900 note is taken of what was called a religious boom taking place in New York, Boston and parts of Canada, and which was nothing other than the Christian Science movement. Mormonism had always been slightly wary of religious revivals since the time of Joseph Smith, whose own religious transformation occurred in reaction against, though deeply in the context of, the revivalism of New York State. From the outset Mormonism thus possessed an implicit negative orientation to mass enthusiasm. The curious aspect of the Christian Science "boom" was that those involved were largely "cultured" people: and in particular the cultured of no mean cities, perhaps especially Boston, (1900:311). While mass revivalism presented a fixed image of uncultured crowds, even a high degree of religiosity struck the *Star* as strange. The wider judgement seems to be that while "faith in its larger sense is on the increase ... belief in religious dogma is rapidly declining", (1900:225). The following year there is an awareness that the Free Churches in London were preparing for new religious success in revivals, (1901:152). Similar reports also came of discussions on revivalism in Boston in 1902. This contrasts with a relative lack of interest in, for example, the Sankey and Moody evangelistic crusades in Britain and in Boston in the 1870s and 1880s.

It was during the new period of relative weakness in the church that closer attention was paid to events in other churches. The editorial for December 1904 makes the Mormon analysis in a clear way and with a telling historical analogy.

It is, it says, at just those periods when people reject divine revelation that they become open to whatever malevolent spirits are abroad in the world. Rejecting truth for half-truth results in being deceived. This was what happened at the birth of the Mormon church. Those who rejected the restored gospel in its cradle of New York State were open to the spiritualism then engendered by the Fox sisters and which yielded the Spiritualist Church. And this principle of delusion following in the wake of rejection was now repeating itself in Wales. As the Welsh Conference closed so the new revivalism exploded. The editorial is a good example of judicious religious journalism. It talks of a "so-called religious revival" of a "strange spirit" sweeping the country and becoming the talk of the nation. Enthusiasm is tremendous, some even frothed at the mouth and needed binding. No fault is found with any good resulting from abandoning evil habits. What is clear and unquestionable is that "the spirits which tell these people that their proceedings are a means of eternal salvation in the Kingdom of God are but snares and delusions", (1904:793). This pattern of "getting religion" and "confessing Christ" is no novelty to the Mormon experience of fellow Americans in the frontier context and in the "usual sectarian manner" of accepting Christ by "expressing a belief in Him".

This notion that delusion follows rejection enabled Mormons to retain a religious explanation both of the present failure of the Welsh mission and the apparent success of the other churches. The same explanation is given for the success of the Torrey and Alexander mission in England in the same year, though in England there had been no formal closure of church work.

Mormon ideals of conversion differed markedly from this revivalist style. Dr Torrey's work yielded conversions which were believed to be only short-lived. Spurious and unlasting they differed from true conversion which "is usually the result of calm, serious, determined consideration", (1904: 360,373). The fire of Welsh revivalism is portrayed as burning violently and irrationally. The converted football team that ceremonially cremated the ball gave rise to the pun that if the revival fire burnt much hotter, cricket balls, bats and wickets, along with all innocent recreation, would be abolished. "It is unreasonable to suppose that the Spirit of the Lord will incite people to foolish acts" of this kind, and the Welsh would have done better to avoid this confusion by accepting the principles of the Gospel, (1904:794). No better clarification of Mormon thought could be pinpointed than in the opposition between "principles" and "enthusiasm", (1859:3).

Believers belonging to main-line Christian churches often presume in their ignorance of the Mormon Church that it must be a highly emotive and enthusiastic body. This general view of sects presumes them to be even more developed forms of the most extreme Protestantism and is usually quite incorrect. Certainly as far as the Latter Day Saint movement is concerned ideas of conversion are tied more to a rational process of educated change than to a momentary emotional crisis and climax. And this has been so for the duration of its history, in part because of reactions against surrounding revivalism at the time of its birth, but also because of its philosophical framework and ritual base.

The powerful influence from the practice of other churches ought not to be overlooked. This is widely acknowledged for the years of Mormonism's infancy, but it extends further and is an intriguing feature over the period of this early twentieth century Welsh revivalism.

Scenes of religious enthusiasm with dramatic conversions made many question whether all this was not a sign of the close of the age and presaged Christ's return. As so often in the *Star* articles and statements were produced to clarify confused questions among the general membership, as well as to present formal teaching from the leadership. In 1906 one article deals with the "Atmosphere of the Millennium". In one particular respect it is surprising, for in describing the advent of this reign of Christ it teaches that the new age will "come to pass naturally, simply and without any particular heralding". "Only those who take part in that Spirit and power would know of its existence. Others about them should be ignorant of this power", (1906:193). Saints are asked whether the exquisite beauty of the millennium will shine within and about them "as it comes gradually to the earth". All this has, it is said, been told the church by its prophets. And it poses a slight puzzle in interpreting Mormon historical theology.

Superficially it is tempting to argue that the early and mid-nineteenth century church was strongly millennial, proclaiming the necessity of emigration to prepare for the second coming of Christ which all would see dramatically in full apocalyptic splendour. Then to say that over the turn of the century this hope gave way to a belief in a gradual transformation of this world into that of the new order through the developing expansion of the church organization. But the picture is far more complex than that. [49] For despite the initial emphasis on the second coming of Christ, which is of necessity a dogma devoid of any visibly immediate consequence, there was a parallel commitment to the establishment of an earthly kingdom. "Why do we gather?" asked the *Star* in a rhetorical question. Because God commands it, because we have a covenant with God to become a nation and because "God has mercifully pointed out a place wither we must flee to escape ... while at the same time we shall be preparing for the coming of the Son of Man", (1843:44).

Gathering to nation-build and emigration to await the Parousia were dual themes of this early period. So it was not a question of abolishing one concept to adopt another as time progressed. It was to develop one at the expense of the other. The dogma which grew was also the one most open to visible expression. The growth of a Mormon culture in Utah was practical evidence that a nation of promise was being divinely succoured. Preaching and teaching the ideal of a kingdom in which the priesthood is the administrator of God's laws in his earthly realm is assured more easy acceptance, in the face of social facts of growth, than preaching a second coming which did not materialize. So visible was this earthly society that outsiders might wrongly assume its growth to be motivated by "impure motive, political intrigue and a thirst for power".

This dual theme embraced by an adventist-national-preparation shows the half-truth, or perhaps the sociological oversimplicity of the New Testament scholar Ernst Käsemann's assumption that "you do not write the history of the church if you are expecting the end of the world to come any day", (1964:28). He is correct if, as he assumes for Christians of the first century, a sharp dichotomy is drawn between this present world and its earthly life and a future realm in heaven. In a case like the early Mormons, however, there is no such absolute qualitative and spatial divide. The rule of God and of Christ in the established kingdom will make use of the earthly social organization already established. For the early Mormons it is self-evident that the gathering to Zion is no redundant behaviour. There was no expectation that earthly work would be voided when the second advent dawned.

An important theological element in the story of Zion's growth is the place accorded to God as such, and to the relation between God and the figure of Jesus. Early Mormonism was not totally pre-occupied with the specific and narrowly focussed second coming of Jesus Christ. Great care is needed in explaining this statement for that millennial appearance does seem to be at the forefront of the message. It was a vital doctrine but it was set within the wide framework of God's activity. God, as the highest of all beings, was related to Jesus whose progenitor he was, but God was also a distinct "personage" as the Mormons say.

Chapter Nine

God and Kingdom

The concept of kingdom was an inextricable part of the millennial reign of Christ but it also had more extensive connotations. In January 1847 the *Star* published a diagram of the kingdom of God with an account placing the eternal father at its head. The telling point and distinctive feature of this kingdom is that there are very many other kingdoms comprising the total kingdom of God. All the most eminent and distinguished prophets sit at the head of their own particular kingdom. This is a development of the biblical idea in the Epistle to the Hebrews that all believers are kings and priests before or under God. What is critical for our case is that Jesus is counted among the distinguished prophets. He too is crowned head of his kingdom as they are. His kingdom, like theirs, is situated under or within the all-embracing kingdom of God. There are "kingdoms of all shapes and sizes, an infinite variety to suit all grades of merit and ability", (1847:73).

The usual theological motif of the kingdom of God became in early Mormonism a dominant symbol which influenced the growth of belief in a multitude of kingdoms. It was not a single reality, but an overarching frame enclosing smaller and subsidiary kingdoms. In other words, there was no total and complete identification of the kingdom of God with the awaited kingdom of Christ.

If this suggestion is correct it enables us to see how the concept of kingdom could at one and the same time refer to an ultimate ideal and to more proximate ventures. It is a shifting idea as far as particular content is concerned but that very variation gains its power from the ultimate belief that the divine involvement in human life may be likened to a kingdom.

No more changing theological idea exists in Mormon history than this one of kingdom. It is intrinsically related to the allied beliefs of Zion and the Millennium as well as the Parousia of Christ. A brief note will suffice to outline the varied patterns of meanings into which these concepts have been set.

In December 1830 Joseph Smith produced a revelation in the *Book of Moses* contained in the Standard Work called the *Pearl of Great Price*. Chapter seven tells of the Old Testament character Enoch who along with some devotees were called Zion by the Lord because of their unity of heart and mind, (Moses 7:18). Enoch builds a city which is called "the City of Holiness, even Zion", (7:19). God then takes this city up into heaven. There follows on earth the entire scene of history involving God himself weeping for the wickedness of men, God who is designated King of Zion, (7:53) and who speaks of gathering his elect from the four quarters of the earth into a Holy City called Zion, a New Jerusalem, (7:62). A strange verse follows in which the Lord says to Enoch that he and his city will meet these gathered-in believers in one united entity.

A similar uniting of heavenly and earthly derived cities is depicted in the Book of Mormon. The New Jerusalem would come down from heaven and another holy city, "like the Jerusalem of old", would be built on earth, (Ether 13:2, 3, 10, 11). Mormons have generally adopted one particular style of interpretation which sees linkages between things as one way of talking about the fulfilling of former promises or events in Latter Day events. In this case the heavenly Jerusalem once existed on earth but had been transposed until such time as the desire to build a holy city to the Lord should well up amongst mankind. At that point the two cities would be linked.

One difficulty in this whole scheme is that elsewhere in the *Doctrine and Covenants* Joseph Smith is given what we might call the code name Enoch, (78:1) and is told he will be made a ruler over many kingdoms and receive a crown prepared for those obedient to God. If that code name also applies to the Enoch in *Moses* there is then a hint that the heavenly Jerusalem is the church originally founded by Joseph, taken to heaven until a further earthly Zion is ready to be combined with it. But Mormons have not followed this speculative possibility.[50]

Historically Missouri was revealed to be the geographical Zion with Independence as its focal point or centre place. This was said to have been disclosed to Joseph in July 1831, (D. & C. 57:1-3). The whole tenor of contemporary Mormon thought concluded that the Parousia was near and that preparation of an earthly Zion at Independence would be vitally necessary for the divine advent. But force of circumstance meant that by the winter of 1838 the Saints were forced to leave the whole Missouri area under Gentile oppression. This enforced geographical relocation demanded a re-working of the theological link between the Parousia and a specific location.

Though the town of Nauvoo in Illinois became the next community focus it was never viewed as Zion. In fact it was during this period that Joseph Smith openly stated that Zion was to be the whole of America even though Independence remained the centre place, (History of the Church 6:318, 319).

Throughout the refining, elaboration and transformation of Zion ideas, there is great significance in the context of pressures informing the leaders. Joseph Smith never lived to see the great Salt Lake Valley. The proclamation that all America was Zion is intelligible as a reaction to the loss of Independence. This generalization saved the faith which hitherto had been particularized at the specific site in Missouri. But after Mormons had suffered Joseph's martyrdom and the privations of migration to the Salt Lake Valley it is not surprising to find that dramatic habitat impressing them with the idea that Zion is better viewed as a real place than as an idea. And as we have already suggested, the earlier revelations of Smith provided appropriate warranty for seeing Zion as both a heavenly and earthly, abstract and concrete, reality.

It also seems likely that Mormons in Europe were not overly concerned with detailed debate on the precise location of Zion. That it was in America was sufficient as a goal motivating emigration. Not only so, for the death of Joseph Smith in 1844 stimulated Mormons in serious reappraisal of their position both geographically, historically and theologically. Potential emigrants are exhorted not to linger on account of this murder but to come and strengthen a proved and disciplined church. At Merthyr there is certainly no complaisance or sense of witnessing from a distance the mobbing of Joseph Smith. In fact there are suggestions that similar hostilities to Mormons might soon break out. "The whole town and works ... are actually drunken with infatuation and rage for or against Mormons", (29 September 1847). This at a time when Merthyr boasted some six hundred members. Throughout Wales about one hundred and fifty a month were being baptized, and in the middle of 1848 this matched about ten per week at Merthyr which felt justified in calling itself the "mother branch of Britain", (30 March 1848).

This intensity of missionary work was not to be stopped by Smith's martyrdom and was not subject to relatively detailed doctrinal dispute. The broad sweep of Mormon thought had Zion, however defined, at its centre and this exerted a dynamic pull on socially deprived but optimistic Welshmen. When that broad message itself changed and Saints were discouraged from emigrating, the attraction of Mormonism waned. It had been extremely successful for more than fifty years and it would take nearly another fifty before the church again flourished at Merthyr Tydfil. Meanwhile revivalism came and begged interpretation at the very moment of Mormon collapse. It was no wonder that Saints saw revival as a deceit and deception.

Sporadic meetings took place in Wales during the first two decades of the twentieth century when in official terms the South Wales groups were organized as part of the Bristol Conference. Some seventy eight meetings were held in 1906 throughout Wales, a very small number. Yet there was some dedicated work carried out as when president Smith and elder M. N. Reynolds walked through Monmouthshire and Glamorgan visiting isolated Saints and carrying out some baptisms. There are but few with only some six at Goytre, for example. When there is reference to Christ as one to be revealed, it is vague and merely asserts his destruction of the wicked and his reigning "in Zion and Jerusalem", (1907:149).

January 1908 witnessed two district meetings in Cardiff with twelve travelling elders present, (1908:78) and in August an open-air meeting in Cardiff was well received, with the only opposition coming from "the Reorganites", (1908:559). Fragmented groups around Abertillery were formed into the Pontypool Branch of the Bristol Conference. In 1909 Cardiff hosts a gathering of Welsh Saints, some of whom were said not to have been at a meeting for over five years. There is an article on the second coming which stresses the most literal meaning of that event and a discussion of patriarchal blessings. These individual proclamations, given by an official church patriarch, offered a kind of private insight into God's will for that person. An extension of the Old Testament patriarchs' blessing their descendants this office became institutionalized in the church. The blessings being given indicated that many church members actually belonged to the tribes of Israel, and in particular to the house of Ephraim; this was seen as evidence that God was actually restoring the tribes of Israel through church membership, (1909:700). But information like this was not very functional in Wales. Similar treatises on the female prototype in the Godhead maintain the profile of distinctive Mormon doctrine, (1910:620). A convention of Conference Presidents held at Liverpool in February 1911 reiterated the necessity of keeping converts in Britain. Practically all church Sunday Schools are said to have lost able teachers through emigration. This same issue dealt with plural marriage reporting that while in 1890, when the manifesto forbidding plural unions was announced, there had been two thousand five hundred and forty one plural families, this had dropped to one thousand five hundred and forty three in 1899 and down further to eight hundred and ninety seven by 1903. One of the consequences of these social reorganizations was a lack of husbands for the maritally free women thus made available, (1911:89, 117). Wales was in no position to help for membership now existed more as a residual element than as any strategic population. We learn of a social evening held at the Park Hotel Hall Pontypool on 12 March 1912 with about seventy five Saints and friends present including elders H. R. Thomas and E. E. Wait from the Merthyr Tydfil area, hinting at the maintenance of links between Glamorgan and that resourceful centre in Monmouthshire, (1912:706).

The *Star* makes other passing comment on Wales, but not on the revival activity there. In 1913 the focus is on the debate over Dissestablishment of the Anglican Church. This hotly contested political and theological issue does not elicit any polemic from the editor. England has more of an interest in some anti-Mormon crusading afoot at Ipswich over Christmas and New Year of 1912-1913.

There are continued reflections on the nature of the church and its practical management. A. C. Lambert talks of it as a body springing into existence without any parental sect or motivating theological controversy. This rather idealistic rationalization may be passed over in order to note how he describes that "dispensation of the fulness of times" which the church exists to proclaim. The dispensation is a system or body of laws given by God for governing his children. The implication is that the growth of church discipline through the revealed procedures of organization affords a focus of divine authority which all may see, rather than a cataclysmic millennial revolution which simply has not come about. On the details of church life, as an example of such a structure, members are reminded that children are worthy to take part in the Sacrament Service on the basis of Christ's atonement, whether or not they were born to church members, (1913:346).

The *Star* was also used to clarify, express and formulate more directly theological ideas. Some of these would have been strange to the ears of many British Mormons whose initial religious education had been in the mainline churches. Jesus Christ, for example, is said to be "one and the same person" as Jehovah. The one being the New Testament equivalent of the other in the Old Testament, (1914:8). There is little justification offered for assertions like this, they are simply made rather than argued. The interesting aspect of that particular identification lies in the aligning of New Testament with Old. Whereas most orthodox believers interpret Christ as the incarnate Son who advances the divine work into the future, this Mormon reworking of doctrine regresses the Christ into such a close association with the God of the Old Testament as to merge their identity. But there is an additional subtlety within Mormon theology which alters the apparent meaning of this linkage. For the God who has dealings with mankind in the Old Testament was thought by some, and notably by Brigham Young, to be none other than Adam.[51] So to link the Christ with both Jehovah and Adam left opportunity for a higher and less involved God. But Mormons differ much over interpretation of deity, especially in the later nineteenth century. To a large extent it was a problem of bringing systematic order to a large and mixed body of vaguer sayings of Joseph Smith and other leaders.

It is a fact of Joseph Smith's literary style that one biblical image, name, or person, suggests and triggers references to others. Many hundreds of examples could be cited for it is the underlying matrix of both *Book of Mormon* and the Standard Works. Citing only the connection or stylistic association of Adam with Michael the Archangel we have in D. & C. 27:11, "And also with Michael, or Adam, the father of all, the prince of all, the ancient of days". At D. & C. 107:54, the Lord appears and those who see Him rise up and "blessed Adam, and called him Michael, the prince, the archangel".

Though these flowing titles afford much opportunity for critical analysis the fact that they occur in what Mormons believed to be revelations means that such criticism is seldom forthcoming. Mormons saw this large body of revealed material both in the *Book of Mormon* as well as in the *Pearl of Great Price* and *Doctrine and Covenants* as the foundation of the restored gospel message. Any potential internal inconsistencies within the texts were of little import. Positive direction was sought in these revelations rather than any source for critical scholarship. These Standard Works of the Church of Jesus Christ of Latter Day Saints were armaments for a battle and not books for leisure criticism.

Criticism came from outsiders and was always directed at the written revelation of Mormons. Their social life attracted especial Gentile virulence.

Tom Roberts could write from Pontnewydd, Pontypool, about a serial story entitled the *Sin of Utah* written by one Winifred Graham. This "bitter attack" on Mormons was matched by a "well-known moving picture" called *A Victim of the Mormons*. It was clear to Mormons that this propaganda was used because opponents had practically given up focussing criticism on Mormon Scriptures. Capitalizing on the publicity the Saints gained permission at several places, including Edinburgh, to distribute tracts to the general public attending these films, (1912: 206, 233, 248).

Even so the total amount of anti-Mormon propaganda was small when compared with earlier periods. In Britain the decades of the eighteen fifties and sixties for example witnessed a spate of books, booklets and pamphlets, directed against the church. That was to be expected given its high level of social visibility and success in evangelism at that time. Nor perhaps was it strange that attention be paid it again after a period of quiet, since Mormon religion in Britain was one of the rare examples of an imported message whose church base and organization was still significantly influenced by Americans. While British religious history had had a long tradition of sectarianism, especially of the Millennarian type, it had usually been founded and directed by Britons.[52] Because of Mormonism's peculiar links with Utah there was a constancy of exposure to American visiting elders and authorities despite an ever-increasing growth of indigenous British leaders. The occasional attention given to Mormons in Britain as the new century advanced had little effect apart from increasing publicity. *The People* newspaper might accuse the Mormons of masquerading as members of the Reorganized Church, and Mormon authorities might deny it, but the consequences are minimal, (1912:572).

To say that social consequences were few should not, however, blind us to the rôle played by passing minor conflicts with the press and pamphleteers. From accounts of antagonism Saints could still perceive that important boundary between them and the world of their Gentile neighbours. At a time when emigration had greatly diminished, and church activity in Britain was at a low ebb, there was a real need to see membership as a distinctive commitment. Boundaries were maintained and attitudes reinforced as much in the pinpointing of adverse publicity as in formal mission of the church itself.

Encouragement was taken from church endeavour even though much had to be made of insignificant events. In this phase of quiescence, a period of little things, every sign of success was welcomed. Three persons baptized at Porth in the Rhondda Valley is real news from South Wales just as is an anti-Mormon meeting in Norwich Market Place, (1912:559). British Saints might be isolated and in a phase of retrenchment but there is for them a bigger Mormon world beyond, for which the statistics furnish evidence of life and purpose. The *Star* for 1914 shows no emigration from Britain for the previous year but indicates a British membership of eight thousand five hundred and seventeen. In the total world, church statistics are presented showing a birth rate of 37 per 1000, a death rate of 9.3 per 1000 with thirty eight being the average age of death. The rate of marriage was 15 per 1000 and of these only 8 per 1000 were performed in temples. This was thought a low performance to be corrected as soon as possible to indicate the significance of temple ritual; the number divorced was one hundred and sixty three and of these fifty nine had been married in a temple ritual as opposed to the one hundred and four who had not undergone the sealing of temple unions, (1914:341).

The March editorial of 1915 strikes a note which tells both of the long-standing millennial message of separatism and of the recent transformation in that exhortation. Repeating the warning to come out from Babylon and not delaying in so doing, prospective converts are called to "seek safety in the acceptance of the gospel". The novel theme is that the Church of Jesus Christ is that to which people must flee. Babylon is the world and refuge is the church wherever people are. Thus is exclusivism proclaimed and Zion relocated. The church institution replaces the geographical Zion in the minds of those now hearing the message, (1915:153).

Even so there remains a stream of opinion hinting at or more directly confessing faith in "the day of the Millennium" which "is dawning and will soon be here in all its splendour", (1915:425). Mormon opinion was mixed during this transitional period: as the first world war had its devastating effects in Europe the Mormons were unsure of what it foreshadowed or portended. Glimpses of a continuation in this mixed view of Zion and millennium may also be gained some decades later. In 1930, for example, the *Star* expounds the meaning of Zion in three ways. Firstly, in terms of the Book of Moses as we have ourselves discussed it above, then secondly, as Jerusalem and finally as the "city yet to be reared on the Western Continent which will be known as the New Jerusalem ... in the neighbourhood of the present city of Independence in the State of Missouri". Further details are added to say that "this city will in time be built and the Lord Jesus Christ will dwell there, (D. C. 45: 66-67). When the plans of the Lord are consummated Enoch's city of Zion will be merged with the New Jerusalem", (1930: 729). But the editor added that for general purposes the word Zion refers to the Church of God "irrespective of locality".

Meanwhile, authoritative announcements are made on the correct spelling of the word Melchizedek and at Goytre, South Wales, four people are baptized, (1915:376, 770). Such interests mark the institutional and local levels of church life. Mission work worldwide is said to be very good, but Wales stands out as a poor exception.

Chapter Ten

Evan Stephens and Mormon Hymnody

Almost as a sign of a Welsh chapter closing in the history of the Mormon Church 1916 witnessed the resignation of Evan Stephens who had been born in Pencader Carnarvonshire in 1854. He had become conductor of the Mormon Tabernacle Choir in 1890 and wrote about one fifth of the tunes in the church hymnbook and words for numerous of its hymns. Himself the tenth child of David Stephens he has been referred to as the "tithing of his father's house". Baptized when eight years of age and emigrating at twelve he affords an interesting example of a boy growing into Mormon life as his prime religious commitment and cultural focus whilst also having a background in a Welsh ethos. Unlike his fellow countryman, Dan Jones, who left behind him six children, two by each of three wives, Evan Stephens was a lifelong bachelor.

His contribution to posterity remains solid. Not only in the musical tradition of Mormondom's great choir, but in the Church's Hymnbook. The 1948 edition contains a dozen hymns whose words he wrote and more than twice that number of tunes. His themes in these Latter Day hymns are broad and varied.

There is an underlying sense of security in Utah as a land of promise. This expresses itself as a love for Zion and gratitude to God for bringing his Saints there and for protecting them. *O Home Beloved* depicts a place of ordinariness which draws and attracts the wanderer wherever he may be; "On foreign land or distant sea, As time goes by my heart grows fonder and yearns more lovingly for thee". It is the kind of song which is almost entirely secular and could certainly have been written as a Welsh folk-song. Given the context of a Mormon hymnbook we understand it to refer to Utah, but had it been located in a British national songbook we would be justified in interpreting the longings as rooted in Wales. Practically the same could be said for *O Happy Homes Among the Hills*. In, *Shall the Youth of Zion Falter*, with its long established chorus, "True to the Faith", there is a slightly more obvious Mormon content, but even so it hangs on a proper reading of the word Zion. Similarly with *Raise your Voices to the Lord*, a hymn of praise; *Let us all Press On*, which is exhortatory; and the Christmas Carol *Glory Be To God in the Highest*. Written and with a choral setting composed by Stephens for women's voices this last hymn reads as an ordinary Christian item. For many converts to the Latter Day movement these hymns which we have just mentioned are likely to have served as useful emotional links with prior Christian commitment across wide denominational boundaries. Words and phrases echo biblical concepts and re-echo traditional hymnody. Distinctive doctrinal understanding can be found in them if a grasp of the dogma has already been learned elsewhere.

The overlap between former commitment and new Latter Day fellowship involved hymns as a major element along with the bible. The distinctive Mormon teaching on the Restoration of priesthoods, on prophecy, temples with their covenants and ordinances, as well as the *Book of Mormon* and Standard Works, was something into which new members grew more or less quickly and to an unequal degree of insight.[53]

Evan Stephens and other hymnists assisted this transformation into Mormon identity by writing hymns both in the style of traditional Christianity and also in the firm perspective of the Restoration. This is an important point because the Mormon Hymnbook is quite catholic in taste embracing many well-known hymns which would have been familiar to non-Mormons. *Rock of Ages, The Lord is my Shepherd, Lead Kindly Light, O God our Help in Ages Past, A Mighty Fortress, Abide with Me* and others, drawn largely from Protestant traditions.

Despite its conviction of the undoubted truth of the Restored gospel Mormonism thus retained the use of some Gentile hymns. In hymnody at least Mormonism was not exclusivist.

The key factor still is the fact that Mormon theology allows the singer to interpret many traditional concepts in distinctively different ways inasmuch as he possesses knowledge of the doctrine. In the early days of the church just as in some contemporary contexts of conversion, individuals joined the Restoration movement without necessarily possessing theological knowledge of any depth. It is likely that the familiar hymns encouraged them in their new religion whilst the distinctively Mormon hymns were able to extend their grasp of the new teachings.

Evan Stephens also made his mark in this direction with the hymn *The Voice of God Again is Heard*. Announcing the final dispensation it speaks of the voice of God breaking a long silence and withdrawing the curse of darkness. Missionary messengers must proclaim this new word and both the living and the dead may benefit from it. Not only so but they must prepare for the coming of the King of Glory.

Still more direct is a hymn for which again he furnished both words and music, *We Ever Pray for Thee*. Set for women's voices it addresses the Prophet at the head of the Church telling him how the Saints ever pray for him and that as God surely hears their prayer so will God's prophet be strengthened to lead the people: "As the advancing years furrow thy brow, still may the light within shine bright as now". It is to each and every prophet that the hymn applies and not solely to Joseph Smith, for of course that founding prophet had been killed on 27 June 1844 almost ten years to the day before Evan Stephens was born on 28 June 1854.

Having a hymn directed to a prophet marks out the importance of that rôle in the whole Restoration. In fact the 1948 church hymnal contains five other hymns touching on the prophetic office as focussed in Joseph Smith. John Taylor's *Oh Give me back my Prophet dear"* recalls the killing at

Carthage, asserts the innocence of Joseph but sees his death as the outcome of his faithful testimony to God's prompting; it also refers to the machinations of Christian leaders opposed to Mormonism: "It is because the priests of Baal were desperate their craft to save, and when they saw it doomed to fall, they sent the prophets to their grave". Indeed a clear identification links Joseph with the ancient prophets of the Old Testament. John Taylor's other hymn *The Seer, Joseph the Seer* is more full still of Mormon doctrine. Joseph is the chosen of God and the friend of man who brought the priesthood back again. His pre-existence is a noble one and his coming to earth is a blessing for men as he opens mysteries with keys provided by God. The prophet loved the Saints, and the town of Nauvoo, like the sun he spread a light and opposed crime: "unchanged in death, with a Saviour's love, he pleads their cause in the courts above". This intercessory function would appear strange to Protestants though not necessarily to Catholics. But the final lines would be unintelligible outside Mormon circles as Joseph is depicted as having his home in the sky where he dwells with the Gods. This plural noun hints at the Latter Day Saint belief that all men are gods in embryo and that some have already developed divine status, amongst whom is Joseph Smith.

But it is the hymn of William W. Phelps that brings prophetic hymnody to its culmination. *Praise to the Man* is a full exaltation of Joseph Smith which is liable to complete misunderstanding by non-members. The chorus to this four versed hymn would only be sung with reference to Jesus by mainline Christians and even then the reference to "gods" would make it practically unsingable; "Hail to the Prophet ascended to heaven, traitors and tyrants now fight him in vain. Mingling with Gods he can plan for his brethren, death cannot conquer the hero again". Once more we have the plurality of Gods with Joseph amongst them. As such he is a representative of other Mormons since all members of the Restoration have this high calling. Yet Joseph is a focus and prime example of the many truths of religion which all could experience. To non-Mormon Christians it seems odd and even blasphemous to sing "Praise to the man who communed with Jehovah! Jesus anointed that Prophet and Seer. Blessed to open the last dispensation, Kings shall extol him and nations revere". Odder still to use blood references in relation to sacrifice and Joseph's death; "Long shall his blood which was shed by assassins plead unto heaven", and "sacrifice brings forth the blessings of heaven, earth must atone for the blood of that man". This makes an echo of the Mormon idea of blood — atonement lying far beyond the conventional Christian notion of atonement. For murder it was believed, as we have already noted, that the murderer's blood needed to be shed before he might be forgiven the sin of killing others. This was one reason why execution by shooting was permitted under later law in Utah, for hanging did not shed blood. So here in Mormon thought certain forms of atonement could be brought about by human means, unlike the traditional Christian idea which restricted atonement to Christ's death. Mormon ideology incorporated more Old Testament motifs which involved atonement through the shedding of animal and human blood.

It is within more conventional areas that Evan Stephens made his other contributions to Mormon spirituality. Three sacrament hymns, or communion hymns, exemplify the distinctive Mormon ethos in connection with this rite.

In Remembrance of Thy Suffering sets the firm tone of Mormon theology of the sacrament as it is called; it is a memorialist theology. "In remembrance of thy suffering, Lord, these emblems we partake". The word emblem itself asserts the directness of reference and the avoidance of that kind of symbolic knowledge which permits vague thought and ease of identifying bread with body. The emotional stress falls more on the rôle of the Spirit in the contemporary believer than on the inner sacramental working of the bread or water. The sacrament also speaks of the future coming as the millennial kingdom:

> When thou comest in thy glory, To this earth to rule and reign
> And with faithful ones partakest of the bread and wine again,
> May we be among the number, Worthy to surround the board
> And partake anew the emblems, Of the suffering of our Lord.

Similarly in his hymn *Sacred the Place of Prayer and Song* Stephens touches on the atmosphere of peace, silence and contentment when "Each come to taste the power from above, The inspiration and the glow, Of holy love". This very same mood is picked up in his last sacrament hymn *Sweet is the Hour when thus we Meet*. The focus of divine activity is in heavenly realms for "Sweet are the songs we gladly sing In harmony and love, The echo of diviner things Heard in the Courts above". The repercussions of heavenly dynamism lie not in the bread and water, nor yet in any sacramental mysticism related to the cross and death of Christ, but in the subsequent work of "Thy Spirit pure, To hallow every deed".

This pneumatic theological motif has come to typify many aspects of Mormon life and is a most appropriate expression of the corporate commitment of the Saints. While the doctrines of God as Father, or of Jesus Christ as an historic redeemer, lie behind this sacrament rite, they are not the most obvious, nor even the most direct way of identifying how Mormons feel about their corporate act of remembrance. The Spirit is quite different. Being an invisible power known by the effect on the stirred and aroused heart, the Spirit can be experienced directly and as part of a larger group of people. Part of the truth of Mormon religion comes to Saints through their sharing in the sacrament. They feel themselves, and they see others, moved by the Spirit and this has a convicting certainty to it. Mormon piety is a corporate piety first and foremost. Frank I. Kooyman's sacrament hymn is the best example of how the Spirit motivates the Mormon community for action.

> Thy Spirit, Lord has stirred our souls,
> And by its inward shining glow

> We see anew our sacred goals
> And feel thy nearness here below.
> No burning bush on Sinai
> Could show thy presence, Lord, more nigh.
>
> "Did not our hearts within us burn?"
> We know the Spirit's fire is here.
> It makes our souls for service yearn.
> It makes the path of duty clear.
> Lord, may it prompt us, day by day
> In all we do, in all we say.

Alexander Schreiner, for a long time the organist at Salt Lake City's Tabernacle this century, wrote the tune for this hymn which has become well loved by Mormons as a fine musical grasp of the ethos of emotional but restrained and corporate spirituality. As a final and complementary comment on sacrament hymns mention must be made of Hugh W. Dougall's *Jesus of Nazareth, Saviour and King* which does focus on Jesus as its title so fully shows. Its middle verse tells how the broken bread leads the Saint's mind to the bruised, broken and torn body on Calvary's hill, a suffering still powerful in its effect upon the contemporary believer, yet firmly rooted in the past. So too with the cup:

> 'As to our lips the cup, Gently we press,
> Our hearts are lifted up, Thy name we bless,
> Guide us where'r we go, Till in the end
> Life evermore we'll know, Through thee, our Friend.'

Here in Mormon spirituality of the Sacrament is to be found a deeply reverential and emotionally touching yet restrained piety which is as thoroughly memorialist as any eucharistic scheme can be. It shows that there is no necessity for a sacramental theology of the usual incarnational type before profoundly convicting emotion is triggered. But these very theological terms associated with sacramental thought need much more careful treatment in the light of Mormon theology than we have given them in this chapter. To that task we now turn in the hope of showing something of the emergent subtlety of Mormon religious ideology.

But as a final comment on Mormon hymnody mention must be made of the 1985 edition of the *Hymns of the Church of Jesus Christ of Latter Day Saints*. A new collection with musical settings somewhat easier for average accompaniment it omits four of Evan Stephen's hymns which have been treated in this chapter. *O Happy Home, Glory Be To God, Sacred The Place Of Prayer*, and *Sweet Is The Hour*. The first three of these were originally set as choral pieces and along with the fourth they all express general Christian sentiments rather than any distinctive Restoration doctrine. By contrast it is interesting to observe that John Taylor's, *The Seer*, and, *O Give Me Back My Prophet*, which were clearly Restorationist, have not been included. One distinctive feature of some newly added hymns is the stress on genealogical work and family life, as typified in the hymn title, *Families Can Be Together Forever*.

Chapter Eleven

Comparative Theology of Sacraments

One particularly vital theological comment must be made at this point for it is not easy to use theological terms from the mainstream Christian traditions when evaluating or describing Mormon ideas. Especially is this true in the theology of the Lord's Supper or the Sacrament Service.

In that broad stream of Catholic theology where sacramental theology is well developed a firm distinction is drawn between the nature of God and the nature of the created cosmos, including mankind. God has created the cosmos, *ex nihilo*, from nothing, and it has a nature distinguishable from God. The universe is not an extension of God, it is different. Matter itself can, however, come to be a vehicle of and for divine communication as God chooses to use it. In such sacramental contexts there is a bridge formed in the sacramental material between the matter of the universe and the divine nature of God. This traditional sacramental outlook presupposes the initial difference between God and matter and then the subsequent use of matter to convey spiritual messages.

For the Restoration movement of the Latter Day Saints that initial divide between God and the cosmos is quite improper. The Mormon theory of matter regards everything that exists as belonging to one class. The God to whom men pray may be tremendously greater than his worshippers, but they both belong to the same material realm. Divine entities are far more highly evolved or differentiated than men on earth, but these same men have the opportunity to develop their own lives until at some point in the post-resurrection world they too will be as divine personages now are.

For this reason Mormon doctrines of Jesus Christ are intrinsically different from traditional Christologies which distinguish between the very essence of God and of man, and which argue that Jesus possessed both human and divine natures in his one personal identity. The theologically and historically important expression that Jesus as the Son of God was "of one substance" with the Father, or *homoousios* as it is in Greek, is quite redundant in Mormon theology. For, as we can now appreciate, all divine and human and even inanimate things are of one substance, they all belong to the same material — spiritual continuum, being refined and transformed over time but still possessing the same substratum.

But there is another reason why the sacrament service held in local Mormon chapels is not sacramental in the normal Christian sense of the term. It is because the ritual of the temples assumes the role performed by sacraments in main-line Christian orthodoxy. In the light of what has already been said about Mormonism's non-duality of matter and spirit some care is needed in explaining this further suggestion of temples as Mormon "sacraments".

Temple as Sacrament

In normal Christian sacramental theology the distinction between spirit and matter which we have already emphasized is overcome in some object which is thereby transformed.

Baptismal water is blessed and consecrated as is the bread and wine of the Eucharist, and after consecration it is deemed to have changed in some way. The outward and visible sign then conveys as it also symbolizes an inner and spiritual grace. What sacramental Christian traditions do in their specific sacraments is to confer spiritual quality upon ordinary matter. Mormon theology does not follow this pattern, it cannot do so because of its conviction that all matter is actually spirit in some degree. But even though Mormons do not make qualitative distinctions between levels of spirit-matter evolution they do make qualitative distinctions between, as the phrase has it, time and eternity.

Time and Eternity are categories which replace the normal dichotomy between matter and spirit in orthodox churches. If Roman Catholic sacramentalism is exemplified best in the doctrine of the Mass, then Mormon "sacramentalism" is best viewed in its doctrine of the Temple. For the Catholic bread and wine under the hands of the priest traditionally become the very body and blood of Christ: matter and spirit are united in the spiritual food of the elements. For the Mormon, rites performed in temples by Melchizedek priests transcend time in the dimension of eternity. Each temple in its spatial reality is a zone of eternity. It is set in contrast to the numerous local chapels which are expressions of time, of the present mundane order of reality.

So the temple on the one hand and the local meeting place or chapel on the other constitute two distinct contexts of religious reality. What goes on in the local chapel or Stake House takes place under the motif of time and pertains to the period of man's mortal existence on earth. This includes many group activities of education, leisure, administration and worship. It may seem odd to include worship in this category, and odder still to add the sacrament service to this domain, but this needs to be done to reflect the Mormon scheme of reality. It was within the time framework of this present world that Jesus was incarnated and was obedient to the point of his death. The memory of this event belongs to the same present world order.

What goes on in Mormon temples, by contrast, opens out the entire flow of cosmic duration far beyond the period of life on earth. Not only is the pre-existence of human souls a central idea in teaching given at temples, but that soul which has to exhibit its continued obedience through a mortal life, has to be prepared for its existence post-mortem. For after death and the final resurrections men and women will obtain an eternal state of ever progressive development and fulfilment in their own deified state. Temples furnish the appropriate context on earth in which to prepare for and initiate eternal duties and outlooks.

Insofar as we are correct in seeing rites as sacraments when they effect a linkage between the natural and supernatural worlds of religious schemes of reality, then for Mormonism, sacramental action must be restricted to the temples. Thus we can see why the chapel-based "sacrament service" of the Lord's Supper cannot in non-Mormon theology be classified as a sacrament, while many rites performed in temples could justifiably be deemed sacramental.

This short excursion into comparative theology will have helped show how distinctive a scheme is Mormon theology and practice, and how the church itself came to be a vital focus of religiosity. What I mean by this is that the restored message is one and the same as the restored church organization. While all church bodies view themselves as important, some tend to make the message a distinct and separate entity from the proclaiming institution. But just as the Roman Catholic Church sees its own existence as the basis for maintaining the truth of the faith as it interprets it, so the Church of Jesus Christ of Latter Day Saints believes its very existence to be the framework of the restored truth of God. This is a distinctive feature in the world of Protestant thought since it does not follow the general Protestant definition of a valid church as a gathering in which the word of God is truly proclaimed and the sacraments administered.

In Protestantism there is an assumption that the very independent existence of the bible, which is not the possession of any particular church or denomination, and the existence of the rite of baptism and Lord's Supper as autonomous events, means that many groups can utilize these things and thereby be authentic churches. The Mormon movement entirely disagrees with such a stance. For it, the church organization, with its rites and ordinances, along with the message, are both uniquely restored by God to mankind. The Restoration movement cannot produce and train believers as Christians in some general sense and such that a believer could sever his membership to go and join some other group. Authenticity of faith necessitates participation in the total life of the Restoration.

This is why the concept of "activity" in the life of church members is significant. It became all the more obviously significant as the twentieth century began to unroll and to demonstrate that no millennial advent of Christ had taken place. In the nineteenth century, activity had been directed towards mission preaching and the cultural establishment of Utah as a Mormon society. That having been accomplished the twentieth century set an agenda for maintaining and extending this Mormon organization which was also a physical manifestation of the principles of the restored gospel.

President Francis M. Lyman in a powerful address at the Salt Lake Tabernacle on 6 October 1916 spelt out the Mormon rationale of activity underlying which is a theory of life as process.

Passivity represents death and darkness as a purely negative aspect of reality. There is no such thing as a neutral state of existence. Mere inactivity itself conduces to destruction. Activity, by contrast, leads to animation, to life, and under the right influence of teaching, to salvation. The call for action is all the more pressing for those bearing the priesthood. They, after all, share in the very attribute of Godhead. Priesthood is an attribute of deity, and so is activity. There is, therefore, a great requirement that priests should be active. No narrow list of events can be made by which to measure activity, for all ordinary life of a quality worthy of imitation counts as activity. But for the most part it is wise to create things for people to do, especially those not holding particular office in local congregations who are themselves kept busy enough. The boys should be encouraged to do jobs alongside the older men and given opportunity to express their religious commitment. Study of the scriptures is itself a worthy activity, as are the many church events.

"Men grow by activity" while their participation in the life of the church confers "peace, security, life and salvation", (1917:150). This attitude has prevailed and flourished in the church up to the present day. It enshrines the Mormon ideal of progressive development which is the central philosophical perspective of Mormonism and embraces a theology of divine evolution, but it also expresses a psychological dimension touching child rearing in an atmosphere of achievement motivation. The Mormon use of the word "opportunity" is quite distinctive and speaks of a divine provision for self-advancement if only the individual avails himself of its possibilities. The church itself as the focus of the Restored Gospel is the prime arena of opportunity as of its ultimate consequence in salvation.

There may also be proximate consequences as in the rather unusual suggestion that church activity on the part of converts drawn from the North American "Red-Indian" led to a change of colour in their skin. This needs to be explained both literally and metaphorically.

In a 1917 editorial entitled "Indians Becoming White and Delightsome" there are positive suggestions that the North American Indians who are being educated are, in an obvious and literal way, becoming "white" in their life-style. Their occupations, ideas and aspirations are changing in such radical ways that some profound significance may lie behind the transformation. The prophetic nature of the *Book of Mormon* is drawn upon to explain this, for in the Books of Nephi there are both prophetic foretellings and descriptive accounts of dark-skinned people becoming fair. One text believed to give account of events between B.C. 588-570 tells of the Lord God cursing disobedient followers of Nephi for "the Lord God did cause a skin of blackness to come upon them", (2 Nephi 5:21). A similar text is directly prophetic: believed to have been spoken by Nephi between 559-545 B.C. concerning the post-resurrection period of Christ's life it declares that converts will believe the truth and that "their scales of darkness shall begin to fall from their eyes", (2 Nephi 30:6). On its own, that reference could be interpreted in terms of a mental enlightenment, but it immediately adds the rider that "many generations shall not pass away among them, save they shall be a white and delightsome people". A passage in the third Book of Nephi, which is deemed to have originated in A.D. 10-14, furnishes a direct form of this purifying process. Nephi the Third, whose putative ancestor had featured in the 6th century B.C. texts, tells how those darkened Lamanite peoples had thrown in their lot with the white Nephites and because of this pact against attackers they were blessed. "Their curse was taken away from them, and their skin became white like unto the Nephites. And their daughters exceedingly fair", (3 Nephi 2:16).

The *Star* editor expressed something of a general opinion in seeing the culture contact with American Indians as producing a radical change in their culture and was being intrinsically Mormon in interpreting this transformation as a spiritual metamorphosis following the prophetic promises of God.[54] For him it was "impossible to contemplate the great change that has come upon the red race in America without feeling convinced that the prophecy of the *Book of Mormon* has begun to be fulfilled", (1917: 72, 74).

Participation in the life of this church was thus seen by Mormons as a participation in the very acts of divine fulfilment. This same conviction which made it possible to believe that converted red-skins would yield white skins, also led members to see their church involvement less as a filling of bureaucratic offices than as an "organization of kings and priests", (1917:185).

Mormon Elders as Ministers

One of the most interesting episodes which illustrates several quite distinct attitudes towards church membership arose in 1916. It focussed on one William Thomas Hawkes of Ashford in Middlesex, in England, who claimed exemption from military service on the grounds that he was a minister of religion. The Military Service Act granted exemption from active service in the forces for those who were ministers "of a recognized church".

In September 1916 elder Hawkes had been convicted at Feltham magistrates court for failure to respond to his call-up by the military authorities. The magistrates had supported the military's view that the Church of Jesus Christ of Latter Day Saints was not a religious denomination but rather was an alien group too small to lay claim to valid recognition. Hawkes appealed against their decision and in April 1917 the case was heard before the King's Bench Division. Their Lordships came to the decision that the magistrates were not justified in law in stating that the Latter Day Movement was not a church. Having now granted that the L.D.S. group was a proper church the Lord Chief Justice's Court sent the case back to the magistrates for them to decide whether Hawkes was a recognized minister of this body now deemed a valid church. After much deliberation ending on 30 April the magistrates were equally divided and the case returned yet again to the higher Court of Mr Justice Darling, Mr Justice

Avory and Mr Justice Bailhache on Friday 9 November 1917. Mr Justice Darling extended this case even further by returning it yet again to the magistrates instructing them to sit in an odd number to decide the case without yet another equally divided court. This was finally accomplished on 2 January by the Spelthorne Bench of some seven magistrates. After a two hour hearing they decided that elder Hawkes was a regular minister of the Church of Jesus Christ of Latter Day Saints. An amicable ending saw elder Hawkes presenting copies of the *Book of Mormon* and *Articles of Faith* to the magistrates. This decision was finally confirmed and costs charged to the Military by the higher Court on 5 February. For the *Millennial Star* this marked the final victory and justification of the church as a valid religious body, (1917:301, 764. 1918:42, 121).

But in saying that the church had gained a legal victory we must be careful to identify carefully the nature of the victory. The precise triumph was in gaining legal validation of the church as a recognized and acceptable body. That such a body could possess authorized ministers was of secondary importance, and what was of even less importance to the church itself was the issue of exemption from Military Service.

In fact an editorial of 17 May 1917 goes out of its way to announce in no uncertain terms that the Latter Day Saints are not opposed to serving their native country when required to do so by the military forces. As a general rule the Saints are to be loyal to the governments under which they live. This is a question which we will encounter again when the Second World War brings to the stage of human history that painful picture of Mormons set against each other because they are faithful to those respective nations of their birth which now were at war with each other.

For the moment the *Star* presses its opinion and conviction that the church is no more alien to Britain because its headquarters are in America than is the Catholic Church because its centre is in Rome.

The Mormon belief in individual persuasion and conviction underlay the situation in which active military service was left to private conscience. The principle was that church members were faithful to their country, whether they believed warfare for their country was right was a separate question.

As the twentieth century was now well under way and the church entered this period following a shift of millennial emphasis numerous detailed issues arose which served to integrate the movement anew. The Hawkes case demonstrated the legal standing of British Mormonism, demonstrating at one and the same time the free will of individual members and the basic church ideology that members ought normally to be faithful patriots.

Part of the tension of being a British Mormon lay in the absence of a British temple. We have already shown how vital temples are to the Latter Day Saint cosmology, and increasingly its importance was noted in the *Star*.

One specially interesting paradox was examined in 1918. It arose from the fact that since Mormon living is underpinned by the belief in using opportunity to demonstrate faith and obedience, a lack of opportunity could easily become a cause for religious frustration, so the absence of a British temple alongside the call to perform temple rites might have occasioned a dissonance for many Saints.[55]

Two avenues were presented as a means of eliminating this unfortunate eventuality. One was to say that whenever the Millennium came then there would " be temples in all the great religious centres of the world and not only Zion and Jerusalem in which ordinances will be performed" for all those "who have no opportunity in this life" to hear the gospel or benefit from gospel rites. Opportunities would thus be provided in the fulness of time. The other way touched more directly on Mormons with ancestors felt to be in pressing need of vicarious rites. They are told that arrangements had recently been made for "Saints residing abroad" to have temple ordinances performed for their dead kinsmen which could be organized through their mission presidents, (1918:169). A few rules are added as basic information or instruction, such as the necessity of the dead having attained their twelfth year before endowments could be performed for them, and that at least one year should elapse before vicarious rites are accomplished for the dead, (1918:310). British readers are informed that endowments for the dead occupy a great deal of temple time and that the proxies are remunerated for each session, seventy five cents for men and fifty cents for women.

In and through these rites and the discussion of them the church members were increasingly made aware of their Mormon identity. They are asked whether they refer to other Saints in their branch as "they or we", their answer being viewed as indicative of their commitment. "Your answer will indicate whether you are a social being or a prig, a lover of your people or a fault finder", (1918:796). Accounts of church members who have left the movement also reinforce the need for devotion through the implied desertion of the unfaithful. One such was Bishop R. C. Evans of Toronto. He had joined in 1876 but had now resigned to form a church of his own called "The Church of Jesus Christ", (1918:665). By contrast the parent body, the Church of Jesus Christ of Latter Day Saints is said to be no such sect, or offshoot from some other group. It is, most certainly, a social institution and no apology is made for that, but it is deemed to be a social institution divinely originated. James Talmage writes in no uncertain terms about the institutional nature of the church and in so doing reflects a longstanding Mormon tradition of acceptance of the fabric of the movement as both humanly rooted and divinely cultivated. "The Church of Jesus Christ, as an institution both earthly and heavenly, that is to say, having vital relation to mortal life and to eternity, cannot have originated at human instance. That Church is not the fruitage of man's planting, neither the offshoot of other and older institutions. The Church of Jesus Christ therefore is not, nor cannot it be a sect", (1919:76).

As a social institution it enabled individuals to flourish, to develop their powers and potentials through participation. It also set a framework within which the family might flourish; not least important in connection with which was the fostering of the home-evening whereby each family might spend one evening each month together, (1919:171). Immodesty in dress was thought so prevalent in general society that church members were encouraged not to wear low-cut and high-hemmed dresses, (1919:200). Orson Pratt, who had of course been editor of the *Millennial Star* in 1856-57, is quoted extensively on the approach Saints should adopt to family life.

Men are to learn how to control and govern themselves, not least in the choice of a wife; a woman who should be modest, industrious, honest and with integrity, clean in her appearance as in her cooking and every kind of domestic labour.

Above all she is to be genuine in her religion. It is her duty to teach and instruct her children from their earliest years, when between one and two they are capable of being made to understand much. She is, in fact, said to be more directly responsible for the children than is the father. She is to conquer their crying in anger to prevent them harming themselves, and to bring them into subjection. Once obedience is firmly won it will then endure. One's word is always to be kept and the mother ought never to deceive through threats or promises. Love is the moving principle, parental company needs to be enjoyed, and at all times justice must be tempered by mercy.

When the father does undertake to correct his children the mother ought not to intervene for that would only conduce to strife and bespeak weakness. But besides all that, it would be a rebellion against the order of family government which is divinely established, (1920:58). It is precisely this divine source of origin which gives additional point and depth to the father's power within the family, that same origin also validates the church as more than a human institution. The zeal of the Protestant Reformers like Luther might and should be commended, yet their endeavours must inevitably be qualitatively different from the Restoration which God achieved through Joseph Smith, for Luther had lacked the Lord's authority, (1920:292).

To rehearse this form of argument was to encourage the Saints during an essentially lean period. The branch at Cheltenham, for example, was composed entirely of women, these sisters ran a large group of the Mutual Improvement Association but could only enjoy the Sacrament Service when visited by male holders of the necessary priesthood as in June 1920. In July the Welsh Saints, who now were actually members of the Bristol Conference, held a meeting at Cardiff which also attracted non-members, or "investigators" as they are called for the first time, (1920:495). The Saints at Pontypool were not going to miss this occasion and hired a charabanc to get there.

Nearly a year later on 22 May 1921, Merthyr held a branch conference. Elders Fred R. Morgan, Richard Williams and Gomer D. Thomas are mentioned as being there along with President R. C. Thomas from the Pontypool Branch. President Rossiter of Merthyr gave one of the addresses and elder H. G. Day another, both on general gospel topics. There is no particular doctrinal theme picked out for special attention: perhaps this is to be expected at a time of general striving to maintain a skeletal presence in the Principality. It should also be remembered that this was the immediate period of the National Coal Strike which would not have facilitated church endeavours, though the editor of the *Star* takes the opportunity of this phase of church life to point out to members the real advantages of being a Latter Day Saint. It is not for seeking and obtaining wealth, though he alludes to the point that many have prospered after joining the church to an extent they would not have expected beforehand. Yet it is not such advantages which the church exists to afford. Even the hope of an office and power within the total framework of the movement is not a worthy desire, (1921:456). Compared with participating in the Restoration movement all else is of lesser significance.

Chapter Twelve

Wales Reorganized

A moment of change was now about to fall upon the church as far as Wales was concerned, and all these issues of authority in family and benefit from church association sharpened up as it was decided to organize Wales into a separate Conference. This was proposed at the Semi-Annual Conference of the Bristol Conference held at Cardiff on 9 October 1921. President Whitney presented the idea which was then unanimously sustained. Elder Fred R. Morgan, then clerk of the Bristol Conference, was sustained as President of the Welsh Conference. It was said to have been a gathering long to be remembered, (1921:667).

After seventeen years the land of Wales once more powered its own Conference and organization. Almost as a celebration, and certainly as a mark of new life, there was a baptism in the Taff Fawr river at Merthyr on 30 October, carried out by elder Frank Lockyer. The same day witnessed a branch conference and among those present was brother Morgan Jones, listed as a graduate of the University of Wales, who gave a talk to others on the history of Morlais Castle which the delegates visited as part of the festivities. These ended in a social gathering arranged by the Relief Society, (1921:667, 720). Mormon life was slowly reviving in the Welsh valleys for in addition to the resurgence at Merthyr there was a similar move at Pontypool, a branch which had retained faithful local members throughout the period of disorganization in Wales. Their branch conference was on 27 November 1921. Only a couple of months later, on 29 January 1922 a Welsh district conference was held at Merthyr. The seventy five Saints present give a hint of the level of interest. Three news reporters attended.

The Welsh Annual Conference at Cardiff during 1922 saw Fred Morgan honourably released as President of the Welsh Conference and elder James A. Western appointed in replacement. In his address on this occasion elder Western emphasized the need for co-operation among all Saints if the Lord's work was to proceed. He urged upon his hearers the message that the Lord had declared the present time to be "a day of warning". The Saints were to warn their neighbours for the seed that they now sowed would be harvested in later years, (1922:220).

It was now a time of realistic assessment of the church and its situation, not least of the way in which it related to the world at large. When the Restoration message had first come to Wales it had met with increasing acceptance despite the periodic and often intense opposition. Much had happened since then which now demanded reflection and reappraisal. Yet there is in the life of religious movements a strong tendency to see the present as the prime focus. It is the here and now that matters and which draws the commitment and energy of believers. And this seems to be the case even in this Latter Day movement with its tremendous centre of activity in Utah and early nineteenth century period of revelation.

It is always difficult to generalize over religious movements, and it would initially seem sensible to agree with someone who might say that Mormonism ought to have been a spent force in Wales in the early twentieth century. Such an exodus had been attained through emigration, so many elements of the nineteenth century message had now been removed, that no attraction would remain. But to agree with that analysis would be to fail in accurate evaluation. It certainly was true that this religion would never again send thousands more away to a new religious, economic and social world, but it would go on to construct a church community with a strong appeal to a new local generation.

A 1922 editorial in the *Star* spelt out in detail the formal structure of church organization. The church of Christ on earth is a "reproduction, so far as mortal conditions will permit, of the church of Christ in heaven", (p.344). The heavenly prototype had been disclosed in a vision and became the model for earthly bureaucracy. The phrase, "so far as mortal conditions will permit", is quite significant not least because of the whole episode of plural marriage and its suppression in 1889-90. This was perhaps the clearest example of the church confronting the political power of the world. The *Star* explained that event as one where the "Church, in General Conference assembled voted — not to please the world but to conform to the Laws of the Land — to do away with the practice of plural marriage", (1922:214). The cumulative history and experience of Mormonism, as of any religion, demands explanations which earlier members simply did not have to consider. With this explanation after the event comes a kind of realism grounded in necessity which yields its own logic. At its worst it involves a total rewriting of history, at its best it furnishes a richer awareness of the inner rationale and potential of the faith and its doctrine. For there is a real sense in which the theology of a faith only comes into systematic order as answers are demanded by new problems.

The early twentieth century church was just such a reconsidering body of believers. Its convictions and self-evaluation rehearsed with considerable emphasis that "unlike the churches of the world" it was "not founded upon books and traditions. No book however holy is good enough to preside over the church of God". Thus was the Protestant principle of biblical authority outlawed. "No tradition however trustworthy is firm enough to be its foundation. It rests upon a rock, but that rock is not the Apostle Peter, nor the Bible", and thus is Roman Catholicism denatured. But then, and perhaps to the surprise of *Star* readers the discussion continues and adds the *Book of Mormon* and any record of God's dealing with man, no one account can be foundational for faith in church government. Authenticity and validity "rests upon Christ himself, living and ever present with his church", (1922:8). Here is the clearest expression of the principle of present significance. Here and now validity is to be found, and it is located in Christ's presence with the Church leaders.

Principle of Present Significance

It is important when reflecting on this phrase "principle of present significance", which we have coined for the purpose, to realize that we are not dealing solely with a theological idea. When the Mormons of the 1920s placed both the bible and tradition in a secondary position as far as church validity was concerned they did so to underline the vital aspect of religious experience which they felt dynamically within themselves and which stood out as a source of power. Power for motivating individual life, and power to fuel the dynamic life of the church at large. Religious experience is a notoriously difficult concept to discuss in an abstract way, most especially when looking at past moments in history, since there is no guarantee that all members of a movement felt the same thing or experienced impressions of a similar kind. All that can be said with any degree of certainty is that in their public accounts of religion Mormons have focussed on the power of experience encountered by individuals in the congregation as the means through which certainty of divine presence and authority have come.[56]

Even so, religious experience requires a focus before it assumes any purposive significance. Some religious groups single out the bible, the preaching from it, its reading and study, as that point which roots experience. Yet others locate their experience in persons or rites enshrining tradition.

The Latter Day Saints saw, as they continue to see, the central leadership of the church as the focus of their experience of God. It is the First Presidency of the Prophet which guarantees the validity of their experience. It is because the Prophet originally was called by God and received the Restored Gospel and Ordinances that the contemporary Saint can feel secure in his experience of God. His own sense of the presence of the deity is framed by his belief in the vocation of the Prophet as the true Prophet of God. When the Latter Day Saint "sustains" the leadership of his Church he thus expresses something both about his own religious experience and about the focus he gives to it. Even the very fact of distance between a Mormon far from Salt Lake City and the President based there is overcome by the local leaders whose authority he also "sustains".

The Prophet stood, both historically and in a contemporary way, for the dealings of God with mankind. And, what is more, the Prophet's office was no static entity. It was already becoming an historical institution and a focus for the faithful. There is no easy way of talking about this process yet it is a vitally important one in Mormonism. In essence the fact is that the First Presidency of Joseph Smith in the 1830s and the Presidency of later Prophets, whether in 1920, or 1980, cannot be directly equated since each successive age adds a depth of history to its predecessor. This depth of history is important within Mormonism, it is the framework for the church's cumulative tradition and a perspective for perceiving the present in the light of the past.[57]

History is also one means by which Mormonism has come increasingly to be a world-affirming faith.

This assertion requires an explanation for at the outset someone might object and argue that the Restoration movement of Mormonism is world negating. The early hope of an imminent end to the current world order, with the demand to live apart from the Gentile population, would seem to express a world-negating stance. And up to a point it did. But after the Utah expansion and a settlement of increasing success there emerged an attitude of power and control.

It is quite important to grasp this change for the attitudes engendered by it touch events which are otherwise difficult to interpret. For example, Sir Harry Lauder was made an Honorary President of the Salt Lake Scottish Chorus and gladly accepted the honour, (1922:367). Just as Dr Joseph Parry had been a Utah Eisteddfod adjudicator without being a Morman so Sir Harry Lauder is embraced within a "Mormon" Institution. This acceptance of Gentiles into peripheral and honorary association expresses the Mormon sense of expansiveness and success. It is oddly similar to the report that Edinburgh University students tarred and feathered an elder after raiding a Mormon Meeting at the Free Gardiners' Hall. The Vice Chancellor of that great University formally apologized and the church is glad to report this incident as expressing its impact upon varied aspects of the world's life, (1922:427).

There is an odd sense in which world affirmation was, and continues to be, possible. It consists in the underlying and radical difference between the Restoration message and the broad theological outlook of the other churches in Christendom. Precisely because particular items of doctrine were so unlike main-stream Christianity, Mormons were free to be accepting of other aspects of life. The church inevitably viewed its distinctive doctrinal ethos as grounded in revelation, while equally as inevitable was the cry of heresy and falsehood that came from other churches.

The rooting in distinctive doctrines is clearly seen throughout the *Millennial Star* as items of an educative type jostle with mention of encounters with worldly groups. So in the cases of Sir Harry Lauder and the Edinburgh students we find them dealt with in the same covers as an article by Dr James Talmage on "The Eternity of Sex". Sex, in the sense of gender, is something which does not pertain only to this life and this earth. The gender distinction is not transient, neither is it peculiar to mortal existence, it is grounded in the gender of the spirit which animates the body. "There is no accident or chance, due to purely physical conditions by which the sex of the unborn is determined. The body takes form as male or female according to the sex of the spirit whose appointment it is to tenant that body as a tabernacle", (1922:539).

Dr Talmage was a significant power in the church as an educator. He wrote the volume, *Articles of Faith*, which serves as a major focus of doctrinal orthodoxy first published in 1899. Born in Berkshire in 1862 he had emigrated and was ordained an Apostle at Salt Lake City in 1911. As such he was a General Authority of the church, and as such he also served as the British and European Mission President from November 1924 until

January 1928. For all of that time he was also the editor of the *Millennial Star*.

It is interesting to note that Talmage held with particular vigour to the belief in the gender of human beings as an extension of the gender of their spirits, for he also advocated the idea that each spirit was itself the product of Divine Parents. Thomas O'Dea recalls that Dr Talmage represented the Mormon religion at the 1915 San Francisco Congress of Religious Philosophies and spoke of human beings as quite "literally the sons and daughters of Divine Parents, the spiritual progeny of God, our Eternal Father, and of our God Mother", (1957:127). We have already mentioned this belief in a Mother God when considering Mormon hymns; what we should note here is the fact that it has not gained total and official recognition as a fundamental Mormon doctrine. Some believe it along with Talmage but some do not.

What probably ought to be mentioned in connection with Talmage's *Articles of Faith* is the degree to which Jesus is identified with, or perhaps it is better to say, identified as, Jehovah. The distinctive difference is between Jesus as Jehovah, and the God who is Father of Jesus. That Father of Jesus is Elohim. So Elohim and Jehovah are different beings. But more than this, the term "Father" is also used of Jesus in certain contexts. These points are difficult for non-Mormons to follow but are part and parcel of Mormon exegesis, we have touched on these themes when dealing with the *Star* for 1914.

A similarly distinctive exegesis of Mormon doctrine can be found in Talmage's discussion of various temple rites in the *Star* of 1919, (p.34). Vicarious ritual in which the living may undergo rites on behalf of, and for the benefit of the dead, are deemed to be the expression of God's merciful economy. Not only may baptism be performed for the dead but marriage too can take place for their advantage. Not simply that form of marriage pertaining to this world, but a form called Celestial Marriage in which family relationships are "perpetuated by sealing under the authority of the holy priesthood", (1919:34).

This is the clearest example of the Mormon doctrine of marriage and priesthood as central features of the Restoration. Human kinship is basic to life itself just as priesthood is fundamental to time itself. Kinship binds person to person, priesthood confirms that bonding fixing it firmly both in this world and the worlds to come. So Talmage instructs his readers by drawing from the *Pearl of Great Price* and the *Doctrine and Covenants*. Mormonism, more than practically any other Christian ideology, patterned the heavenly and earthly realms into one total scheme. In this sense the LDS theology came to be more totally all-embracing than any other movement of its time. For members drawn from other denominations this may have been an attractive proposition, as vague notions of an after-life were given shape and content as an extension of earthly life.

Meanwhile, throughout the latter part of 1922 and into 1923, the work continued slowly in Wales. At the end of September the Welsh Conference was held at Cardiff and local members were encouraged to assist the travelling elders in their mission. Many visitors attended. September also saw President James Western addressing and being well received at the Varteg Debating Society, (1922:699, 714). Still, the usual peripheral anti-Mormon voices were being raised. President Western had call to write to South Wales papers, the *Cardiff Echo, Express*, and the *Western Mail* to dispute with Lulu L. Shepherd who had been warning mothers to guard their daughters against Mormon predators, (1922:634).

Chapter Thirteen

Active Salvation

Early in January 1923 David O. McKay, of whom we will learn more at a later point in the history of Merthyr Tydfil itself, met with the travelling elders in Wales. He was President of the British and European Mission from November 1922 until November 1924, and edited the *Millennial Star* for the same period. At the outset of 1923 elder James H. Western was honourably released from being President of the Welsh Conference and was succeeded by elder Don M. Rees. At Merthyr brother D. T. Rossiter was replaced as branch president by Fred P. Jones. Morgan Jones and Joe Rogers were his two counsellors, (1923:157). The Welsh Conference met on 11 March at the Stacey Hall in Cardiff. The Merthyr branch furnished a chairman for the occasion at which David O. McKay was also present. Among the statistics rehearsed were the facts that total church membership was one hundred and fifty five thousand six hundred and six, 75% of whom were said to own their own homes, (1923:186). In line with the sense of a growing optimism at this time we find the *Star* dealing quite explicitly with issues of church organization in relation to faith. The world affirmation, to which we have already drawn attention, is reflected and clearly expressed in this attitude to faith and action.

The fundamental assumption is that effort is good. Effort must be personal in the first instance as each individual appreciates how his or her work must be channelled and directed to a worthy communal end. As though to ensure that no-one misses the point the *Star* adds that the very theology of the church, "preaches the necessity of individual effort as a means of eternal salvation", (1922:308-311). Salvation and effort are intimately related. No clearer statement on the power of self-action could be made.

The very same principle which would bring people to salvation would also result in a successful church. Activity was just that principle, and effort its guiding motive. Individual responsibility might have been highly prized as an American virtue but in the church it was also a value of deep religious significance. In addition it became extended to embrace institutional boundaries. The Mormon Church was an institution all of whose separate sub-divisions provided very many opportunities for responsibility. These were divinely inspired tasks through which each member might find occasion for his and her free-will to yield devoted service. From the earliest days in formal church-membership, children had the opportunity to learn duties and to perform them, the graded structure of the priesthood hierarchy guaranteed that progress might be continually made, and doctrines of the afterlife saw to it that eternity itself afforded opportunity enough for constant improvement.

Such sustained emphasis on improvement through responsibility and via opportunity raises one particularly important point concerning salvation and human endeavour. In essence it is this, that Mormonism altered the way human endeavour was conceived as a religious behaviour. Protestant theology had viewed "works", or the striving activity of people, as worthless and negative. God's unmerited mercy and grace counted for everything while human attempts at attaining merit counted for nothing. Within the Roman Catholic domain doctrine focussed attention on the priesthood and sacraments through which grace came to church members from God. Grace could also assist and facilitate human endeavour which would be favourable and meritorious in the sight of God.

Mormon theology altered the entire scheme of this discussion. To put it in a phrase the Restoration movement argued that human endeavour was, in and of itself, meritorious. More particularly it selected out certain religious rituals which took place in temples as works which God required to be done; the doing of them was a religious duty. Being able to do them was an opportunity, and possessing the free-will to devote oneself to them a privilege. These rites or gospel-ordinances became symbolic of the "works" of man.

Church activity in and of itself was thus a key element of life's work in the process of salvation. Action and activity was beneficial in an ultimate sense. The central focus of action was ideally pin-pointed in temple rites but ripples of significance extended much wider to embrace ordinary activities of life. These too were conducive to salvation. At the practical level this means that when the *Star* reports how the Pontypool branch held a successful social gathering for recreational purposes on the hills above the town, with games and music and the like, there is an inevitable overtone of the intrinsic benefit of such things, (1923:367). The total organization of the church provided for "directed service" which is "faith-creating" and through its efficiency "implants a firm belief in its members that revelation is real and that God lives and is near us", (1923:569).

Attitudes to church organization were intrinsically religious, organization was not some kind of second-rate and ignoble necessity. Mormonism was never to spawn the opinion, prevalent in many Christian churches, that bureaucracy is an inferior and unspiritual burden.

The coming and going of new members into particular offices is but one aspect of the high value placed on the formal duty and service within church hierarchy. On 12 September 1923 elder Joseph Orgill became President at Merthyr to succeed Fred P. Jones who was transferred to Sheffield, (1923:604). Further movement was reported for 21 October at the Semi-Annual Conference at Cardiff. Brother William Day was about to leave for Utah with his family, thus continuing that ideal link of Welsh Mormons with the central focus of Utah, (1923:698). At the same Conference the little branches in Wales were encouraged by being reminded that they played a similar part to the small Christian groups in the time of

St. Paul. Small they might be, and few might have been the movements to Utah by migrants but their symbolic power to the Saints was great.

Monthly meetings of the Priesthood at Cardiff now seem to be taking place with a "steady improvement in the branches of the conference", (1924:158). A growing optimism seems to sound in the *Star's* pages at this time, an optimism rooted in the belief that the church organization is intrinsically guaranteed success by its very nature. It is no mere human institution but its form of activities are set fair for times long after this world has ceased: "its activities will endure even when time shall be no more. It possesses this essential feature of perfection — the life principle that ensures advancement", (1924:199). One of the compelling aspects of the church, as viewed by these Saints, is a deep sense of the transcending nature of the church as an institution. To belong and to participate is to share in a dimension sweeping far beyond the present. This future orientation is powerful, more powerful than one might initially anticipate given the historical background of the Restoration. Despite its recent and dynamic history the Mormons still held the future in expectancy, and not because of any belief in a near Advent.

Here is a quite vital point. With many groups committed to a millennial Advent the failure of the divine coming leads to a frustrating disappointment. One reason why the Latter Day Saints suffered no such dismay lies in the value given to the church organization. In the very offices and processes which constituted the church, the members possessed a dynamic scheme of activity which they believed to have a divine source and which would convey them to a more divine future. The Apostle Reed Smoot would speak of the church as having no earthly competitor, nothing matched its organizational perfection whether on the physical plane as temporal concerns or in the spiritual domain. And he, of course, spoke as one who had long served as the very first Mormon Senator on the American Senate, (1925:481). Confidence in church organization was, and continues to be, a real source of hope for the future in the light of there having been no Second Coming of Christ. The potential of the church organization for coping with all future eventualities is well expressed in a *Star* pronouncement of 1926, (p.45). "The Church of Jesus Christ of Latter Day Saints is the most perfect organization in existence. Each quorum and society, of which there are many, operates in its own sphere without infringing on the rights and privileges of others. The church is a progressive institution having authority to create new offices and organizations whenever the need is manifest, as aids in administration under the direction of the Priesthood." Progressive revelation involves progressive organization. There is, here, no static ideal of a revealed blue-print which will never change. Indeed the Mormon concept of truth is itself intrinsically dynamic in such a way that it is not improper or inaccurate to speak of truth as changing through development.

It is not easy for Protestants to understand this Mormon sense of a perfect church organization. Protestant theology has long accommodated itself to a divide between ultimate truths and the proximate necessities of a formal church structure. Mormons, by contrast, believe the concrete realities of church organization to be part and parcel of the divinely appointed progressive movement into the future.

Minor oppositions to this church of eternity had often been seen as a sign of its authenticity, but as times were already changing in a significant and positive direction in terms of the popular acceptance of a Mormon presence, so minor and negative events came to be viewed differently. A new confidence may be detected in the way church leaders took up and coped with items of opposition and conflict. A couple of examples will illustrate this more positive attitude.

The first takes us to Abercarn in Monmouthshire in the March of 1924 and to a council-house tenant who, being a Mormon in a town lacking an appropriate place of worship, held services in his home. The Town Council had been pressed to silence the worshipping family and to forbid this use of their home. In the ensuing discussions one Dr. E. M. Griffiths alluded to the rumour that only some two years previously thirty or so girls had left the relatively nearby town of Machen, and had disappeared. Dr. Griffiths admitted that this particular Mormon was quite respectable, and that he himself had little interest in Mormon doctrine. Even so he did not wish to see any more girls vanish!

David O. McKay was, of course, editor of the *Star* at this time just as he was also the British Mission President. He took it upon himself to write to the Abercarn Urban District Council citing the *South Wales Argus* newspaper report. The communication is interesting because of the parallels drawn between Mormon identity and the Old Testament incident in which the Medes and Persians legislated against prayer and thereby pressed Daniel into apparent disloyalty. But the final tone is one in which McKay expresses disbelief that Welshmen, those of the same race as his mother as he passingly notes, could be so unjust. They simply cannot have explored all the facts which he hopes they will now do, (1924:232-4).

We might add that three years later Thomas Hughes wrote in the *South Wales News* to deny that girls were lured away to polygamy thereby showing the persistence of this popular attitude, (1927:106). In the same edition Lily M. Evans from Abercarn wrote an article entitled, "when Mormonism stirred a Welsh Village", in which she recalled December 1923 as perhaps the worst time the local Saints had known. "Every branch and street meeting in Newport and Cardiff were overwhelmed with a hurricane of persecution", (1927:476). She remembered the testimony of the local doctor for he had been a family friend, and presumably she found his belief in the disappearance of girls in connection with the church a hard blow.

A slightly different example can be taken from Merthyr Tydfil. Again we know about this because of a letter written to David O. McKay and published in the *Star*. On Sunday 19 October elders Melvin W. Grant, Gordon B. Affleck and president John W. Crofts of the Welsh Conference were to hold a meeting at Merthyr's Bentley Hall. Unfortunately the same Hall had been booked for a large political meeting of the Labour Party. Some five hundred party members were reckoned to have gathered outside the Hall annoyed that they had to wait to get in because of the too closely booked time of the respective meetings. Appreciating the potential for trouble, president Crofts went out to the crowd and invited them to come in and wait until their meeting was due to start. This many did and kept the good order to which Crofts had exhorted them. He not only averted trouble but also reckoned to have preached to more in that short period than would otherwise have been reached in several months, (1924:299). But again, and at that self-same Conference, president Crofts stresses the marked improvement in the condition of the church. Even so the missionaries are called to live exemplary lives since the wider community watches them.

One member of that wider non-church public, Mrs Peter Hughes-Griffiths, addressed a meeting on life in Utah and spoke to the many Gentile, and substantial number of University women present, on the benefits and positive features of Mormon life. All to rapturous applause which quite took president Crofts by surprise, (1924:413).

An equally patriotic note was struck on 30 May when Memorial Day was celebrated by Americans in South Wales. The American Consulate at Cardiff officially invited president Crofts who attended along with elders Ralph C. Jones, Joseph M. Skeen, Merlin S. Ellis and Rulon W. Openshaw. Flags from the London American Legion were used to decorate the graves of the four American soldiers buried in Cardiff.

A lighter note was heard in November when at the Welsh Conference the American Vice-Consul, Mr. C. Christiani, played a saxaphone solo, accompanied by his wife. James Talmage presided at that conference and its success was marked. He had taken it upon himself to meet various editors of local newspapers and the general opinion was that as a result "a profound change in the attitude of the press was brought about", (1924:813). Improvement was in the air as D. O. McKay and his wife noted on visiting Merthyr together on 2 August of the same year, (1924:607). At the end of 1924 the Welsh Conference could report the activity of two Seventies, seven Missionary Elders, eight Local Elders, eight Priests and two Teachers, along with ninety one others, giving a total of one hundred and twenty two Saints. Eight had been baptized and two had died.

The relatively small number is not to be taken as an index of weakness. On the contrary much action was afoot. The Welsh Conference of 5 April 1925 was, for example, held at Llwynypia. This small town is part of the long line of industrial towns and villages running from the top of the great and impressive Rhondda Valley down to Pontypridd. It was the first time for fifteen years that Rhondda Saints and friends had met as a single group, (1925:271). A degree of widespread community integration existed among the Mormons in South Wales which is reflected in the items of news considered important. Social evenings at Mountain Ash or the death of particular members fall into this category. On this last point it is not insignificant to see that when Mary Ann Biggs of Varteg died her funeral service was conducted by president Crofts but in the Varteg Wesleyan Methodist Chapel, (1924:304). Permission for this to have taken place must have meant a degree of acceptance on the part of the local Methodists. But this might have been expected since the Pontypool and Abercarn branches, close neighbours of Varteg residents, were the only two fully organized branches in the area. Being of relatively high social visibility it would be expected that other churches would either oppose or accept this presence. Thomas Biggs, whom we presume was related to the woman of the same name just mentioned, was elected as Conference President to replace Peter J. Charles, he stressed this level of organization in Monmouthshire at the Welsh Conference at Varteg Memorial Hall in 1926, (pp.285, 716).

The centre of Mormon activity in Wales now becomes focussed in Monmouthshire with a continuing presence at Merthyr and in the Rhondda Valley. All these were solidly working-class and industrial areas. Although these were the regions of relatively high Mormon residence the Saints ensured that their presence elsewhere in Wales was not passed over unnoticed. The 1927 Full Conference was held at Blackwood, a town central for those one hundred and thirty five members listed as belonging to the Welsh District and to the branches at Pontypool, Abercarn, Pontllanfraith and Cardiff, (1927:717). At the April Welsh Conference at Varteg, president Biggs was honourably released and replaced by elder Raymond Murphy. *The Western Mail* and other South Wales newspapers for 25 April are cited as giving favourable coverage to this event.[58]

The interest in what the papers say is a recurrent theme and shows how sensitive were the Saints over their public image. The overview was that, "this wall of prejudice is crumbling", (1927:3). Numerous non-members were attending meetings and conferences and the Mormons fostered such links. A basic distinction can be drawn between attitudes to Mormonism in these established centres of activity and those triggered in more distant areas by specific missionary endeavours. James Talmage had been encouraging mission work in more rural areas beyond the industrial belt for some time, (1926:287). In September 1928 president Nathaniel E. Parry and Clifton Kerr took a five day trip to farming districts of Pembroke and Cardiganshire. Though these two travelled without "purse or scrip" it is curious to note how the *Star* adds that such a method of travel "is neither recommended by the Church of Latter Day Saints nor generally used by its missionaries", (1928:682). By the summer of 1929 these missionaries had made some headway. In Haverfordwest in West Wales, for example, they felt that interest was encouraged by those who set out to disrupt the preaching. Some seven hundred are reported at one meeting which took place two weeks after a bitter anti-Mormon campaign, (1929:558).

If it is true that acceptance came sooner in the industrial towns than in the rural towns then it is only because the battles had already been fought and prejudices tried and found wanting. In both 1928 and 1929 conferences and public meetings were held at Caerphilly, an interesting and tactical location since it is explicitly recorded that at that time there were no church members in this ancient and historic town, placed as it is between Cardiff to the South, the Rhondda Valleys to the West and the Monmouthshire strongholds to the East. Over 52% of the local South Wales membership attended and some 65% of the evening congregation on 22 April 1928 were investigators. This large number was put down to the fact that an advertising campaign had taken place in this town where "Welsh peasantry is typified", (1929:282). Very similar scenes were witnessed a year later as the church reflected publically on "One Hundred Years of Divine Authority", (1929:285). This degree of openness to the wider public is also reflected in the important and socially significant fact that the church often invited Gentile participation in its communal events. The Dowlais Male Voice Choir, at that time one of the most famous in Wales, sang at the 1931 Conference in Merthyr with the *Star* carrying a long article on these eighty two or so singers. The venue of the Miners' Hall housed eight hundred people for the night, with only one hundred of them being Mormon, (1931:716). Shortly after, three hundred attended a lantern slide show which "helped to allay prejudice and false propaganda", (1931:653). Other groups also served to entertain and build bridges of understanding with the wider world, the Troedyrhiw Apollo Concert Party, for example, at a Cardiff Conference, (1925:303), or the Aberamman Girls' Choir and the Dowlais British Legion at Merthyr, (1932:638, 1933:158). Numerous other examples could be cited, but all would illustrate the central and vital point, that Mormonism was seen by Gentiles to be world-affirming and to praise what was good in the Gentile world by incorporating it within Mormon celebrations.

Chapter Fourteen

Coming into their Own

Through these events of a very practical kind the tide turned as Mormons were perceived to be citizens of worth and goodwill. In large measure the Saints themselves were responsible for this shift in public opinion due to their efforts and application to foster good repute. The one distinctive feature running through Mormon social events and even some religious services is the use of local authorities from outside the church. We have already touched on the local choirs used at events, but we have not mentioned Local Authorities in the form of Lord Mayors, Councillors and eminent persons in general. These should not be forgotten because when inviting them to attend functions the Mormons were explicitly contacting those with a high social profile who could influence wider public opinion. Very few religious movements normally regarded as sectarian would do this. Quite obviously, this form of public association is a regular feature of life in the Anglican Church as also in some of the Non-Conformist denominations. In terms of the sociology of religion both Church-like and Denomination-like movements might be expected to foster close relations and to seek alliances with the institutions of power in their society. The feature of "inclusivism" by which people are counted as members of both church and society at one and the same time, because church membership tends to be co-extensive with being born into a particular society, makes for intimacy between apparently secular and apparently religious institutions. Sectarian movements, by contrast, are usually typified by an exclusivist principle of membership. People must join the group through an act of decisive commitment. As a result the general attitude towards institutions outside the movement is negative. The firm boundary between the world outside and the inside fellowship of truth is maintained at all costs.[59]

But exclusivism on the part of sect members is very often matched by suspicion and hostility amongst the general public. The two attitudes balance and reinforce each other. We have already seen that attitude in Wales in the middle of the nineteenth century. During that period of intense church growth and emigration the lines between church and world were firmly drawn, and in sociological terms there is little difficulty in describing that phase of Mormonism in Wales as markedly sectarian. We have also documented the way in which the call to emigrate turned into an exhortation to remain in Britain during the first decade of the twentieth century. That dual history of call and exhortation was rehearsed in the *Star* by John A. Widtsoe in the early 1930s and can be taken as the charter for the new era which was now beginning to emerge.

> "At first the people of the Lord had to be brought together to give them strength. The prophecies of old have been fulfilled. We have become well known and strong. Now our duty is to spread over the earth. It was not

enough to conquer the great deserts of W. America; we must conquer the whole world. We still have the right if we desire to go to America. There is no force used in the Church of Jesus Christ: but many of you have your missions here", (1932:631).

If one year might be singled out to mark the turn of the tide both in the attitude of the church and in the attitude to the church then let it be 1934. By then it is not particularly appropriate to speak of Mormonism in its South Wales strongholds as sectarian. It is much more like a denomination, one amongst many others as far as outsiders were concerned, despite the distinctive attitude held by members towards their own faith.

A brief sketch of 1934 in the *Millennial Star* will show a picture of the new stability. The conference at Merthyr shows six hundred in attendance, many being friends and investigators. A Sunday School Conference follows at Merthyr in March with much smaller numbers, but the fifty or so parents in attendance mark the educational work going on. The Mutual Improvement Association was flourishing and in April hosts members from elsewhere in Wales for a Ball at which Sister Ivy Forword of Pontypool was crowned Queen of the Ball by the Mayor of Merthyr as guest of honour amongst the three hundred in attendance. The Mayor was not a Mormon. He complimented the church on the honesty and integrity of its members and saw the whole occasion as successfully achieving its goal of helping people make friends. The Mayor said how pleased he was at the work the church was doing in the area. President Frank R. Bennett and elder Robert H. Booth, along with brother Thomas Price and sister Florence Pulman were doubtless pleased in their organization of this event. But not only were these church members named in the report of events, there is also mention made of Mrs. Arthur Walman, Miss M. Reynolds and Mr. Eddie O'Connor as friends of the district who have thrown in their assistance.

Within two weeks the M.I.A. branch at Pontypool holds its Gold and Green Ball, on 26 April at the Varteg Memorial Hall, and there again it is the Chairman of the Local District Council who is invited and who comes to crown the Queen of the Ball.

The Welsh District Conference was held at Merthyr with special stress laid on the vital importance of auxiliary organizations in the church, indirectly we can see this as an indication of growing interest in church structure and organization which was now taking place. Again the occasion is enhanced by Gentile entertainment in the form of the Dowlais Aolian Glee Men.

Outside Conference meetings some baptisms take place in the open air in April at Barry Island and in August at Milford Haven.

October 22 is heralded in the *Star* which makes much of the fact that the Superintendent Registrar at Manchester had granted, for the first time, a certificate of registry to the Mormons thus enabling weddings to be legally performed at the Mormon chapel. What the editor says of Manchester can be taken as perfectly appropriate of Merthyr and South Wales, for now the civil authorities' attitude is "indicative that the prejudice and discriminations which have confronted the Church on every side to delay and postpone the time when it might take its true place in the communities of the British Isles are fast giving way to a wholesome respect and sincere appreciation of the church and its work". The final quotation typifies the transformation which the Saints themselves felt to be taking place: "We now seem to be coming into our own", (1934:827).

As far as the Merthyr Saints were concerned this shift was accompanied in 1937 by the use of a new chapel for their meetings. Even so it was not until 1961 that the ground was broken for the building of a new purpose-built Mormon Chapel, and it was 1960 which the church itself identified as the beginning of a New Era. We will consider this topic in due course, but now we return to the decades following 1920 to see how the Mormon sense of doctrine and church organization was taking shape.

Chapter Fifteen
Cumulative Confidence and Identity

One feature of Mormon life which has constantly played beneath the surface of Mormon self-identity and self-evaluation is that of confidence. In the mid to late nineteenth century confidence took the form of conviction. The conviction that God was calling this people to prepare for the coming of Christ. With the settlement of the Salt Lake Basin and the growth of Utah as a State, confidence assumed the form of a confirmation that the prophetic exhortation had not been in vain. The millennium had not been false. The millennium had not come in any supernaturally dramatic and cataclysmic sense but the Saints did have much to show for their endeavours. Not least did they have themselves as a sign to themselves. In other words, the emergence of a large Mormon population in the form of a Utah sub-culture and a distinctive church proved to the faithful that God had been at work. To look back at the growth of this community was to gain further confidence in and through the visible and undeniable fact that thousands stood as a testimony to the nineteenth century message of the church founders. Mormon confidence is a cumulative factor. Mormon views of history spell this out in various ways, not only in the sense of the Restoration and the prophetic message but also in terms of social evolution.

A speech at the Salt Lake City Conference of April 1925 provides one insight into Mormon self-evaluation. S. L. Richards argued in a way which is worth quoting at some length.

> "We are great by process of natural selection. You have heard the blood of the pilgrim fathers extolled. Sociologists today are saying that the perpetuation of that blood, the blood of those men who came from England and Holland and established this great Republic, is indispensable to the perpetuation of the great principles of liberty, equity, justice which underlie this mighty nation, its constitution and institutions. It is my belief that the men who were drawn from the Old World to found this government have been selected with no more care and to no higher purpose than the people who have been selected from all the hamlets and villages of the Old and New World to come to Zion to prepare the foundations of the kingdom of the living God", (1925:466).

The natural selection referred to here is paradoxical, for in the strictest sense the biological notion of selection and survival of the fittest was not generally favoured by the church. When the *Star* published expressions of disbelief in evolution it did so, in the words of Orson F. Whitney, to stress the idea that man was made, quite literally, in the image of God. God made man as man and not as a monkey, (1926:68). Richards talks of selection in relation to the "qualities of independent thinking, high manhood, power and strength", features of the will and of the intrinsic spirit of individuals, yet even so there is a sense of the Mormon emigrants as excelling others in their volition and action. It is the eternal spirit within each which makes them outstanding persons. The reference to natural selection is more metaphorical than literal, its power lies in the image of the Mormon which it conveys.[60]

And not only were the early Mormons highly motivated, not only could they pass on strength of character to their early twentieth century descendants, but they had received and implemented a divine form of church organization. Reed Smoot discoursed on this at the Tabernacle in Salt Lake City the day after Richards had spoken about evolution. Smoot was convinced that no other church on earth possessed such a "perfect organization to look after the welfare of its members not only spiritually but physically and temperamentally as well", (1925:481). We have referred to this before but it merits repetition to help delineate the pattern of opinion prevailing in the early twentieth century. The Bible, so prized by most Protestants, might be flawed by "errors that have crept into it through faulty translation", yet it might still serve as the word of the Lord, but even so it was "not the source of eternal truth", such truth was located in the perfect church structure of the Restoration, (1926:70). Truth came from revelation which continued to flow, was not restricted to books, and found its channel in the church itself.

As far as British Saints were concerned the *Millennial Star* was the organ of the church which best helped them form a broad picture of the scope of their religion. Historical reflections periodically contributed to a cumulative awareness of progressive divine activity and human cooperation. Doctrinal elements facilitated the growth of an increasing knowledge of the framework of belief. Reports from branches and from Utah helped forge a unity of purpose and commitment with a geographically expanding boundary. The geography was combined with the history and was doctrinally interpreted as the rise of the kingdom of God focussed on Zion.

Political realities reinforced this perspective. The *Star* interpreted to its readers the fact that until 1931 there had been no quota placed upon British immigrants to America. The barrier on immigration which went along with other wartime constraints in America and many other countries was a benefit, as far as the Saints were concerned, enabling and stimulating them to "build Zion here today", (1937:12). Not only so, but John A. Widtsoe had pronounced his opinion that "it was the Lord's will that the United States should put up a wall against emigration." "Let us not be deceived", he exhorted his fellows. "The Spirit of God acting upon the Congress of the United States led to the action", (1932:631). Indeed by 1930 the view was established that the "destiny of the Church" was to "cover the earth". Unbeknown to themselves the Nations of the World were under divine direction to assist this expansion, while church authorities felt that "as occasion justifies the action, undoubtedly temples will be built in various parts of the earth, for the further salvation of the children of men", (1930:745). Service within the church, wherever one might live, was to be of more importance than emigration to a centre point. From at least the middle of the 1920s and throughout the 1930s the *Star* furnishes much information on church organization and rationale. Although British members were now going to live in their native areas they were not going to forget that very distinctive identity which belonged to Zion's children. The emergent picture is compellingly innovative and would speak at every turn of the ideals of a Restoration Movement whose truthfulness lay in its eternal heritage and origin. At a Semi-Annual Conference at the Tabernacle Orson F. Whitney, who had been President of the British Mission for a year and a half in 1921-22, and who was now in the Council of the Twelve expressed an extraordinary conviction which merits quotation and which shows the degree to which many Mormons believed their church organization to be far more than a human construct which history had generated. "I believe and think I have good reason to believe that this church, so far as it has been developed, is a replica or duplicate of a church in the heaven of heavens, presided over by the Father, the Son and the Holy Ghost, the great First Presidency over the Universe. Joseph Smith having beheld in vision that heavenly church, undertook by divine command to reproduce it on earth", (6 October 1928).

Eternal — Temporal Correspondence

Attention to details of church procedure was thus a matter of religious duty beyond that of other churches. In terms of the history of religions we have here an example of what we might call eternal or celestial correspondence. When the ancient Hebrews or the later followers of Muhammad said that their scriptures were given directly by God and were copies of eternal laws we have a case of divine-human, or heavenly-earthly correspondence. The validity and religious power of the scriptures was rooted in their sacred source. More than that, it could be believed that these objects of scripture, existing as now they did on earth, were a link with heaven. They were channels of religious authenticity, guarantees of genuineness. And this was now the view of many Latter Day Saints living dispersed and away from America. They might not have the benefits of the fully operational church as it was in Utah and they did not have the immediate means of emigration to gain that land, but they nevertheless found themselves in the bosom of divine organization. This particular concept, divine organization, is perhaps very significant for grasping the idea of dispersed Zion. Especially in connection with what we have to say later about the advent of the temple in British Mormon life. It is too simple to argue a sharp distinction between the temple and the non-temple level of church life, though there is some point in that dichotomy once the church reaches a level of temple organization in any geographical area, but before that occurs it would be misguided to introduce too sharp a dichotomy between Temple and Chapel. Certainly it seems that the first four decades of the twentieth century gave an increasingly high, and indeed sacred, status to ordinary forms of Mormon church organization and administration.

One reason why Zion could be said to exist in Britain years before the temple was built there lay in this high evaluation of basic church structure. To be caught up in regular church life was to benefit from a divine pattern of activity. For the first time in the history of Christianity a church was said to reflect God in the immediate sense of divine action. The First Presidency of the Prophet and his two counsellors, according to Orson F. Whitney, mirrored the First Presidency of the Universe. His way of alluding to the Holy Trinity. Joseph Smith, having viewed the heavenly structure, undertook to replicate it on earth. As time went on, more and more elements of church life were introduced according to the pattern of a president with two counsellors, so that even Auxiliary Associations were led by such triadic units. These Auxiliaries are complements to the various priesthood groups and embrace the very important Women's Relief Society which affords great scope for active leadership by women and has assured that Mormonism did not develop a large and passive following of women. The Auxiliaries also serve the young men and women of the church in Mutual Improvement Associations, and through Sunday Schools for all ages and genders.

Chapter Sixteen

Institutions of Salvation

As though this echoing of divine patterns throughout the entire church structure of organization was not enough, one other important feature was stressed in the total scheme of divine-human interaction of church members. It is that of personal divine assistance which argues that every member of the church who fills some church office has the right to a degree of inspiration and guidance of the Spirit to fulfil that calling. Here too there is a form of echoing or reflection at work, for just as the Prophet, Seer and Revelator of the Church, to give the prime leader his full title, is the perfect type of a person in full receipt of divine guidance for the task of running the whole church, so the apparently lowest office holder has the same benefit. In other words the model of office-holder and the task of leadership is the same at whichever level of church structure we look. One of the benefits inherent in this view is that each person functions to the best of their ability in relation to God and other members. Hierarchical structure in this case seeks to enhance the duty of all and not to isolate or alienate anyone by distancing them from the divine source of government. But at the same time it is ensured that no individual can usurp power or extend his influence over the area of responsibility which belongs to any other office holder. Thus is a degree of power guaranteed whilst it is also contained and restricted to particular spheres.

Mormon theology developed in a way which combined beliefs and practices in a total form of life endeavour. The theology was also a sociology, beliefs about ultimate reality were inextricably combined with proximate duties. An individual's sense of salvation lay in the total set of appointed duties in the hierarchical framework of the church in a way which did not allow belief to become unduly abstracted.

To be called to an office was to be personally part of the work of salvation in and through extending the church's influence throughout ever broader circles. Unlike many other churches, and unlike most of the mainline Christian traditions, the various grades of the Aaronic and Melchizedek Priesthoods existed as largely separate entities from the particular offices an individual might fill. In fact most offices were, and are, held for relatively short periods of time. To be called into this kind of position for a few months or, more likely, a few years, was something that a person should accept "with the understanding that it is not a permanent appointment, and should be relinquished when the release comes with joy that another is to have the precious privilege of official experience", (1931:73). Release from office should be sought with an honour in mind. Honourable release is the opposite of a desire to resist release. Nor in word, nor in feeling, ought one to oppose release, (1928:200). The democracy of ethos inherent in a relatively rapid turnover in personnel fulfilling specific official duties parallels the firm Mormon assertion that it has no priesthood class nor theological colleges in which to train a professional clergy, (1930:225). This, it was thought, did away with "office-seekers" and ensured greater sincerity of commitment in service. One incidental consequence of the lack of formal training lay in the procedural instructions which the *Star* now found it necessary to furnish. To consider a variety of these is to help portray the ethos of Mormon religion as it entered the phase of acceptance in British society, and as British Mormons grew in self-knowledge as Latter Day Saints.

To be a Mormon was to bear a name given to the movement by outsiders, just as the early followers of Jesus had first been called Christians as a term of derision and contempt. The name "Mormon" was to be accepted in this spirit, (1926:310). It betokened people possessing a style of life and not merely a doctrine. James Talmage expressed the thought of many that those who steadfastly enacted the Mormon life-style would "live longer and be healthier and happier than other people", (1926:285, 162).

The "Word of Wisdom" served as the prime expression of healthy teetotalism and was used, occasionally, as a form of missionary outreach. Some three thousand, including civic leaders, are reported as having heard this particular aspect of Mormonism during a week-long programme at the Pontypool Town Hall in September 1935, (p.621). The *Star* at one point indicated the awkwardness of local branches informing newspapers of "what are termed 'teas' that are held in our homes". At the same time members were requested "not to play cards", (1926:290, 292). Dancing was a perfectly acceptable practice and a long-standing custom in the church, as long as too close a bodily contact was avoided so as not to excite sexual passion, and as long as costume was similarly restrained. Virginia Reels, Minuets, Folk-Dances and even the Waltz and Two Step were all acceptable, (1933:792). Concern over dress and modesty was the inevitable undercurrent of a group aware of its special vocation as God's distinctive people. President Heber J. Grant expressed his own concern with the way women dressed and reminded Latter Day Saints that when the Young Ladies Mutual Improvement Association was first formed it was under the title of the Young Ladies Retrenchment Association and with one aim in fostering modesty in dress, (1926:288).[61] Modesty of this kind went hand in hand with family ideals, ideals which elevated the family into a high place in the Mormon scheme of things. It is no accident that when Stephen L. Richards of the Twelve Apostles spoke of the two great institutions at the heart of the Latter Day movement and its advancement he placed the family alongside the priesthood, (1926:453). When readers of the *Star* were told that Brigham Young had possessed nineteen wives and fifty six children they could only reflect on the seriousness of the family as a pivotal institution in the history of the church, (1926:537). Divorce was, accordingly, not taken lightly. It was not forbidden. In general terms it could be called an evil but it was not regarded as an evil in itself. Evil lay in the causes that might make a particular divorce necessary, (1932:482). One of the tasks of good church leadership was to support people in their marriage to prevent it developing or degenerating to the point of divorce.

Nowhere in the entire scope of Mormonism was marriage and priesthood, or the family and priesthood, more clearly united than in the concept of salvation. Or, more particularly, in the highest and most desired level of salvation which Mormon theology designates as exaltation. The Celestial Glory of the supreme category of heaven may only be attained by married Melchizedek elders along with their dependent wives. Celestial marriage is the distinctive form of union belonging to the Celestial Kingdom in the life after death, but it is initiated through temple rituals on earth (Articles 13). Unmarried persons in the after-life can only attain the status of those who serve the exalted married Melchizedeks, (MWW:313). In formal terms the unity of priesthood and gender relations is expressed ultimately in the Mother-God doctrine to which we have referred much earlier. God bears the priesthood, it is an attribute of Godhead, and He is also united with a mother God: together they have procreated the human race.

Mormons in Britain were reminded that the temples in which rites for Celestial and eternal purposes were performed were not to be confused with the cathedrals of other Christians, nor with Mormon chapels. Mormons possessed corresponding places of worship but no other group could claim temples of eternal consequence, (1928:184).

Patriarchal Blessings

Another distinctively Mormon institution was the Patriarchal Blessing. Originating in the *Doctrine and Covenants* it denoted a hereditary office extending back to the days of Adam and continued thereafter by lineal succession. In the Restoration the Apostles were given power to ordain Patriarchs and this reordering of the office was to yield a new succession of Patriarchs. Though there would be one Patriarch for the whole church at any one time the Twelve also held the authority to ordain regional Patriarchs — or evangelical ministers as is their alternative title in the *Doctrine and Covenants*, (107:39).

In 1931 Patriarch James H. Wallis was sent from Utah to serve in Britain. In fact he was the first so ordained in America for the very purpose of fulfilling this calling overseas. But he was not the first Patriarch in England, for very early in the Mormon mission Heber C. Kimball had seen the need for Patriarchs and as a consequence Peter Melling and John Abberton were ordained in 1840, (R. L. Evans, 1984:130). Practically a century elapsed before the arrival of Patriarch Wallis and the resumption of blessings. That itself is an aspect of the decline of the Mission in the later nineteenth century and its slow growth into a much smaller, but more integrated Mormon organization by the 1930s.

Two points ought perhaps to be made in connection with the Patriarchal office and its blessings. The first raises an interesting concept only recently described in social anthropology, that of dual sovereignty. Rodney Needham has argued that there sometimes occurs within the institutions of a society a balanced distinction between legal or jural power and what he calls mystical power.[62]

Jural power covers the authority by which a society is governed, it involves the right to determine social behaviour and it speaks of the control which exists over people. Mystical power, by contrast, refers to the influence one person may have upon another which helps the flourishing of an individual and which touches upon the sense of well-being. Some care is needed in understanding this concept since the term "mystical" can very easily be identified with the idea of the mystic or with mysticism. Such a connection is not intended. The stress is more upon the personality and sense of individual strength or weakness. So for example, in some cultures it is especially important to receive a blessing from one's maternal kin.

Even though that kinsman may have no legal power he may exert much influence on the individual concerned. To be blessed by one possessing mystical power is to be strengthened and to flourish in a sense of personal well-being. To be cursed has the opposite effect. It diminishes a person in his own eyes, his sense of stature in his self-evaluation declines. These two elements of jural and mystical power reflect both the social and the psychological dimensions of life. And they would seem to be reflected in the structure of the Mormon organization. The priesthoods are the centres of jural power in the church, the patriarchate the centre of mystical power. If we were to speculate a little we might suggest that in the Mormon family there might be some evidence to see jural power located in the mother while the mystical power is centred in the father, (cf R. Hill in B. Porter, 1966:324). If there is any truth in that then it might be possible to see the Patriarch as a father within the otherwise more hierarchical church structure. This would explain why it is said that "a patriarchal blessing is as it were a father's blessing", (1931:504). It is suggestive to see Thomas O'Dea, whose study of Mormonism is academically judicious, say that the "office of Patriarch is somewhat different from the others and stands a little to one side in the hierarchy of leadership", (1957:178). It would be easier to see this office in relation to the priesthoods as the balanced relation of mystical to jural power.

If we accept this analysis then even more sense is made of the highly personal element pertaining to the giving and receiving of patriarchal blessings. The substance of a blessing is a statement of the benefits which will befall the individual during the rest of their life, if they remain faithful members of the church in their manner of life. It also discloses the tribal connection with Ancient Israel owned by the person concerned. All this is possible because the Patriarch is under the immediate guidance and direction of the Holy Spirit. It is very often the case in the history of

Christian religion that emphasis is given to the role of the Holy Spirit when the personal religion of the individual is at the forefront of attention. The Spirit is the divine person which best expresses the sensitive privacy of personal religion, especially when the nature of experience is such that it cannot accurately be told to anyone else. The intimate nature of the patriarchal blessing is just such a phenomenon. Although the blessing is actually written down with copies going into church archives and to the person blest, it is not a document for public consumption. Although we might speak of them as secret, it is better to follow the Mormon designation of these blessings as "sacred". As with temple rites the description of events as "sacred" implies secrecy, but it is easy for non-Mormons to misunderstand the significance of this word. "Secrecy" can imply shame. For people to be secretive is for them to have something to hide. A great deal of early anti-Mormon apologetic was of this persuasion. It was, or so opponents were convinced, because Mormons got up to shameful things in their temples that they wished to keep them secret. The early overlap of Mormon and Free-Mason activity in the 1830s and 1840s has been dealt with elsewhere (D. J. Davies, 1972:109), but it did feed the fire which welded secrecy to hiddenness. In later, and in the modern period we are now considering, secrecy is better understood in connection with privacy and mystical power. It is precisely because temple rites are profoundly significant at the personal level that Mormons speak of them as sacred. Sacredness is itself intimately associated with self-authentication and with that validation which gives to self-evaluation the highest degree of power.

It is just because of this personal sphere of significance that the second point on patriarchal blessings needs attention. It is the question of superstition. When patriarch Wallis was set to work in Britain the editor of the *Star*, John A. Widtsoe, cautioned the readership on the way to approach their blessings

> "Patriarchs are not fortune tellers. A Patriarch, under the guidance of the Holy Spirit, points out some of the blessings, among the many promised the children of Abraham, that may be attained through a righteous life. The fortune teller merely predicts coming events, and usually deceives. The one, with the authority of the Priesthood, connects all blessings with the eternal plan of salvation; the other, foretells by some unknown power, the future, with no reference to the divine plan. One is of God; the other of Evil. To go to a Patriarch as to a fortune teller is to commit sin", (1931:504).

Widtsoe saw the danger of misunderstanding which the more simplistic might fall into. Yet the possibility of superstition here is but one outcome of an over-personal interpretation of the patriarchal blessing. The individual views it in ways unintended by the church authorities, or may do so. Hence the need for guidance. Two years later the Church Historian's Office announced new rules not permitting copies of the blessings to be made, to prevent any possibility of them becoming public property, (1933:222). More than another decade later Joseph F. Smith, a descendant of the prophet and at the time the First President of the Church, explained at the Semi-Annual Conference of 1944 at the Tabernacle one aspect of patriarchal blessings which might strike the casual reader as distinctly unusual. He said that Joseph Smith had argued in connection with the work of patriarchs that " one of the functions of the Holy Ghost is to purge the Gentiles of their Gentile blood". He acknowledged that most people possessed mixed blood originating in diverse ancestries, "but a Gentile born of full Gentile lineage, accepting the gospel and receiving the Holy Ghost, through his faithfulness, according to the Prophet's words — and these are not my words — according to the Prophet's words, will have his Gentile Blood completely purged and he will become literally of the blood of Israel", (1945:222).

Given ideas of this kind it would be understandable if some people went beyond church directives and viewed both their relation with the patriarch and the content of his blessings in an idiosyncratic and potentially superstitious manner. With this in mind it is worth mentioning another anthropological concept which may help explain the caution shown by church leaders towards the way members view patriarchal blessings.

The concept is that of "dual-purpose rites" which I introduced in order to analyse rituals which church or other institutional leaders use for one purpose and goal but which some of the people for whom the rite is performed use for other and somewhat different ends, (D. J. Davies, 1986:53). The patriarchal blessing would seem a good candidate for being a dual-purpose rite. The very fact of church circumspection over it hints at the fact that some may misuse or misunderstand its intended purpose. It may also be the case that the jural-mystical relation of priesthood and patriarchate is reflected in the priesthood's hierarchical caution over the patriarch's more personal exchanges with individual members. What certainly is the case is that any point where private interpretations of what the Spirit is reckoned to say occur is a point in need of moderation and control. Idiosyncracy is always a problem for formal theological systems. This is especially true for the Restoration movement in its clear assertion of the principle of guidance by the Spirit whilst also clearly delineating the boundaries of guidance. In historical terms the Restoration made an interesting pattern of inspiration and authority which took more austere forms in Protestantism with its characteristic principle of an open bible freely available to individual interpretation on the one hand, and the Roman Catholic form of strong hierarchical authority on the other. But behind or throughout the Restoration movement's integration of inspiration and authority, Spirit and Priesthood, lay the relation between time and eternity and also that between the individual and the group.

Chapter Seventeen

Individual and Corporate Religiosity

This very last point, the relation between the individual and the group, deserves some comment for it is one of several themes which the non-Mormon is likely to misunderstand most easily. Part of the very fabric of life, and especially of intellectual and religious life in the West of Europe, and by extension in much of North American thought, is the relation between the individual strand of existence and the totality of society. Especially in religion with Martin Luther's radical sense of the individual before an individually concerned God, and in philosophy with Renée Descartes' notion of the isolated thinker, the West has spotlighted the self as an arena of prime significance. The negative aspect of the isolated self involves uncertainty and doubt which arises from critical self-reflection and results in a profound sense of loneliness. Uncertainty and loneliness combine to produce the pain of modern life.[63] Attempts to escape this condition embrace many avenues, extraordinary stimulation of the senses in drugs, sex, or visual and auditory light and sound have afforded one major channel. Another has been the fundamentalist religious desire for certainty in the intense fellowship of sectarian groups. Yet another has turned towards the body in its supposed natural alignment with the world and has stressed healthy living through diet and exercise. Many groups have taken one of these elements and organized life in relation to it, many fads, fashions and transient lifestyles have thus passed before the twentieth century consumer of ideology and truth.

While very much more could be said about these trends our purpose is more limited and specific. For Mormonism did not build into its original system any preoccupation with the individual. Initially this assertion may appear quite wrong and misguided, but in spelling it out it may be possible to arrive at a deeper appreciation of Mormon thought as the church entered the twentieth century.

First it must be acknowledged that Mormon theology is clear on the fact that individuals are responsible for themselves. Personal responsibility is foremost in heeding and responding to the Restoration message of salvation. Anyone who fails to attain salvation will fail through his own lack of endeavour. The Atonement in Christ's work has a general and universal effect in freeing all from the consequences of the Fall. But there is also an "Individual Effect of the Atonement" by which personal sins are forgiven by Christ as the individual invokes or petitions pardon in, through, and by means of repentance and solid works of moral value, (J. E. Talmage, 1952:89). The socialization of Mormon children and of converts makes plain the duty and responsibility placed upon them as now they face the future in all its eternal splendour. But to talk of duty and responsibility is, perhaps, for many non-Mormons a slightly daunting or even a slightly negative thing.

As far as the Saints are concerned nothing could be further from the truth. The word "opportunity" is probably a far better way of referring to what Mormons mean when they speak of duty and responsibility. It would be unusual if someone spent much time with Mormons, especially at their religious events, and did not frequently hear the word "opportunity" used. Mormons regularly thank God, their Heavenly Father, for the "opportunity" to do this, that and the other. Opportunity is a distinctive feature of the relation which a Mormon sees as existing between a Saint and God. To talk of opportunity is to talk of the individual with all his and her possibility in the eternal plan of salvation. But, and this is where we must now qualify our first point on the individual, opportunity presupposes vital relationships with others. The plan of salvation, like eternity itself, is relational. Thus though the sense of the individual and the scheme of achievement motivation into which Saints are socialized are important, they do not bespeak individualism. In Mormonism individuals take the God-given opportunity to interact with others to enhance the possibility of the salvation of as many as possible. Individual or privatized salvation makes very little sense in Mormon theology precisely because the individual person plays a relatively small part in the Mormon concept of man and woman. The human being is of significance and worth because each person is a child of God, a child of human parents, a parent, and so on, to many degrees of kinship as we discussed earlier in this book. It is as a particular individual within the total church community and the extended family of eternity that sense is made of life. It is that framework which ultimately contains private inspiration and priesthood control.

One particularly interesting aspect of the relation between the individual and the group emerges in instructions given in the *Star* on burials. In a very explicit editorial Saints are told that "funeral services are held for the good of the living rather than for the benefit of the dead". This is perfectly intelligible in the light of temple ritual. The temple, not the grave, is the focus of rites bearing eternal consequences. Accordingly the funerary practice is of benefit to the bereaved. The priesthood, as such, is little concerned with these rites in any necessary way since eternal consequences do not arise in the act of burial: 'the Church makes no provision for any ordinance of dedication (of graves) to be administered as a function pertaining to the Priesthood'. The concluding prayer can be offered by "any suitable person whether he be a bearer of the priesthood or not", (1927:440). In a humane way it is also said that the sermon can usefully contain "well deserved eulogies while known faults may decently be left unmentioned". So in funeral rites the Saints were reminded of the higher relation between life and death, between time and eternity which is rooted in priesthood and the corporate nature of temple work. Unlike other churches they were not to set too much store on the actual rites of interment.

We have touched on burial rites not only to dwell on the eternal and corporate aspects of Mormon life but also to show how the *Star* was giving itself to instructing the Saints in basic patterns of church life in this period of growing institutionalization. Another similar example along with burial and patriarchal blessings covered the judicial system of the church, which consists of peace officers for routine maintenance of order, of the Bishop's Court, and of the high council to which appeals may be made. The presidency of the church serves as the ultimate court of appeal, (1931:118). As a final example, and one of a slightly different order, there was instruction as to the mode of performing "The Hosanna Shout". This act of solemn worship "is voiced by the LDS only when they are assembled in special and exalted service of worship at times of extraordinary solemnity. The words given are repeated thrice as a congregational shout of adoration, each completed utterance being accompanied by the waving of white handkerchieves. Hosanna, Hosanna, Hosanna, to God and the Lamb, Amen, Amen, Amen", (1927:728).

Commitment in Several Forms

But we should not think that Mormons were only concerned with Church organization. The question of attitude and commitment was also important. One of the most telling comments ever made in the *Star* voiced the worry that amongst the young people in the church in America there was only a low degree of religious commitment, so weak was their faith reckoned to be, and so "shallow their testimonies", that church stalwarts wondered whether the desire for pleasure and the influence of modernistic trends of thought might result in a disintegration of the church to the point at which it would cease to exist "as in the post-apostolic days", (1930:715). One practical response to these deep seated fears was the founding of the Mutual Improvement Association Conference of June 1930. Another vital contribution to the increase of commitment emerged from the missionary endeavours of the post second-world war period.

Though such fears may have had a point in Utah they were not applicable in the same way in Britain. This is probably due to the quite different situation of the church in each place. In the history of religion it is not unusual to find greater degrees of religious activity at the periphery of a religion than at its centre. Or, perhaps, it would be more accurate to say that one finds a greater degree of religious commitment at the periphery than at the centre. Certainly this seems to have been the case in Wales, and within Wales, at Merthyr Tydfil. Towards the end of 1936 the Merthyr Saints held their first sacrament service in the new chapel, with 74 year old elder Arthur Evans as the preacher, (1937:16). The Welsh District Conference was also held both there and in the larger Miners' Hall.

By 1938 the British Mission was composed of the following Districts, London, Bristol, Norwich, Birmingham, Nottingham, Manchester, Sheffield, Hull, Leeds, Liverpool and Wales. Each tract embracing very large areas in geographical terms. Socially speaking the over-arching canopy under which the British church inevitably existed was that of the Second World War. From approximately 1940 to 1946 there were no

American or overseas missionaries in Britain, their place being taken by local people, home-missionaries as they were called. This was heralded as a "new phase in the life and progress of the British Mission" as ever increasing responsibility devolved upon local Saints to ensure a continuity. Some four hundred or so home missionaries were active in the early decade of 1940, (1941:441, 518). In Wales this number yielded three hundred and sixty six missionary hours in the first seven months of 1941, compared with nine thousand eight hundred and eighty three in London, two thousand nine hundred and twenty one in Leeds, two thousand one hundred and ninety in Birmingham and one hundred and forty one in Bristol. At this time the *Star* is constant in furnishing statistics of many aspects of church life, something that was likely to be encouraging to British Saints in helping them to know that they were very much part of a world-wide body. Total church membership in 1941 was just under nine hundred thousand with the British Mission recording nearly six thousand five hundred members. The fact that home missionaries put in twenty eight thousand seven hundred and forty six hours in 1942 indicates the degree of active commitment in Britain. Care is still given to practical items to the point of noting that more heating needs to be provided in many chapels since the cold was causing a decline in attendance, (1943:72). On the more grim side of life nine hundred and eighty six Mormons are listed as having died in the armed forces in the War. And here, of course, it cannot be forgotten that as with many Christian groups those who were brothers in a particular faith could still find themselves enemies as patriotic demands fell on them. Unlike the Jehovah's Witnesses who paid allegiance solely to Jehovah as their God and to the Kingdom which He would soon introduce in a divinely revolutionary way, the Latter Day Saints in the twentieth century fully encouraged members to pay full service to the nation to which they belonged. This is clear evidence of the sense of change in the view of the kingdom and of the commitment needed to allow that kingdom to emerge through the life of the church in every nation. At the local level Welsh Saints were reminded of this allegiance when President and Sister George Q. Bennett visited the German Prisoner of War Camp at Neath, where Alfred Newman, a German Latter Day Saint, had been imprisoned, (1947:185). The same statistics draw attention to the rise in the divorce rate in America not only as far as the general population is concerned but even within the ranks of Church members:

1920-22	1	divorce for	38	weddings in Temples	13	civil unions
1923-25	1	for	33	and	15	
1935-37	1	every	28	Wards	12	
1938-40	1		26	and for every	10	
1944	1		17		7	

(1945: 229)

The editor is not slow to remind readers that this increase in divorce is especially bad once they realize that it betrays the three things to which every child is entitled. A respected name, a sense of security and an opportunity for development. To what extent military service might have influenced divorce can only be speculated since there is no internal evidence in the *Star*. The stress on failure to give a child all suitable opportunity to develop is, as we have already discussed, a typical Mormon attitude.

The British Mission returned to a sense of customary life with the return of missionaries from America in 1946; some one hundred and twenty seven in all, (1947-8:175). The Welsh District was said to be doing well, especially at Merthyr under the influence of elders T. Lawrence Oliphant and Fred W. Mason. The Sunday School, Priesthood and Sacrament Services all being well attended. A Relief Society had been reorganized at Varteg in April and that same branch opened a new hall in June. Pontypool witnessed the opening of its own Mutual Improvement Association in September, while Merthyr now began a Boy Scout Troop as part of its general programme. Merthyr also received two women missionaries, this was quite acceptable not only because there had been unmarried women missionaries in the church since 1896, in fact Inez K. Allen, the first one, only died in 1937, but also since women had been stalwarts in mission work during the war period, (1937:414, 1947-8:346).

A special report on Wales appeared in the 1948 *Star* under the heading of "Welsh District Advancing". It rehearses ideas of Welsh religiosity and of a yearning for truth but all lost beneath a cold and bland indifference. This, rather than opposition of any sort, was the problem encountered by missionaries. At the official and formal level they were well received by civic authorities, but the popular response was slow and rather apathetic. Yet the growth of church Auxiliary bodies was laying an important foundation while the various conferences and concerts had afforded considerable opportunity for friendship with non-members. The prevailing attitude is one of expectancy. In 1947 an exploratory visit to North Wales resulted in the beginning of renewed mission activity at the outset of 1948. The report ends optimistically, "The future looks bright and the possibilities are unlimited, so keep your eyes on the Welsh District", (1948:13).

One feature dwelt on at length much earlier in this book was the power of American influence in the local British context. In this second post-war period that influence was again of peculiar import. Although most of the Welsh branches were solidly under local leadership, and not that of American missionaries, the total bureaucracy and form of church organization caused a perpetual feedback of information, encouragement and support between Utah and Wales. This external stimulus was, of course, not present in the life of other major religious groups in Wales. They suffered from that kind of introverted pessimism which post-war, post-depression and post-revivalist conditions engendered. The Latter Day Saint cause had flourished in Wales in the mid and later nineteenth century because of the American promise and call to Zion, now in the mid twentieth century the American stimulus was again not inconsiderable. Perhaps this is most obvious in what otherwise might be seen as a surprising resurgence of the will to emigrate to America. Despite numerous and clear statements that Zion was, in the present phase, a universal concept and that members should serve God wherever they happened to live, a small but socially significant number of Mormons felt attracted to America. In 1948 nearly two hundred Britons so journeyed Westward. The *Star* repeats the official desire that members "remain in their mother countries", whilst also saying that "we are sorry to report that we are losing some of our very fine members as the way has been opened for them to emigrate to the States. It has been their decision to take advantage of this opportunity. We wish them the best of luck". Some five members leave Pontypool, while Cardiff and Varteg also suffer depletion, (1949-50:208, 92, 123). A small but significant part of this more recent emigration is made up of young women marrying Mormon missionaries.

On 26 June the Merthyr Branch was reorganized by the Welsh District President, G. Q. Bennett, elder William T. Davies becoming Branch President and William E. Pulman and Thomas Price his two counsellors. A Relief Society had been established and was increasingly flourishing while various concerts and parties for young and old were the order of the day. Explicit mention is given to the fact that many investigators and friends also attended these occasions. For actual members it can be noted that, for example, throughout the winter of 1948 the MIA average attendance at Merthyr was twenty seven, (1948:186). Slowly but surely new members were being made, four at Pontypool and five at Merthyr where they were baptized in the Public Baths on 24 August. The use of these Baths became a feature at Merthyr for the next few years, (1949:29).

Another feature of life in the Welsh District was that of basketball. The American missionaries formed a basketball team during 1948 and proceeded to arrange matches against several Cardiff teams, and soon reached the top of the Welsh league, (1948:346, 1949:29). This was following a pattern which had begun a year or so earlier in other parts of Britain and which was beginning to yield useful links of friendship and to foster, through public relations, the image of healthy and good living young manhood which was to become the characteristic feature of the Latter Day Saint Missionary for decades to come. The *Star* records that through both their playing and coaching not only had friends been made but cottage meetings had been organized which means that a degree of mission work inevitably followed on from the initial sporting contacts. The high profile of basketball even led to scores being printed in the *Star* of 1948 along with the team photograph of the Newcastle District Team. What is interesting is the variety of opponents, and at this time the fact that church teams won every game they played. The London team would, inevitably, have a wider choice of partners than those in the Provinces; this was, in fact, the case and their listed opponents afford an interesting group: U.S. Navy, Royal Air Force, London Central YMCA, Polish Students, Latvians, Oxford University and London Polytechnic. The only place in Britain where the Saints were pressed to only a few points lead was in Nottingham and by its YMCA, (1948:12).

The visible activism of basketball and the success of Mormon teams demonstrated to church members the significance of the Word of Wisdom in producing fit and competitive individuals. A *Star* feature in 1936 had given an account of Chauncy D. Harris a Latter Day Saint Rhodes Scholar from Provo, Utah, who was now at Lincoln College Oxford and who was active in clarifying Mormonism to his contemporaries, not least "the strict moral code" involving abstinence from tobacco and alcohol. As though to prove the point Harris was a member of the University Lacrosse Team which had first defeated Cambridge, (1936:309). Later in the 1950s, when Le Grand Richards' famous book *A Marvellous Work and a Wonder* was published, the Mormon public would be familiarized with an earlier Oxford exploit of Paul C. Kimball, also a Rhodes Scholar but from 1927. He had taken on the task of coaching one of the rowing crews of his college but on the condition that they, too, observed the dietary codes of the Word of Wisdom. The resulting success of his crew following this discipline was complete and thus justified the sacrifice he had asked these non-Mormons to make, (Richards, 1958:376).

For the great majority of Mormons who continued to live in Britain the observation of the food laws of the Word of Wisdom stood as a constant reminder of their distinctive identity. In the history of religion such food rules often accompany a religion whose identity is marked out in a distinctive way from that of neighbouring peoples. The dietary laws in the Old Testament have been seen by numerous subsequent Christian groups as affording a vital example and model for their own social life. In our own day the Seventh Day Adventist Church is one of the clearest exponents of it as they see themselves as heirs of much Old Covenant practice.[64]

Eating and drinking are among the most fundamental human activities which make it easy to see why the equally fundamental values of religion are often linked and associated with them. Eating or not eating particular things becomes second nature to people and in the process a whole world of values is implicitly acknowledged. Within the broad tradition of Christian culture it may also be true that the idea of food as either very good to the point of being sacred, or else of being taboo, has been facilitated by the existence of the Sacrament of the Lord's Supper. At least we can say, as I have argued elsewhere, that eating is one form of "thinking", one way of communicating a point in the realm of religion, as well as being one means of distinguishing between one group and another.[65]

Members of the Latter Day Movement consider the Word of Wisdom to be a revelation given to their founder by God. In fact it is precisely dated to 27 February 1833 and located at Kirtland, Ohio, as explicitly stated in Section 89 of the *Doctrine and Covenants*. It enjoins abstinence from alcohol whilst allowing wine for the Sacrament Service as long as it is home-produced. In fact the clause on wine echoes the revelation of August 1830 which exists as section 27, 1-4, of *Doctrine and Covenants*, in which Joseph Smith sets out to buy wine for a religious service only to be met by a heavenly messenger who tells him that, "it mattereth not what ye shall eat or what ye shall drink when ye partake of the sacrament, if it so be ye have an eye single to my glory". Accordingly the Saints have used water as the sacramental element rather than wine. As a convention this certainly distinguishes the Restoration movement from all other Christian groups which use wine. Beyond wine, hot drinks are forbidden, usually interpreted as tea and coffee, while tobacco is deemed fit for use only as a "herb for bruises and all sick cattle". In general terms vegetarianism is praised, with meat as a dish "to be used sparingly". In these rules and principles Mormons have the opportunity to reflect upon their distinctive identity as recipients of divine revelation. With the increased scientific opposition to smoking, alcohol and stimulants in general, there is added opportunity for seeing the truthfulness in the Word of Wisdom and thereby of gaining an additional sense of its validity. Mormonism in the scientific twentieth century was thus believed to be increasingly credible.

As the 1940s ended and the turn of the half century took place there was no blowing of trumpets in an attempt to identify this moment as of especial significance to the Mormon Church. There were nearly six thousand British Saints, some three hundred and sixty six had been baptized during 1949, and two hundred and fifteen missionaries had been at work in the country at large. Of the total membership, just over one thousand three hundred were tithe payers so approximately a fifth of the total church was committedly active, if we accept tithing as an index of dedication. The decade of the fifties presented a relatively low profile with a steady base being laid for what would be a most remarkable decade in the 1960s. Endeavour on the part of missionaries and local church members did not meet with an equal popular response. In 1949 large bill-board advertisements were employed at Cardiff and Barry to publicize the facts of Mormon religion. These were paid for by both local elders and some sponsoring wards in Utah. The basketball teams continued their triumphant progress, and slowly the number of British converts at large moved into the above three hundred a year number from 1948. In Wales the generally favourable attitude to Mormons even led to some elders leading the services of other denominations. President V. L. Terry and elder D. W. Widmer conducted Christmas services in the Aberdare Congregational Church while others preached at the Brethren Church at Pontypool, (1949:29, 90, 122). One Thomas Reese Jenkins, who had been a leader in the Church of Christ at Bridgend for many years, was actually baptized and ordained into the priesthood of the Mormon Church in the summer of 1949. In May of that year the Welsh District also held a Genealogical Conference at Cardiff which indicates that a mature Latter Day Saint perspective was becoming established in the Principality, (1949:233). The Millennial Chorus, a church choir of missionaries which had sung on the BBC in 1936, continued its work in 1949 both on the BBC and in public concerts, drawing an audience of one thousand five hundred at Merthyr in July of that year. Merthyr also witnessed a number of baptisms as the 1940s ended with seven baptized in the Public Baths in September with some sixty in attendance, (1949:365).

Merthyr, Pontypool and Cardiff continue active, and work at Bridgend begins to open up and improve into 1950 with four baptized at the Baths there, with nineteen others present; a small occasion but a significant one precisely because the Restoration movement is intrinsically committed to expansion and development. If no progress occurs, then the very raison d'être of the church is called into question. Every advance is significant so that when, for example, Merthyr Saints gathered for a banquet, their social spirit of pleasure could have behind it the knowledge that the real basis of the movement was sound and slowly edging forward. The humour of the Pullman brothers, a church family, which was said to have "had the crowd in stitches", symbolizes that recreational and communal nature of the church which accompanies the dedicated endeavour of mission. In the Welsh District during 1951 there were thirty seven baptisms and in the *Star* there seemed to be a general stress on the importance of homes and families. Symbolically appropriate to this was the fact that in January 1952, of the five baptisms at Merthyr, three were of one, the Osborne, family. At Merthyr more than 50% of the members were by now subscribing to the *Millennial Star*, as compared with 24% at Cardiff and 27% at Pontypool.

Instruction in aspects of church life continued to come through the *Star* and show a sense of growing intensification of congregational life. In retrospect this can be seen as a useful maturing of the church prior to its growth and influx of new members in the 1960s. The Sacrament Service in particular was discussed and described over the 1940s and 1950s. This is quite intelligible since, obviously, no temple ordinances were performed in Britain in the absence of a temple, so that chapel life, and this one important rite set within it, might be expected to attract more particular attention. Not least because converts joining the church from other churches would already possess an attitude towards this particular ritual from their prior religious practice. So when the Saints were reminded that in this church members did not kneel to receive the sacrament and did not exhibit signs of piety in public they were in effect being given a comment on the way in which Mormon behaviour differed from, for example, the Roman Catholic and Anglican tradition of the day, (1939:276). Further direction instructed that perfect silence should follow the main prayer of blessing until everyone present had partaken of the elements, (1946:211), and that "when taking the sacrament it is proper to take it with the right ungloved hand. It is also proper that the tray should be held and passed with the right hand", (1953:13). Thus was custom and convention fostered, though at the same time the largely chapel oriented population of British Mormons were reminded of temple rites and benefits. The sealing ceremony which "perpetuates family relationships" in the total scheme of salvation was one such case, while on the daily level of moral behaviour young Mormons were warned that "petting is harmful" to good personal relations and development, (1952:95, 111). Explicit guidance was quite in place for many reasons, not least the fact that a steady growth in baptisms and increased membership was currently taking place. In 1950 five hundred and ninety three baptisms in the total British Mission; in 1951 almost double at one thousand and forty three; 1952 some eight hundred and nine; 1953 three hundred and forty five; 1954 four hundred and five; 1955 six hundred and six; and in 1956 six hundred and ninety eight.

The consolidation which had taken place during the 1950s, and which had itself been furthered through the responsibility shouldered by Britons for mission work during the period of the two World Wars, took its most concrete shape in the English Temple. Its corner-stone had been laid on 11 May 1957, a ceremony which had ended with the singing of "God Save the Queen", and it was dedicated for use by President David O. McKay on 7 September 1958. This was the fourteenth Mormon temple now existing across the world. Enshrining the importance of regional Mormonism this was the clearest symbol of Zion as the pure in heart wherever they might live.

New branches at Swansea and Newport answered to the new British Temple. In other words local and national development was taking place and reminded the Saints of their success, (1957:61, 356). The Merthyr branch inaugurated a local Eisteddfod which itself shows a sense of local and Welsh pride, (1957:192). Not too far away the children of the Blackwood Sunday School in Monmouthshire paraded through the streets of that small town with their banners, (1958:254). One article, in particular, in the *Star* illustrates this profound sense of corporate identity which marked the Mormon Community. Entitled the "Peculiar People of Little Utah" it characterized the attitudes which Mormon community life engendered in its members. In many ways it might be read as a description of how new converts might perceive the group into which they were drawn. A culture, or at least a sub-culture of its own, this was a place where nobody argues with one who slips from eager service. Rather are such individuals given new tasks to perform in the knowledge that involvement will shape and mould them until their thinking reflects that of the group. The rather closed world of members becomes a new world to the newcomer, and its total activism stands paramount. "Mormons must always be doing something, accomplishing something. Drama is training for public appearances. Dancing is healthful exercise and a means of fostering marriages between young people of the church. The human beehive must always be gathering honey. Among the members of the tight little group there is almost a feeling of family", (1958:127ff). As far as Wales was concerned that family feeling was about to undergo even greater intensification as this decade gave way to the 1960s. But before looking into that decade it is worth pondering the nature of this family feeling for it should not simply be passed over as the experience of a close-knit sectarian body. At one level it is precisely that kind of experience, but for the individual concerned to be part of the total movement is to have a sense of being a Mormon set within an extremely comprehensive plan of salvation.

Chapter Eighteen

Mormon Homo Religiosus

In terms of the history and phenomenology of religion we can approach this area by asking just what it is that comprises the religious person, *homo religiosus*, in Mormonism? Whilst many answers are possible one stands out in the Mormon concept and category of a "testimony". [66]

Testimony

A testimony is an individual's personal and private conviction of the truthfulness of the Mormon message. It is not, primarily, his knowledge of the doctrine and history of the Restoration, though it presumes some such knowledge. Rather it is the intuitional aspect of mind and life brought to an emotional grasp of the teaching and yielding a commitment to the focus of identity as a Mormon. The Prophetic leader of the church is that focus for the office of the Presidency embraces ideas of the Restored Gospel, of the events which surrounded the genesis of the church, and of the contemporary social organization of the church through which the truth comes to life as experience. [67]

Whilst a testimony is a radically personal reality, it is also fundamentally part of the social reality of the church. It is within the church community that a testimony arises, develops and matures. It is through close personal relationships with others who themselves possess strong testimonies that new testimonies are engendered. And especially is it through service to the church that a robustness comes to underlie the young Mormon's grasp of his or her religion. To "gain a testimony" is an intrinsic part of Mormon spirituality. For people not belonging to the Church of Jesus Christ of Latter Day Saints this needs to be carefully explained for one very particular reason. Namely, because Mormonism is not a "conversionist" religious movement. It does not follow that well established pattern of Protestant evangelicalism in which stress is placed on the evil, sin ridden, human heart, lost through the Fall of Adam and redeemed through Christ in an act of repentance and direct regeneration by the Holy Spirit. This kind of conversion grounded in a new birth into Christ is not part of the Mormon scheme of life. We have seen earlier in the book how Mormonism turned from Protestant evangelicalism. It does not preach for conversion in this rapid sense of psychological descent into guilt and ascent into freedom of forgiveness. So the gaining of a testimony is not the experience of a momentary conversion. But this is not to say that testimony is an emotionless thing. On the contrary, it involves quite powerful emotions, but they are more cumulative in their effect and depend on the awareness that all Mormons are united in their shared commitment to this cause whose truthfulness God has revealed to each one. In a testimony the solitary individual becomes profoundly aware that the centre of his or her life consists in a truth which has also become the centre of other people's lives. This knowledge leads that individual to empathize and sympathize with those fellow believers who stand in a similar state of mind and heart. A testimony is thus an aspect of group membership believed to be rooted in the eternal nature of that church group. In our final chapter we will return to the theme of testimonies of faith promoting experiences to reinforce the nature of this group spirituality.

At various church meetings members may talk about a great variety of topics but it is not unusual for a person to conclude an address or exhortation on a particular topic by a general formula which constitutes a testimony. Examples are often of the following type which I take from older editions of the *Star* though contemporary cases would be similar and show the degree of custom which has become associated with this declaration of commitment and identity.

> "I close my remarks by bearing my testimony to the world that I know, as I know that I live, that God lives, that Jesus Christ is His Son, the Redeemer of the world, who came to the Earth with a divinely appointed mission to die on the cross for the sins of mankind. And I bear my testimony that I know that Joseph Smith was a prophet of the true and the living God", (1936:308).

> "Brothers and Sisters in the British Mission, may I close with a testimony that I know God lives and in this latter day has again spoken to His people through the Prophet Joseph Smith: that this, the Church of Jesus Christ of Latter Day Saints, is His Church and that through it and our obedience to the Gospel which has been revealed to us we can obtain exaltation in His Kingdom which will be reestablished on this earth when it shall be renewed and receive its cleansing and preparation for us, that God is our Father and we are His children. May He bless us and help us all to do His will is my sincere prayer for us all", (1948:62).

Finally a testimony from a Prophet while in office. President David O. McKay on his 95th birthday had the *Star* print:

> "I know that Jesus lives. I know because I have heard his voice and I have received His guidance in matters pertaining to His kingdom here on earth ... I know that His Father, our Creator lives. I know that they appeared to the Prophet Joseph Smith", (8 September 1968).

And the *Star* editor added; "Even so we know for a surety that President McKay is the Lord's Prophet, Seer and Revelator here upon earth today ... for we have stood in his presence, felt of his spirit". The very use of the verb "know" is utterly characteristic of the Mormon sense of the knowledge of God. For that, in essence, is the nature of a testimony, it is the sense of the knowledge of God as an intuitive grasp of the church-taught doctrine of a Restored message of planned salvation.

Not infrequently the person giving his testimony will show some sign of emotion. The flow of speech will be interspersed with an intake of breath, a rising in the throat, or even some tears, as it becomes obvious that the sincerity of this person expresses deep private meaning. The rest of those present respond to this in powerful but quite silent ways. As the person returns to his or her seat they are likely to be gently touched by others as a token of their understanding of the unspoken as well as of the spoken communications.

It is characteristic of Mormon leaders to speak in a certain tone of voice when talking about matters of faith and life. It is one of quiet and calm certainty with little of that brash loudness which typifies certain fundamentalist sects. So marked is this style that new converts sometimes comment on it. It may well have been this distinctive form that was noted in print as long ago as 1891 by Brigham H. Roberts who referred to a "New School of Mormon Oratory" which depended "for its excellence more upon the presence and power of the Holy Ghost than upon the skill and art of man", (*Era*: September 1970).

Key leaders come to serve as models for new and for young Mormons as they grow into the values of the faith. For values do not exist as abstract principles but in lives committed to them and enshrining them. This is the special significance of the Prophet in the church. Not only in the historical sense of Joseph Smith as the original vehicle for the Restoration, but of all his successors to the present. The idea of the Restoration is encapsulated in the extensive scheme of leadership beginning in the Prophet of the past, through the Prophet of the day to other leaders.

A most significant attribute of leadership in Mormonism is humility. It is a prized attitude of life. It is, obviously, a virtue in the general sense of Christianity, but within the structure and organization of the Latter Day Saint movement it takes on an additional significance because of the non-existence of a professional priesthood and because members are called in and out of office in a regular way. We have already considered the background to this acceptance of and release from office, we can now see how it relates to Mormon spiritual values. Humility embraces the acceptance by the individual of the authority of leaders to call and release members in terms of positions of power in the church, especially in the local community. Humility thus includes belief in the guiding power of the Holy Spirit over leaders engaged in making decisions of this type.

The Mormon idea of humility is intimately linked with processes of development of the personality and accords with Mormon ideals of progressive change. It involves increasing sensitivity and gentleness as personal assertiveness yields to service. Emotional warmth in social encounters accompanies the sense of brotherhood within the total movement. Mormons say that church membership makes people more sensitive to emotions. And that sensitive humility is believed to be increasingly visible in the face of believers.

But this takes time. And it is also closely linked to two specific institutions in the church, the period of missionary work, and engagement in temple rites, especially the former.

When young men and women are called to serve a two year period of missionary work they are usually in their late teenage. If they are drawn from established Mormon homes and communities where the basic truthfulness of Mormonism is generally accepted by the majority of people, they may find the move to a part of the world where few accept the faith to be a considerable challenge. Instead of their faith and religious practice being implicit, it now becomes demonstrably explicit. They must challenge outsiders with the message and in so doing they meet with polite rebuff, bland indifference, or rejection. At the same time they are something of minor celebrities within the Mormon congregation where they serve. All this adds up to a challenge to self-identity at a deeply personal level. For many of these young people the outcome is a positive advance in self-awareness, an added degree of self-confidence and a deepened active commitment to the beliefs of the Restoration. In other words the missionary either "gains" a testimony or has his existing testimony "strengthened", while at the same time there begins to emerge that sense of dependence upon God and fellow believers within the total church organization which can best be described as a sense of humility. At this stage in life it is very limited in effect but it nevertheless exists and a foundation is laid on which subsequent experiences will help raise a sound attitude of humility.

In descriptive terms the sense of passivity, of being acted upon, features prominently in the phenomenon of religious humility, and this is in no sense lost in Mormonism despite its activist approach to life. The expression of thanks for the opportunity of service is one aspect of that mutual dependence on leaders and peers that befalls the missionary and which belies passivity. When events seem to work to the advantage of the missionary they convey the providential guidance of God. In these ways the missionary learns that in and through his activism he too is acted upon. This tempers pride of the grosser sort and sets endeavour within the total endeavour of the church.

When the mission period ends and the much matured young person returns home and to normal life, he does so as a more useful member, prepared for future service through having been called to and released from office in that attitude of grateful humility which the institution itself needs if it is to succeed as a lay-hierarchy.[68] The missionary experience can be viewed as a model of and for all other offices in the church. It confers a prestigious and highly socially visible status on someone for a specifically restricted period of time, after which a form of institutional anti-climax sets in.

If humility is associated with the mission period it is also linked, though in a different way, with the temple and its ritual. Much has already been said about the place of temples in Mormon theology and practice, it now remains to show something of the contribution made by temples to Mormon spirituality. In Wales, as in Britain in general, the decades following the opening of the London Temple in 1958 were crucial in the formation of a temple-based church membership rather than a very largely chapel-based membership. This took time and is still in process of accomplishment. As might be expected young converts to Mormonism found the temple ritual easier to accept than many older members whose Mormon identity had been forged within local chapel circles. Our immediate task is to relate temple practice and Mormon spirituality. In a study I carried out at the very beginning of the decade of 1970 among members of the Latter Day Saints Student Association in Britain three broad patterns emerged as responses to questions concerning benefits gained from temple attendance. We can summarize these reflections as benefits of peace, knowledge and achievement.

The category of "peace" is the one most directly linked with what I am calling the humility dimension of Mormon spirituality. These students spoke of a spiritual rejuvenation, of inner peace, of sacredness. They sensed themselves as being out of this world, bathed in serenity and possessing a greater appreciation of the love of God. Many other Saints have made similar comments, and all stand in an appreciation of what has come upon them at the temple. They have been privileged to be in receipt of blessings. Indeed the very word "blessing" is widely used in the church and hints at the receptive mode of religious existence. In and through some aspects of temple ritual there is a growth in religious identity, a moulding of experience, an increased sensitivity to the breadth of fellowship in the church both in time and in eternity.

The more active dimension of life is also in evidence in the category of "knowledge". Church doctrine, or some parts of it, seem to come to life and take on a compelling aspect when learned in the context of the temple. Most especially is this so in connection with genealogical ideas and vicarious baptism for the dead. Almost as an extension of "knowledge" is the category of "achievement" since through vicarious rites and other rituals for self and immediate family, ends are attained. Saints spoke of their sense of service, of their "super-constructive use of time", and of the knowledge that they were helping others.[69]

The November 1970 edition of the *Star* not only had a leading article on temple involvement but also other material reminding readers of the work waiting to be done, and exhorting them to do it. Readers were reminded, in no uncertain terms, that "there is no full salvation for the living without vicarious service; we would not be sufficiently qualified and prepared for that salvation".

At this same period the actual state of temple involvement on the part of members in Wales, in the South West Mission as it then was, could not be described as extensive. The following table gives some impression of the state of transition between pre and post-temple organization as then prevailed.

Members in Branches of South West Mission (Early 1970s).

	Merthyr	Aberdare	Pembroke	Pontypridd	Swansea
Total	359	89	116	115	460
Average at the Sacrament Rite	70	10	41	27	44
% Attendance	20	11	35	23	19
Number with Temple permits	22	3	0	2	12
% Possession	6	3	0	2	3

For our present purposes these figures show that only a relatively small number of people could be called temple-goers, and therefore only a small number would have reaped the benefits of the particular processes of spiritual development we have been stressing here. But that is not to say that ideals and examples of humility were lacking. Not only were they found amongst some of the better instructed temple-goers, but constant contact with Utah brought living examples into the local communities on a regular basis. Once again we see that the universal distribution and contact of church members facilitated the fostering of Mormon ideals.

But we have now moved ahead of our chronological progression by dwelling on the mixed nature of the 1970 Welsh group, at least as far as the temple was concerned, all before considering the decade of the 1960s. Yet there is some merit in that leap since it will place a degree of restraint upon the temptation to over-eulogise the decade of the 1960s which was so successful in so many respects. To it we now turn.

Chapter Nineteen

A New Era: The Decade of 1960

At the very outset of the 1960s high optimism filled the church as it viewed the immediate future. This, it was said, would be a special time. 1960 was the "first year in the New Era", it was a fulfilment of the text in the *Doctrine and Covenants* that, "this is the time of the hastening", (1961:1), and it echoed David O. McKay's autumn pronouncement of 1958 that with the new British Temple a New Era was heralded in the British Mission, (1961:32). What the *Doctrine and Covenants* text actually says is, "Behold, I will hasten my work in its time", (88:73). A broad enough text which in context lacked any particular reference, it was, nevertheless, taken up by these modern Saints to express the excited immediacy of anticipation which they now felt. It might have been expected that ideas of the Second Coming of Christ would recur as the prime means of formulating religious hope; they did not. The established nature of the church world-wide and the powerful weight of its organization enabled members to see the existing institution as itself pregnant with possibility in fostering an even more extensive kingdom of God on earth.

Nowhere were these hopes more insistent, nor more immediately realized, than in Wales and at Merthyr Tydfil in particular. The Prophet-President of the Church, David O. McKay, came to Merthyr on 2 March 1961. It was a visit of deep significance and of many meanings. The prime purpose in this one day visit was to unveil a plaque on the house where his mother Jeanette Evelyn Evans had been born and lived as a girl, prior to emigrating to America with her parents in 1856.

The Prophet had been to Merthyr much earlier in 1899, some twenty or so years before he had become President of the British Mission in 1922. But, since those days, he had been ordained an Apostle in the Church and had become its Prophet, Seer and Revelator in 1951. It was now ten years after acceding to that office that he came in an act of filial piety to mark his mother's birthplace. He was himself an old man. At 87 years of age, white-haired, and the leader of a powerful institution, he impressed many who attended the several events of 2 March.

At the unveiling he dwelt on the theme of motherhood and sonship, and was touched with emotion to the point of having to stop to recollect himself. As we have already seen, an emotional halt of this kind would be totally understood by church members as a sign of genuine concern, and also of piety. In and through his address on that occasion it is quite apparent that piety and filial piety are far from separate phenomena in Mormon experience. The very corporate nature of salvation grounded in temple ritual, and which unites family members, ensures this to be the case. But even so, there was a distinctive ethos surrounding his words on this occasion, he tells us that he had his speech written down that very morning in preparation for what he was going to say publically. It moves from a more abstract and impersonal to a decidedly more personal tone as he begins with an objective and ends with a totally subjective focus. In fact he ends as though talking to his mother rather than talking about her. Some parts of that speech merit rehearsing.

> "If departed loved ones are interested in our mortal strivings, anxieties, failures and achievements, and by means of some spiritual power they be cognisant of our actions, I hope Father and Mother share the joy of this inspiring occasion ... I now unveil this plaque as a feeble expression of our gratitude for life, love, watchful guidance, care and protection that Mother gave us ... As one of those children who in childhood and youth gave you, my Mother, greatest cause for worry and anxiety, I stand at your birthplace ... May we lowly children, your descendants, be guided by Kind Providence, which shaped your life, Mother, and be ever blessed and inspired that we may always keep your name in honour", (1961:188).

Whether or not the Prophet intended to stress in any doctrinal way the dynamic links binding the departed and those living on earth we cannot say, but it is at least obvious how significantly he took them to be within his personal life. No act could have been so intrinsically Mormon, and few acts could more appositely encapsulate more than a century's history of Mormon culture in and between Wales and America. Here the nineteenth century missionary preaching had converted and caused a young family to emigrate. One of its offspring had not only grown in the faith and become a missionary himself, but had risen to the prime office in the Restoration. Not only did he unveil a plaque in concluding his duty as a son but he broke the first soil in preparation for the first chapel to be planned and built by the Merthyr Mormons. In so doing he was turning from the emotional recollection of his family past to look into the future of the even wider family of his church. Elder Hugh B. Brown, himself a member of the Council of the Twelve and by now 78 years old, had given a dedicatory prayer at the plaque unveiling in which he spoke of the President's parents as having emigrated and "established a kingdom within the Kingdom of God". That phrase well caught the twofold element of the Prophet's duties in his visit to Merthyr, as it also soundly reflects Mormon theology of family, church and eternity.

David O. McKay gave a considerable address at the ground-breaking, which embraced a variety of issues. He lamented the fact that he had never learnt Welsh despite the fact that his mother used to speak it at home during his boyhood. The local authorities in the form of Merthyr's Mayor were thanked for their support and goodwill towards the church, as demonstrated that very morning when the visiting Mormon party had been given a civic reception by the Mayor.

Sir Thomas Bennett was present and thanked for his part in having built the very central Mormon Chapel in London and who had designed and was now about to execute the construction of the Merthyr Chapel. The Prophet interpreted the intentional erection of specifically Mormon-planned places of worship as a significant step forward from the long-standing necessity of using hired halls.

Yet he was aware that as branches flourished within the new buildings there would, inevitably, be some fault-finding and dissent, so the Saints needed to be warned and prepared for such things. Not least since the goal of the church was universal brotherhood which the local church and the visiting elders had the duty to engender by their mission work. At Merthyr this new church building, the first in Wales, was a sign of that missionary activity which had gone on in Wales for more than a century. Indeed one of the earliest and certainly the most famous of the Welsh missionaries in Wales, Captain Dan Jones, was an ancestor of brother Ralph Pulman, a staunch member at Merthyr and whose organizational capacities had enabled this special day-visit to go particularly smoothly. The *Star* report concluded with the thought that through the events of this visit President McKay had not only honoured his mother but had actually instigated the opening of a New Era.

Certainly this seems to have been an important time in Mormon self-evaluation and in the local Mormon sense of history. No longer was the living prophet of the church only a name applying to a dignatory living half a world away. Not only had many Merthyr members now seen, heard, and been impressed by him, but the local history of Mormonism had been made all the more alive and dynamic in and through the ceremony of his honouring his convert and emigrant mother.

Throughout the summer of 1961 Mormons in Wales and many parts of the British Isles adopted a high social profile. The *Star* reports numerous regional newspapers carrying accounts of the church. *The South Wales Echo* for 4 August reports on the £32,000 paid at Cardiff for six acres intended for a new Chapel at Rhiwbina as well as noting the earmarked £120,000 for the building at Merthyr. *The Belfast Telegraph* for 17 June covers the fact that local Saints there are about to have a ground-breaking ceremony on a £5,000 plot which was to carry a £60,000 church. All this for an Irish membership of about six hundred and twenty. It also tells of interdenominational stress in Belfast resulting from the missionary programme which involved young people in the church through initial sporting contact.

In the *Scottish Daily Mail* of Edinburgh the growth of members in Scotland from one thousand three hundred to two thousand six hundred in six months of 1961 is emphasized, as is the similarly projected £60,000 chapel for Glasgow. Here in Scotland and in Ireland, but not as in England or Wales, there appears to have been a degree of opposition from other local churches. In England we find elders presenting the *Book of Mormon* to local dignitaries, as to the Mayor of Brighton (*Brighton Argus* 12 July), while in many places they gave interviews to raise the general level of popular awareness about the church. The profile presented was heavily accentuated by youthfulness in the Elder missionaries, as by the activism of the sporting programme they fostered. This sporting life was touched on in a *Star* interview with Marian D. Hanks at that time in 1962 among the First Council of the Seventy in the church. Presented with the fact that for some two years many youngsters had been baptized after being contacted and fostered through baseball games and had then entirely fallen away from the church a few weeks later he responded by placing the real emphasis not on baptism as such and as a goal, but on that conversion of life which is a longer term process. On as important an issue he was asked about the high number of young women over young men in the British church. His personal response was that women unable to find LDS men should "keep company with young men whose standards are honourable and decent in every respect", and that they should "do all in their power to involve young men in the programme of the church", (1962:84). This was an obvious social problem because many of the younger men and boys baptized through the baseball programme had subsequently fallen away, and since Mormon membership did tend to foster a more closed group for recreational purposes.

As a social problem this became increasingly significant throughout the 1960s for the yet further reason that permanent chapels were being built in many parts of Britain for the first time. Once erected they were much more than places of worship, they were designed quite specifically to house recreational halls alongside the formal chapel area, as well as furnishing classrooms, offices and kitchens. These were among the first significant group of all-purpose religious buildings to be constructed in Wales, and to a certain extent also in England. What was certainly true was the fact that Mormons themselves contributed much to the actual labour of building them; one English case will suffice though many examples could be furnished.

The new Latter Day Saint Chapel at Nottingham in the East Midlands was opened on 15 December 1963. It had taken two years to complete and the voluntary church labour that went into it was thought to have saved £17,000 in costs. A craftsman from Salt Lake City, elder Floyd Nielson, had supervised much of this work and was assisted full-time by four young Mormons from widely differing parts of the country. David Bourne from Liverpool, George Simpson from Dundee, Christopher Crabtree of Bristol, and Trevor Charlton from County Durham. Together they had worked some seventeen thousand hours, and they, in turn, had been helped over some four thousand two hundred and eight hours by Nottingham Saints. The total cost of construction was £70,000. Of this, 80% had been furnished from general church funds (*Nottingham Guardian Journal*, 16 December 1963).

It is obvious from this that the chapel represented two major facts. On the one hand, it enshrined local commitment and energy so that it was not surprising to find the Saints using the building as a focus of their religious activity. It also encapsulated a final and concrete realization of the hopes that had carried people through more than a century of church adherence apart from permanent places of worship. Here, finally, the doctrine of Zion, as the universal pure in heart, took on a firm reality. We argued earlier that it was the building of temples across the world which established the doctrine of Zion as a universal reality, and that is true, they did and do serve that end; but during the 1960s, and in many places today where temple attendance may be sporadic or difficult, it was the local chapel which marked the significant religious place around which life could revolve. For Mormons the chapel became as much a social as a religious focal point; indeed in the Latter Day Saint understanding of life it is hard to distinguish between these perspectives. As long as the Saints met in hired halls they could think of themselves as pilgrim-migrants, or certainly as pilgrims, and potentially as migrants. But once buildings were planned and erected members could see themselves all the more easily as locally fixed Saints.

But, on the other hand, the chapel was also a mark of the international nature, the universal nature, of the church. The Merthyr Chapel, for example, was quite explicitly built of and from Welsh materials wherever possible. One of its distinctive features is the slate roof which, aesthetically speaking, sits very well in the Merthyr valley being fully in accord with its context, despite its otherwise modern lines. But in its opening and life the American presence was real, as is the influence of Mormons from other parts of the world when serving their mission there.

To possess a church building is to have one's religious outlook transformed to a degree. It is a sign of success and achievement. Mormon theology copes well with that, a fact worth heavy emphasis, since some Protestant traditions can engender anxiety over success. Success is worldly and ungodly, it shows the approval of sinful others; and all this despite the often rehearsed "Protestant Ethic" theory of Max Weber that religious men sought material gain as an indirect means of being persuaded that God was blessing them, and therefore they were, probably, amongst the divinely decreed elect aimed for salvation.[70] Mormons had abandoned theories of election, predestination and depravity which meant they could cope more easily with success. This may well have contributed to the church's success in the 1960s and 70s, especially for the upwardly mobile.

At the same time, the existence of a chapel could lead to the movement being identified as one group amongst other similar groups, one chapel amongst others. The relativism of a cosmopolitan setting might be feared. To a degree this did occur and local leaders needed to be sharper in maintaining distinctive identities than hitherto. When David O. McKay spoke at Merthyr's ground-breaking his speech could, at a rapid read, be understood as an interesting example of general Christian piety. On closer inspection it qualifies itself in describing the chapel as a place for worshipping the true God "who founded the Church in the Meridian of Times", a distinctive Restoration reference. So too, for example, at the Nottingham Chapel just mentioned. In 1966 its bishop, A. S. Green, addressed the Nottingham Cosmopolitan Debating Society. He reminded them that Mormons had been in Nottingham since 1843. They now had three hundred and seventy five members and their new chapel but they should not be labelled as just another Christian group. "Despite the drive for Christian Unity it was impossible for Mormons to join with any other Christian group", (*Nottingham Guardian Journal*, 24 January 1966). The very logic of the Restoration was against such an acquiescence in the jumble of many denominations. The pressure to missionary activity, not least in the visiting missionaries themselves, has served to maintain this distinctive feature of the Restoration as a dynamic group set amongst many other groups.

Chapter Twenty

Other Restoration Groups

We can take this opportunity to refer to other Mormon groups which have scarcely been mentioned throughout these pages but which, historically, are quite important, and which, sociologically and theologically differ to a degree from the Utah-based Church. We first consider the Reorganized Church of Jesus Christ of Latter Day Saints and develop the rough sketch already given in chapter three.

The most obvious feature of this movement is the fact that its leader and prophet is a lineal descendant of Joseph Smith. Joseph Smith Junior, the original prophet of Mormonism, had a son who became the Reorganization's first prophet in 1860. Developing in Iowa in the 1870s the church moved its headquarters to Independence Missouri in 1921. Symbolically this was a return to Zion. This church has been, in the American courts at least, declared the legal continuation of Joseph Smith's original movement.

Doctrinally it is quite unlike the Utah Mormon Church. In fact the theological difference is startling. The Reorganized Church possessed an orthodox Christian view of God as a Trinity of co-eternal persons, denying the evolving nature of God and rejecting the Adam-God theory quite expressly. It has never practised polygamy nor secret temple rites. Whilst it believes in temples being constructed after specific divine command in revelation, there are no secret or vicarious rituals. In other words it does not follow the dichotomy between time and eternity as does Utah Mormonism. The Reorganization believes in contemporary revelations and each year new truths or directions are given through the prophet to the Church and added to their distinctive *Doctrine and Covenants* book.

Work began in Britain within only a few years of the reorganization of the Mormon movement. Charles Derry was a leading figure, and in 1863 there was a conference held at Penydarren, an area of Merthyr Tydfil. In 1864 Llanelli was its venue. Further conferences at Merthyr were held in 1866, and in the course of time other branches were formed in South Wales, notably at Skewen, Neath, and at Penllergaer near Swansea. The movement was never numerically as large as the Utah Church, perhaps because there was relatively little to distinguish between the Reorganized Church and other Protestant churches, of which Wales had many, at least this was correct on the doctrinal front. Despite possessing a living prophet, continuous revelation, and an unusual priesthood structure, the teachings were largely those of more evangelical Protestantism. There was nothing of that qualitative difference which sets the Church of Jesus Christ of Latter Day Saints apart from other churches in the Reorganized schema.

The Penllergaer Branch when it was set up a century later, in 1954, comprised only eleven persons, in two families, who rented a chapel building from the Welsh Methodists, finally buying it in 1963. Even by 1971 membership stood at only eighty eight, so there had been nothing of that dramatic increase which the Utah Mormon Church had experienced in Wales and elsewhere in Britain. For example, the Stockport group began in 1902, had sixty four members by 1914, although the site of meeting changed, the membership in 1972 was only eighty. A similar picture emerges at Leeds. Organized in 1885 with fourteen members, in 1972 it recorded approximately thirty eight. Joseph Smith the third visited the Leeds members in 1904.

Although some emigration took place in the nineteenth century with this church even developing its own Emigration Fund there was nothing on the scale of the Utah migrations. This brief comment on the Reorganized Church must suffice as a note that the Restoration movement is a dynamic and complex one with several different sections sharing a family likeness despite numerous vital differences. In sociological terms the Utah side of the Restoration movement has, by far, been the most successful in generating large numbers of members within a distinctive sub-culture. From the brief sketch of Reorganized doctrine just painted it is obvious that the Utah persuasion became quite markedly different in teachings as in the entire framework of intellectual outlook. That very difference may have assisted in strengthening identity and fostering community success, while the broad similarity between Reorganized Mormonism and mainstream Christian churches has certainly not conduced to numerical success.

One other Restoration movement can also be mentioned in this context even though it has not been of any significance to British Mormonism as such. It is the group called The Church of Jesus Christ with its headquarters at Monongahela, Pennsylvania. It traces its authority to and claims a distinctive validity as a Restored movement from Sidney Rigdon who was First Counsellor to Joseph Smith at his death. One William Bickerton joined Rigdon when the latter organized a group after Smith's death, a group which quickly disintegrated. It is believed that God then called Bickerton to lead this group, which he did, being followed in its Presidency by William Cadman, 1880; Alexander Cherry, 1905; William H. Cadman, 1922; Thurmin S. Furnier, 1964; and Gorie Ciaranino, 1965. By the early 1970s this total movement could count only six thousand members. It too, like the Reorganized Church, resembles more some Protestant churches than it does the Utah Mormon movement. It does not accept the *Doctrine and Covenants*, celestial marriage, baptism for the dead, high priests, degrees of glory attained through temple rites, and it never fostered polygamy. On the side of assertive difference these Mormons practise a foot-washing rite at least four times a year; engage in mutual embraces in religious fellowship, and above all believe their movement to have the distinctive mission of converting the American Indians whom they regard as one of the lost tribes of Israel.

But perhaps the most distinctive feature of this church is its heavy emphasis on the immediacy and effect of the Holy Spirit in dreams, visions, appearances and healings amongst ordinary members. The second and seventh of its articles of faith and doctrine illuminate this point.

The second article of doctrine describes the Holy Ghost as the "mind of the Father and of the Son, the unseen power and glory which emanates from God and can, at his will, manifest itself in various forms". The seventh deals with divine inspiration needed for preaching and any successful work in the Church. It is categorically stated that while some theological education may be useful it is no real necessity for ministry. Not only so, but "formal schooling or practical training which fosters the belief that inspiration and the gifts of the Holy Spirit are unnecessary in the Ministry of Christ's Gospel is erroneous and harmful".[71]

This church publishes a regular broadsheet, *The Gospel News*, and, at least throughout the decade of the 1970s and on through the 1980s it has regularly contained reports on significant dreams, healings and examples of guidance, which are all deemed to express the vital activity of the Holy Spirit. It is fairly common for church members to report seeing angels. At the summer camp of the church in 1971 the elders met each day, fasting and speaking in tongues, and at one such gathering one brother "saw an angel in the circle that was formed. The power of God fell upon the Elders, confirming the wonderful experiences", (Vol.27, No.9, p.1). Interpretations of tongue-speaking are also furnished and tend to be of the exhortatory type: "Jesus is the hope of all who come to Him", (Vol.29, No.6, p.11, 1973).

In several respects this church resembles the dynamic spirituality of earliest Mormonism in retaining a sense of the miraculous. Its present interpretation of past events in the *Book of Mormon* shows this. For example, in the Third Book of Nephi there is an account of an exchange between Jesus, in his American resurrection appearance, and the twelve disciples chosen there to parallel the twelve in Palestine. When asked what they would ask of Christ as their heart's desire, nine request a full life and then rapid entry in the kingdom of heaven. This is granted them. To the silent three Jesus grants what they inwardly wish, to remain on earth to continue their gospel work. So it was that these three remain unnamed but transformed through a transfiguration and a visit to heaven, and are said to remain on earth until the kingdom finally comes. All this following from, and is based on, the aside at the end of St John's Gospel where the beloved disciple's future is left undecided. To Peter Jesus says of John, "what is it to you if he remain until I come?", this rhetorical question is used by the Johannine writer in the Bible to emphasize the personal calling and discipleship of Peter rather than as a directive of the future course of John's existence.

Be that as it may the *Book of Mormon* develops a doctrine of "The Three Nephite Disciples" as just outlined. Subsequent Utah Mormonism has generally tended to ignore this episode, but not so the Monongahela group for whom it serves as a minor yet significant reminder of the mysteriously spiritual nature of the world. Mabel Bickerton, writing in the *Gospel News*, December 1971, could rehearse the story and add that "we believe ... these three Nephites ... are still here ministering to people and helping to bring souls to Christ. It is a great blessing," she adds, "to know that they have visited some of our brothers and sisters in the Church of Jesus Christ". Her wish is that living church members, and here she was writing for the children in the church, would "meet them sometime and receive a great blessing".[72]

This idea is quite remarkable for one particular reason. Not only does it authenticate this church as an arena of mysterious spiritual activity, but it also validates it historically. It is of passing interest to note that in the 1790s the Monongahela region was popular among American Welsh ministers in connection with the Madoc myth of Welsh Indians.[73]

It is not easy to speak of the Three Nephites in terms of a doctrine, nor yet as a pragmatic fact. They are believed to exist but in the mundane form of ordinary mortals, for their bodies have been transformed so as to afford a transitional stage between earthly life and life in the kingdom of heaven which still is to come. They constitute quite a distinctive category of religious phenomena, marking a contemporary historical-mythical continuation with the assumed life of Jesus in America. So while most forms of Mormonism have firmly identified themselves with New Testament times, only through the *Book of Mormon* and the Restoration of Priesthood through Joseph Smith, the Monongahela group adds to these beliefs the tradition of living, though anonymous, persons. They are "living doctrines", mysterious yet powerful as symbols of the past as of the anticipated future.

It is but one idea which finds its fuller significance in the visions, dreams and messages of regular religious life. In a very direct example recorded from Detroit, Michigan, in October 1971, some women members had presented a programme on the American Indians and during the singing of the hymn, "O Stop and tell me Red Man", one sister, "saw a man seated on the rostrum". "She felt that this man was one of the three Nephites", (Vol.27, No.9, p.8). Other visions have included seeing dead members present and smiling in church, as well as the face of Christ, and shining lights. More private disclosures usually come in dreams of the dead, or giving confirming validation to forthcoming church events. So the formal ritual activity through which the church hierarchy is perpetuated is enhanced by personal and mysteriously spiritual means. On other occasions, as at some ordinations, for example, speaking in tongues takes place, or voices from heaven are received to predict future events or to validate the task in hand.

In this form of the Church of Jesus Christ in its Latter Day Saint variety, we have a good example of a charismatic authentication aligned with a fixed ritual practice. It might be seen to resemble the Utah Mormon Church a century before, when the intrusion of the Holy Spirit into mundane and church affairs was more frequent. It is interesting to see that among existing Latter Day Saint groups it is the numerically smaller bodies which are certain that the Spirit is free to act in obvious ways, while the much larger and institutionally more complex Utah church gives considerably less scope for such charismatism. And it is to the larger, Utah, body that we now return for further analysis of church development.

Chapter Twenty One

Reflections on the Decades of 1970 and 1980

The decade of the 1960s had been a success in Britain at large and many members would find it easy to agree with George W. Cornell's interpretation of Mormon history to date:

> "Such were the humble ridiculed beginnings one hundred and thirty five years ago, of a movement that today has become one of the most prosperous, diversified and fast expanding religious groups in the world ... that it should have reached its present stature from its most unpromising origins is a modern paradox!! Some wonder why. It is the eternal work of God, re-established in proper order and authority in this last Dispensation of the Fulness of times", (M.S. 1969:12).

Now that the world membership was moving from the three to four million mark with a powerful and international structure its sense of identity was secure as far as most were concerned. Ezra Taft Benson, himself an American national figure in President Eisenhower's Administration, could write of the church, in May 1969, as suffering greater hindrance from cliques within than from persecutors without, a sure sign of the establishment of Utah Mormonism worldwide.

Further strengthening followed throughout the 1970s. The extremely well organized and large Area Conference for British Saints took place in 1971 and was the occasion for a profound explicit awareness of Mormonism's presence in Britain as a permanent witness to the Restoration. But permanence did not mean temptation to stagnate in established patterns of action. New names and thus altered identities for church groups, new teaching schemes, and the receipt and reception of new revelation, all betokened the vitality of Mormonism. On this last point we must stress the revelation of 9 June 1978 which now opened the Priesthood to men of all racial groups. Hitherto the negroid races had been prohibited from ordination. This was a sure sign to the membership that the Spirit of God was dynamically active among the First Presidency of the Church.[74]

At a more popular level the 1970s witnessed the widespread fame of the pop-music group The Osmonds. Their six-man group came on the early 1970s' stage as a striking example of morally sound family life enjoying itself. The ideal of family life and marriage was stressed and the pop-image of teenage romance was handled in as non-erotic a way as possible under the circumstances. *The Sunday Times* featured this phenomenon in January 1973 describing the teenage music market as "flooded with cuddly, clean-living teenage (and even sub-teenage) heroes brought over ready-made from the United States". Donny Osmond even featured in a running cartoon story carried in the magazine for teenage girls called *Mirabelle*. In its 1973 Christmas edition Jay Osmond also starred in a special feature which highlighted him and his family's commitment to Mormonism. A commitment in which their household "is run on discipline and love", and which is sure that "you can celebrate with a glass of milk or fruit juice" rather than alcohol.

Just over a decade later, Mormon church magazines were announcing one Utah church member as the winner of the Miss America title.[75] For British and other Saints to read of this young woman, daughter of Robert E. Wells a member of the First Quorum of the Seventy, as one at the centre of media and popular attraction, is a sure sign that the church is successful in today's world. Success and relevance stand easily together alongside conservative religious positions. More specifically it could be argued that achievement is viewed as the crowning of endeavour. With a long historical perspective it is instructive to set this kind of popular music and cultural triumph against the early nineteen-century Mormon message calling members to flee from the world and its cloying interests. Though it would be easy to agree with Mark P. Leone's idea that there is a certain 'memorylessness' in contemporary Mormonism which obliterates past ideas in the process of establishing a more developed form of truth for the present, I prefer to see the conservatism carried along by such media stars as the continuation of the historical commitment of the Saints. They are concerned to see how bright and successful performers can frame their faith with their public acclaim. Even so there is an obvious shift from the centripetal call to prepare for the coming of Christ so evident in the nineteenth-century to the centrifugal and world affirming attitudes of the later twentieth-century.

Perhaps it is no accident that the journal we have now touched on for each decade of its existence and whose very name, *The Millennial Star* describes an epoch, finally ceased publication at the end of the 1970s to be replaced by the new church magazines, the *Ensign* and the *New Era*. Both these latter titles indicate something of the recognition of new times and new attitudes. The star which had sought to announce the new reign of Christ fades as the existence of the extensive society of Mormondom came to serve as an ensign of a new era already existing.

The nineteenth-century was the period in which the theological concept of eschatology first came to be widely used in Europe and America. This idea referred to the doctrines of the last things, of matters pertaining to judgement, death and the eternal kingdom of God. Nineteenth-century Mormon thought fully reflected the major trends in this widely-shared doctrinal expectation as we have seen. Later, in the twentieth-century, some Protestant theologians came to speak of what they called realized eschatology by which they meant that values of the ultimate kingdom came to be enshrined in contemporary existence among the faithful.[76] If there is one way of glossing the history of Mormon theology and practice, as far as the eye of the world is concerned, it might be to say that there has been a radical change from a belief in an immediate coming of Christ to a realized eschatology. It is a shift from imminence to immanence.

Throughout this study I have sought to show how the growth in temple spirituality has conduced to a form of piety which relates the mundane and the supernatural worlds on one single continuum. The emergence of a theology of salvation which is grounded in an extended family and set within a framework of pre and post existence has meant that the framework demanded by an act of judgement in the near future became increasingly unnecessary.

It was not until 1975 that the Merthyr Tydfil branch of the church, the branch which had so much earlier been called 'the mother branch of Britain', finally gained the status of a Stake. Maturity as an area of Zion did not come until new notions of church purpose had been established. It is fitting that this change occurred after the demise of the *Millennial Star*.

It is not hard for contemporary Mormons in Britain to understand why so many thousands migrated to America in the last century. They can see it as a response of faith, much as they see their own commitment to the church today. It is unwise to interpret such a view as an act of memorylessness. It does not involve any sort of blindness to the fact that once a doctrine was preached which is preached no longer, rather it engages in an imaginative association of faith with faith.

Chapter Twenty Two

Restoring Transcendence

We have left uncharted the more specific details of church life in the 1970s and 1980s in the belief that some future date will afford a more balanced vantage point for analysing these recent times. It will, for example, be interesting to explore the part played by the church through its Mormon Tabernacle Choir in the broad realm of civil religion in America.[77] And many similar items will offer future scholars ample scope for reflection. My final concern is with the theme of Mormon spirituality which has run throughout this book. It is a theme which touches very deeply the life of church members over the last two decades as much as in any earlier period, and for that reason I conclude by making some tentative suggestions about the nature of Mormon faith and religion as it has developed into the present day.

Three scholars will help make some key points, they are Thomas O'Dea, Mark Leone and Jan Shipps. Having criticized each I will end by offering an alternative perspective on the dynamics of Latter Day Saint spirituality and religion.

Thomas O'Dea published his well-known sociological analysis of American Mormons in 1957. In it he stated quite categorically that, 'a receptive, contemplative relationship to God is not found as part of Mormon prayer and worship', (1957:154). However true this might have been in America in the 1940s and 1950s in the public aspects of religion, it is certainly questionable now, and is largely incorrect as far as much British Mormon life is concerned. The question of comparability is important, especially if O'Dea, Roman Catholic as he was, used the devotional attitude to the Mass in his reckoning. As I have argued earlier in this book it is the temple and its rites which serve sacramental ends in Mormonism and not the more public forms of religion, not even the Sacrament Service of weekly use. The pragmatism of Mormon church life is obviously important but it should not be allowed to mask the feelings and sentiments which help fire the life of faith for Saints.

Mark P. Leone's more anthropological study is also potentially misleading on this issue of spirituality because of the way he uses the concept of sanctity. It is quite a key idea in his book, *Roots of Modern Mormonism*, and he develops it from Ray A. Rappaport. The unfortunate fact is that this concept is really none other than the sociological notion of plausibility. It concerns the way in which ideas are legitimated and given validation in a society. 'The quality of unquestionable truthfulness', is how Rappaport defines sanctity, (Leone, 1979:84). Leone explores how church leaders have used Mormon scriptures and rule of thumb under changing social circumstances to maintain a degree of power and authority over members.

There is nothing wrong with this particular application of theories of legitimation, the confusion comes when sanctity is introduced as a mode of discourse. Not least because Leone later goes on to say that 'transcendence collapsed' for modern Mormons as they reduced the historical past to an aspect of their contemporary experience, (1979:213).

It is my contention that the growth of temple ritual and of a church membership whose full bureaucratic involvement required temple participation has led to a distinctive form of spirituality generated by the temples. It could be argued that far from transcendence collapsing it has been regenerated as the temples assumed the symbolic and experiential position which the kingdom of God had been expected to occupy by nineteenth-century Saints.

Sanctity could then be read as a validation of Mormon ideology springing from the self-authentication of religious experience. It is a theoretical tendency of social science to focus on the social source of power, but in terms of the phenomenology of religion it is always important to explore the individual as the arena in which truth is recognized.

Transcendence as the sense of being confronted by or related to a source of religious power which marks life as good is a widespread phenomenon in the Latter Day Saint world. It may be true to say, with O'Dea and Leone, that Mormons developed a view of the world which did not distinguish between the sacred and the profane in traditional ways, and that the secular was sacralized or the sacred secularized, but any thought that through this process all individual religious sense of another order of life and experience vanished must be halted in the light of what some Mormons say. They say, as we saw in chapter eighteen, that through their temple work they have gained a new dimension of faith. New levels of awareness have dawned upon them. And this is not simply a passing moment but is something which enters into their wider life as Mormons.

This sense of a religious aspect of existence is well portrayed in the last scholar I wish to consider. Jan Shipps has argued that Mormonism constitutes a new religious tradition which is as different from Christianity as Christianity was different from the Judaism out of which it emerged in the first place.

Published in 1985 her approach shows a similarity to this present study due to a common interest in aspects of the history and phenomenology of religion. She is not to be classed with O'Dea and Leone with their predominating sociological perspectives. What I seek to do by way of criticism here is a constructive development of a point she makes at the very close of her argument.

As part of her task of classifying religion in Mormonism she introduces the idea of units of salvation and relates them to the goal of the religious life. Mormonism, she says, adopts the individual as the unit of salvation and the family as the unit of exaltation. The goal of life is a corporate development of family groups into their own eternity and not some heavenly worship of a single God. All this is perfectly intelligible in the light of earlier chapters in this present book. The question now is whether such a dual scheme of religious dynamics can be brought together in a more satisfying way. I want to suggest that it can reach a higher level of integration through the concept of embodiment. It is as the individual Mormon comes to a sense of bodily experience of religious ideology through ritual practice and the daily life of families that an integration of salvation and exaltation occurs. I would wish to add a critical point by way of a hypothesis and say that the Mormon idea of salvation, applicable to the individual person, itself belongs to the category of 'time', while the idea of exaltation, applicable to the individual as a member of a sealed family, belongs to the category of eternity.

The religious ideas of most other churches are placed by Mormonism in a preparatory stage of experience. Mormonism is, in this sense, a Christian ideology as far as time is concerned, but is its own scheme of thought in its own terms of eternity. This goes some way to solve Shipps' problem of two apparently irreconcilable schemes of religion in Mormonism.

Her passing references to myth and story as the framework of Mormon religion can also be developed in the category of narrative theology as the perfect form for the cumulative and developing content of Latter Day Saint thought and practice.

So to portray modern Mormons as solely pragmatic bureaucrats running an efficient organization with a membership of some five million people would be to ignore the way their faith appears to them. While it is true that there has been an extensive elaboration of church structure and practice across the world over the last twenty years and that members see this as sound and judicious endeavour, it does not rule out the interface of the individual with the church community as a faith community.

Ordinary church members talk about 'faith-promoting experiences' in relation to their testimony. These in and of themselves add useful information to our picture of Mormon piety. For some informants these events are what the non-member would merely call coincidence but which the eye of faith sees as a divine assistance, though perhaps of only a low order of magnitude. For others it is a question of healing through a blessing by the elders whilst the sick person is also taking medicine prescribed by the doctor. Some comment on more marked cases of healing, while yet others recall stories of chains of coincidence while seeking to establish their genealogical tables.

Whether in a faith-promoting experience in the mundane world, or through events in the temple, not a few Mormons have come to a religious experience which gives them a testimony and personal assurance that divine powers are at work through their church. It is worth observing that during the 1970s and 1980s many religious groups have witnessed a growth in more obviously supernatural trends in their pattern of religiosity. The dramatic rise of the charismatic movement in many major denominations attests to a resacralization of the world following the more secularized age of the 1950s and 1960s.[78]

While the Roman Catholic and Anglican communions had to cope with this re-enchantment of the spiritual worlds of their people as best they could in relation to the normal world of daily life, it is possible that the existing and growing temple scheme of Mormonism permitted this re-enchantment of otherwise secularized individuals with less of a disruption to normal church activity.

Having made this appeal for an inclusion of an emotive piety in Mormon spirituality, it is quite unnecesary to argue that it needs to be balanced by that institutional activism which has been documented throughout this book. In the course of time the various dimensions of church life have seen to it that both the reflective and effective, the more symbolic and the more obviously pragmatic aspects of human personality have conjoined to make this religion a force at the heart of private and corporate life.

But I have also stressed the theme of spirituality in several chapters to redress an imbalance often found in sociological studies of religion. When institutions and processes are the focus of attention the individual is easily overlooked. More particularly the question of the mood or sense of embodiment as a believer is avoided. Yet for the individual few things are more important than this awareness of identity in belonging to a fellowship of the truth.

We have shown how the chapel and the temple each in their different way contribute to a Mormon sense of religion. The rise of the temple has particularly impressed many members with the transcendent dimension of faith. It would be easy to argue that temple rites are the perfect context in which personal imagination and private symbolism marries with the intentional symbolism of the church itself, but we need caution here since it is a regular temptation of western intellectuals to separate private and public symbolic systems.[79] The temple is an established cultural symbol in many Christian contexts through its Old Testament primacy. What the Mormon leaders did in the early decades of church life was to take that symbol and invest it with a distinctive ethos in relation to their theology of eternity and the sacred. This is of fundamental significance when debating the place of theology in Mormonism.

Too much time is spent arguing the relation between history and theology. We have already explored this field and suggest that narrative theology might be a more creative area of discourse which avoids the sharp distinction between critical history and imaginative stories of the past. The social anthropologist Ioan Lewis is wise to stress the fact that distortion occurs when beliefs are detached from their normal contexts. Both time and place are the ever changing contexts of belief. This is especially vital when theology as an abstract system of thought is the object of our attention. [80]

It is necessary to know what each writer means by the word theology before any sensible discussion is possible. In some Mormon writing there appears to be a desire for a theoretical and abstract systematic theology which is not merely an historical account of the rise of the Mormon religion.

In mentioning liberation and narrative theology we are reminded that many believers in churches where formal theologies exist and have developed over very many hundreds of years now wish to develop their own style of more ready to use theology. This leads me to my last major consideration. It is a suggestion on what counts already as the practical theology of Mormonism. For it could be argued that in practice Mormonism possesses more of a pastoral theology than a systematic theology. It owns a theology which guides the piety of its active members. The idioms chosen as the central means of theological discourse by Mormons are, we may suggest, twofold. They are personalistic and iconographic.

Mormon theology is personalistic in the sense that it focusses on specific persons who themselves enshrine divine revelation. Beginning with Joseph Smith there is a succession of specific prophetic leaders who are the visible manifestation of the ideal of God's Restoration of true belief and practice to this world. Mormon theology remains person focussed at the basic level of the church member whose testimony speaks of an intuitive and emotional knowledge of the reality of God. Testimony is more important than testament. Hence the earlier account in which the authority of the church was said to lie in a living prophet rather than in sacred texts. Mormonism is not fundamentally textual and propositional as a theological system. This may sound strange given the fact that the church possesses the *Book of Mormon* along with the Bible and some other Standard Works of a literary kind. The significant point is that Saints use these sources to assist their faith and not as the proof of it. The historical concern that Mormons show in wanting to justify the character of those men involved in the earliest days of the Restoration is one expression of the person-based nature of the religion.

A major arena in which favoured persons function is the Conference. Throughout the first half of this book there is repeated and constant reference to conferences since they were not only actual meetings of the Saints but also the unit of organization in the mission period. Rather like the early days of the Methodist Church, the Latter Day Saints had leaders who were forging the way ahead and creating the life of the church as they went. Conferences enabled them to impress their hearers with the mark of zeal. Conferences enabled the character to be seen through what was heard. In terms of Mormon spirituality leadership demands godliness and that is perceived through contact with people in a direct way. In this sense piety is passed from one to another in an imitative form of learning. Heresy takes the form of immorality rather than of imprecision in formal doctrine. To be in good standing with the church is more important than to have all ideas fully in accord with some abstract ideal. If Mormonism had been a religion whose theology was a systematic theology, then heresy would more frequently have been couched in terms of error in understanding. The history of the church is important in that it furnishes the contexts for the various leaders to be seen as persons with their distinctive aura of godliness. The idea of salvation history does work in Mormonism at the more abstract level of dispensations through which the plan of salvation passes, but there is also need for a narrative theology of individuals through whom that plan is made effective. And it is at this point that our first category concerning persons passes into the second idiom of Mormon theology, the iconographic.

Mormon theology, the handling of its beliefs about God, takes place in temples more than in chapels, in chapels more than in lecture rooms as far as key leadership personnel of the church are concerned. In normal terms Mormonism is seldom regarded as an iconographic movement, in fact its organizational and pragmatic dimensions are very often at the forefront of descriptions of the church. Such an emphasis is misplaced as far as the sense of embodiment of many Mormons is concerned.

Salt Lake City itself, along with its entire valley, is one form of icon. This was where the desert would blossom as the rose and the Old Testament prophetic figure be fulfilled. More than this it was part of the ideology of Zion, the very city of God which would be established in the last days. It was, in other words, a physical context which conferred spiritual benefit. More specifically still the temple, and later other temples, was highly decorated in a variety of ways as a means of educating those performing rites within its walls.[81] Unlike chapels the temple walls, or some specific rooms within it, were painted with murals depicting various aspects of the religious dispensations within the total plan of salvation. The creation, the fall, the world as it is, and the nature of the heavenly glories as they will appear, all these theological ideas were physically manifest to furnish a context for teaching the faith. So teaching verbally as well as by visual cue and by physical action on the part of initiates all conduced to a practical display of theological concepts. If we may expand the concept of icon a little further still we can say that each Mormon becomes an iconographic representation of truth. Special temple clothing and activity allows the individual to enter into the system of ideas which constitutes the Restoration.

At this point it is important to stress that religious art does not easily avail itself of heresy. Art demands interpretation and personal response rather than logic chopping criticism.

Even the foundation story of Mormonism, the account of how the religiously confused Joseph Smith went into the woods as a mere boy to pray to God and ultimately to encounter divine personages, is a verbal picture. This is another reason why the debate about history and theology in Mormonism is of particular complexity. For the faithful these events serve as mental icons. They are images which arouse a response. Pictures of Joseph Smith and his first companions allow modern believers to visualize some possible past and to identify themselves with it. And this is experienced as beneficial.

In this sense the temple is an iconographic expression of Restoration truth. What it demands of the faithful is moral purity of intent and participation rather than doctrinal precision. Experiences gained at the temple help foster and forge experience and ideas within an artistic representation of the great persons through whom God is believed to have established His work in these latter days.

But it must, finally, be said that the total church organization is the ultimate icon. We have showed earlier in this book how the very structure of Latter Day Saint institutions was believed to be a representation of the divine pattern of organization. It will only take sufficient responsive members fully participating in the temple ordinances to make this church on earth appear as the perfect expression of the divine imagination. Sustaining the Prophet and participating in the Temple the Saint practises Restoration theology.

It is precisely because this theology is extended throughout the breadth of this church and has been generated through its history that this book has been possible. Our chosen limitation has been the narrative theological history of the *Millennial Star*, yet despite its basically uncritical account we have still been afforded a framework within which to explore the ideology and ethos of the Mormon scheme of salvation.

NOTES

1. Mary Douglas, (ed). *Witchcraft Confessions and Accusations.* Tavistock, London, 1970.

2. Since a very large number of references will be made to the *Millennial Star* throughout this book, we will use a variety of modes of reference in the text to avoid monotony. Along with the full title we will also use the abbreviated forms of *Star and Millenial Star*, and whenever it is obvious from the text that this journal is the source of material we will simply give a year and page number in brackets. Occasionally reference will be to the month in which a report is made rather than to a page number. This should provide very little difficulty for anyone who wishes to consult the journal in its full form.

    Similarly we will refer to the Church of Jesus Christ of Latter Day Saints only infrequently in this full form. Sometimes we will employ the LDS abbreviation, and at others the title of Mormon will be employed. Quite often we will use the general term of Restoration movement when referring to the church.

3. The church hierarchy is formally divided into the lower order of the Aaronic Priesthood with its internal divisions of deacon, teacher and priest; and the higher order of the Melchizedek elders which also includes the statuses of high priest, seventy, patriarch and prophet. All are believed to have been restored to the earth directly by Jesus to Joseph Smith. It is interesting to note in passing that Ephraim, a fourth-century Syrian Christian, suggested that Christ received the priesthood at his baptism at the hands of John the Baptist who himself was son of the high priest Zachariah, (Robert Murray 1975:178-182). There is no suggestion of any historical link between him and Joseph Smith.

4. Women share in the priesthood of their ordained husbands or prospective husbands. There is also an extensive system of women's organizations in the church affording much scope for leadership and responsibility.

5. The distinction between the sacred and the profane which William Robertson Smith established for religious studies in his famous study of *The Religion of the Semites*, (1894) and which was extended in the sociology of religion by Emile Durkheim's *Elementary Forms of the Religious Life*, (1912) touches on the phenomenological observation

of the duplicity within experience so often categorized within religious traditions in terms of good and evil. Care is needed in employing this distinction since at each stage of religious development the internal dynamics of a movement may focus upon different items as most truly expressing either the sacred or the profane, or the holy and the common as Robertson Smith originally called it. For Mormons in the nineteenth-century the act of emigration provided a means whereby the profane world of Babylon could be transcended by entry into the sacred world of Zion. In the twentieth-century such transcendence is associated with the ritual of the temple.

6. I first developed this idea of pools of potential orientation in my original study of *The Mormons of Merthyr Tydfil*, 1972:28.

7. Protestant hymnbooks of the nineteenth-century often carried extensive sections on the promised land but by that term they referred to heaven. The famous Sankey and Moody hymnbook, *Sacred Songs and Solos*, which went through many editions, had twice as many hymns on the life to come as it had hymns for young people.

8. A classic expression of a sociological theory of religious response to worldly poverty is V. Lanternari 1963.

9. The *Star* renders the hymn in this way:-

Hiraeth y Sant Tylawd	*The Longing of the Poor Saint*
Hiraethu wyf yn Mhabilon Am fynd i Seion wiw Yn disgwyl am y newydd llon Yn amser da fy Nhuw	In Babylon I pine and grieve For Zion far away But I shall go I do believe In God's appointed day.
Dywedair prophwyd Brigham Young In English tongue so grand A welcome you shall have among The Saints in Zion's land.	Then says prophet Brigham Young etc.,

10. The way new religious experience is related to prior religious experience is an extremely complex issue. The anthropologist Dan Sperber's innovatory study on symbolic knowledge may well be of assistance in showing how new symbols are incorporated into the old stock of symbolic knowledge changing it in the process, 1975.

11. B. R. Wilson's *Religious Sects*, 1970, affords one useful scheme for classifying sectarian movements.

12. Edmund Leach's *Dialectic in Practical Religion*, 1968, presents an anthropological view of the relation between formal and popular ideas on eastern religiosity. More recently P. H. Vrijhof and

on eastern religiosity. More recently P. H. Vrijhof and J. Waardenberg (eds), 1979, have explored the field more widely in their *Official and Popular Religion*.

13. In one sense the entirety of this book concerns Mormon hermeneutics, or the interpretation of reality which the LDS view of history progressively generated.

14. This resembles the way in which nineteenth century liberal Christianity saw itself as crowning the partial truths present in pagan religion. This fulfilment model of truth is a typical feature of Christian epistemology and may be grounded in the fact that early Christianity saw itself as emerging from a now fulfilled Judaism, which itself was a progressive and prophetic movement fulfilling Old Testament prophecy. The evolutionary ideas of the nineteenth century were quite comparable with this kind of theological thinking. It is interesting to observe how the Protestant theologian Paul Tillich's *Systematic Theology* classifies infinite process and fulfilment together as forms of the Progressivist idea of history, (Vol.3. p.377).

15. *The Restorer* was published monthly at Aberdare for a short period during 1864-1865. Each issue contained a Welsh section entitled *Yr Adferydd*.

16. This issue tends to resurface periodically. On 30 March 1986 *The Sunday Times Magazine* carried a full account of attacks made upon Steven F. Christensen, a collector of historical documents on Mormonism, at Salt Lake City. He had acquired the Salamander Letter which purported to cast doubt on the Book of Mormon's authenticity and authorship. Similar themes are pursued in chapter twenty-one.

17. For a variety of analysis and comment on the widespread phenomenon of glossolalia see David Martin and Peter Mullen, 1984.

18. The distinction between *kairos* and *chronos* is explored in Paul Tillich's *Systematic Theology*, Vol.3. p.393.

19. Klaus J. Hansen suggested that the former Protestantism of many Mormon converts made them, 'emotionally unprepared for a practice that might have reminded them of popery', (1981:170). I doubt, however, whether Marian dogma and the LDS idea of a mother god are at all closely related.

20. The anthropologist Victor Turner has used this notion of root metaphor to discuss the patterning of symbols in cultures, e.g., 1975:15.

21. As opposed to K. J. Hansen's comment that the Saints explained the deaths of their colleagues in terms of their going to preach to the Gentile dead, the *Star* did not espouse that argument, 1981:109.

22. J. Haynes, *The Book of Mormon Examined*, 1853:12. This idea was later expanded by G. B. Arbough, 1932.

23. A. Willis, 1912.

24. F. Ballard, 1922:14.

25. W. J. Conybeare, 1855:336.

26. E. Clay, 1853:35. J. Masters, 1857:3. J. C. Bennett, 1842:304.

27. W. J. Conybeare, 1955:101.

28. W. Mulder, 1958:347.

29. W. Riley, 1903:73.

30. J. Caudwell, 1965:11.

31. *Aweful Disclosures of Mormonism*. Bodleian Library Oxford, no date or publisher.

32. Routeledge and Company, 1855, no author given.

33. C. H. Clarke, London, 1855.

34. J. Haynes, 1853:5.

35. Edinburgh Review, 1854:107.

36. *The Mormon Imposter*. Newbury, 1851.

37. *The Church of England Newspaper*, 18 June 1971.

38. Work by former Mormons like Jerald and Sandra Tanner offers extensive doctrinal and ethical analyses as in their book, *The Changing World of Mormonism*, 1980.

39. See, for example, Paul Tillich, 1964, Vol.3. pp.317ff. Emil Brunner, 1934:388.

40. D. J. Davies, 1984:96. Rodney Needham, 1972.

41. Edwin S. Gaustad. 'Historical theology and Theological History: Mormon Possibilities'. *Journal of Mormon History*, Vol.11, 1984.

42. Maureen Ursenbach Beecher. 'Entre nous: An Intimate History of the Mormon History Association'. *Journal of Mormon History*, Vol.12, 1985.

43. See note 12. Also Robert Towler, *Homo Religiosus*, 1974. The American expression of the issue has tended to follow the theme of civil religion for which consult R. N. Bellah, 1970. British studies are very limited but see David Clark's study of popular Methodism, *Between Pulpit and Pew*, 1982, and James Obelkevitch on religion in Lincolnshire, 1976.

44. J. Navone, *Towards a Theology of Story*, 1977, G. W. Stroup, *The Promise of Narrative Theology*, 1981. G. Guttierez, *A Theology of Liberation*, 1973.

45. Arnold Van Gennep, *Rites of Passage*, 1960.

46. Gwyn A. Williams, *Madoc, The Making of a Myth*, 1979. Also *The Search for Beulah Land*, 1980:37.

47. This helped overcome any problem of cognitive dissonance in LDS life at that time. Cognitive dissonance is the psychological conflict between firm expectation and its disappointment. It has been used as an idea in studies of failed prophecies in religious movements following from the work of Leon Festinger and H. W. Riecken, 1956. Its applicability to Mormonism is very limited. See note 55.

48. As argued by Whitney R. Cross, 1950. See also Thomas O'Dea, 1957:11.

49. Though this simple position was one I adopted in my paper on LDS Eschatology, D. J. Davies, 1973.

50. The fact that the Mormon historian Richard L. Bushman notes that Enoch was depicted as a seer and powerful preacher but makes no interpretative link between Enoch and Joseph Smith is interesting, 1984:187.

51. *Journal of Discourses* 1. 50-51. See Thomas O'Dea, 1957:122.

52. J. F. C. Harrison, 1979. It is important to recall that Britain engendered numerous new religious movements during the Industrial Revolution which parallels something of America's frontier revolution.

53. Note 10 introduced the work of Dan Sperber on symbolic knowledge. I have also argued along similar theoretical lines to suggest that converts use prior religiosity to good effect in the new structure of symbols gained in the new religious context, D. J. Davies, *B.J.R.E.*, 1985. But this is a complex area and it is certainly true that in Wales Mormon leaders were well aware that well-known non-Mormon hymns contained material that was false to the theology of the Restoration and might hinder the new faith of converts. T. H. Lewis points this out as he compares the several editions of the Welsh Mormon hymnbook initially edited by Captain Dan Jones, and originating in 1847. The first collection was small and expressed an awareness of the unsuitability of some pre-existing Welsh hymns. From the one hundred and thirty hymns of the first edition to the five hundred and seventy five hymns of the third, 1852 edition, there is a marked shift of emphasis. Lewis sees the change as involving a shrinkage in the missionary element and an increase in strictly Mormon themes of temple life, destruction of the Nephites, baptism for the dead and preaching to the departed spirits. This was an area fraught with potential hazard but one in which Dan Jones made a positive attempt to make inroads into established domains of Welsh Nonconformist religion. See T. H. Lewis, *Y Mormoniad Yng Nghymru*, 1956:94ff.

54. Some Mormons of the present day see their 'Lamanite Syndrome' as quite unfortunate since it supports a derogatory view of American Indians. D. F. Green, for example, sees the term 'Lamanite' as of equal force to that of 'Gentile', both denoting those outside church membership. 'Book of Mormon Archaeology: the myths and the alternatives', *Dialogue* IV. 2. 1964:71ff.

55. As we have already seen in another context as in note 47.

56. The concept of power in religious explanations remains as important today as when the phenomenologist Gerardus van der Leeuw published his entire scheme of religious phenomenology based on power in 1933.

57. The paired concept of the cumulative tradition of a religion and the personal active faith of the individual constructed by Wilfred Cantwell Smith (1963) is useful in the Mormon context.

58. *Star*, 1927:278, 287. 1928:733. 1930:363.

59. A long-standing distinction between Church, Sect and Denomination will be found in B. R. Wilson's analysis of sect development in his *Patterns of Sectarianism*, 1967.

60. There is a definite area of varied belief in the Mormon church over the theory of human evolution. Many find the scriptural accounts quite acceptable in a rather direct manner of reading them, but others, most especially those involved in further scientific education, have difficulties at this point. The First Presidency of the church has stated to some individual scientists in the church that no official position exists on organic evolution. Some scientific church members have been worried that statements in books on doctrine which say, for example, that there was no death on the earth prior to the fall of man, were incompatible with modern scientific perspectives. On prompting the Prophet over such matters they were acknowledged and told that the church only speaks officially on things that have been distinctly revealed, and that no revelation exists on specific scientific matters of evolution. This problem is inevitably significant because the church fosters its own institutes of higher learning, most especially the prestigious Brigham Young University at Provo in Utah.

    In 1970 I carried out a brief questionnaire survey of some students at this University including some items on organic evolution. On the small sample of only one hundred and seventy two students twenty five believed that our physical bodies were derived from non-human animals, and one hundred and forty seven did not so believe. But these students belonged to three different classes in terms of academic subjects. These were surveyed on the assumption that the more conservative students, in doctrinal terms that is, would be found in the religion class of a conservative teacher, that the liberals would be in a particular earth-science class, and more neutral students in an education class. It emerged that class membership was significantly related to position on evolution. The following table is included simply as a reflection of varied opinion.
    Do you believe that our physical bodies were derived from non-human animals?

Class	Sex	Number	Yes	No
Geology	Male	17	10	7
	Female	13	5	8
Education	Male	10	4	6
	Female	22	1	21
Religion	Male	45	1	44
	Female	65	4	61
		172	25	147

There was some indication that gender was associated with the belief adopted but in statistical terms it is not as sufficiently significant as the class attended.

61. The name MIA or Mutual Improvement Association was abandoned in 1974 as the Aaronic Priesthood and Young Women's organizations assumed its functions.

62. Rodney Needham, *Reconnaissances*, 1980. The distinction between mystical and jural power is best understood in sociological terms as part of the classification of the world which many peoples construct in their own distinctive fashion. Needham also edited an important anthropological study on this area entitled *Right and Left*, 1973. In general terms the Latter Day Saints do engage in an interesting series of classifications which could be studied further. The major dichotomy between men and women united in the shared priesthood is mirrored in the distinction between the lower Aaronic and the higher Melchizedek orders united in the scheme of priesthood, just as time and eternity are distinct and managed through priesthood ritual. The opposition between temple and chapel follows a similar pattern, so too the divide between the living and the dead is mediated by vicarious temple rites. The right hand is symbolically favoured and specified as that which should take the sacramental bread and used in other church contexts. The fact that every decision-making office has two counsellors attached to it might also be evidence of a similar scheme, as would the balancing of the Bible and the Book of Mormon within the total category of sacred scripture. The firm distinction between negro and white which has more recently been removed was also couched in terms of priesthood. And all this has the mythical-historical context of the old world of Israel and the new world of America mediated by Jews travelling the divide by sea and by Jesus giving separate resurrection appearances.

63. B. L. Mijuskovic, 1979, explores this area in a more philosophical way while David Riesman's famous study of *The Lonely Crowd*, 1950, was more general. See also R. E. Weiss, 1973.

64. The symbolic function of food has been much discussed in recent anthropology. The work of the following scholars is especially helpful. Mary Douglas, 1966, 1975, 1982. Jack Goody, 1982. Together these suggest how food functions sociologically and symbolically. Audrey Hayley, 1980, develops a similar theme for an Indian devotional religious movement.

65. D. J. Davies, 1986:35ff. where I explore what I call the alimentary forms of the religious life. Much of this is applicable to the Saints

through their fasts and Word of Wisdom, and it also applies to the Sacrament Service even though its theology is far removed from the ideology of the Catholic Mass. Mormons place a heavy emphasis upon the significance of matter but in quite a different way from many other Christian traditions which make qualitative distinctions between matter and spirit.

66. R. R. Marett first introduced the idea of *Homo religiosus* in his Gifford Lectures, 1933. I have used this category, now widely employed in the phenomenology of religions, in exploring the Mormon missionary as an example of Mormon spirituality, D. J. Davies, 1984:139.

67. Hans Mol's sociological work on religion and identity, 1976, offers an interesting hypothesis on the way in which the individual believer's sense of identity is related to the source or focus of that identity. In essence he argues that such sources tend to be sacralized, or viewed as beyond doubt and contradiction. In the Mormon case this would apply to the First Presidency of the church whose authority and contact with divine revelation guarantees the truthfulness of the individual's religion.

68. In a brief survey at the Brigham Young University in 1970 some one hundred and three unmarried Mormon girls were asked whether they would prefer to marry a returned missionary than someone who had not served a mission. I obtained the following response.

Strong preference,	49
Preference,	33
No preference,	21

Some of the respondents stated quite clearly that they thought a mission made a man out of a boy. D. J. Davies, 1972:62.

69. Some twenty three Mormon students responded to a questionnaire concerning many aspects of their life. Only six had not attended the temple, and ten had been there several times. Among the specific descriptions of their experience at the temple were those who said it gave them a deeper appreciation of the love of God. A sense of spiritual rejuvenation and a joy in service. An awareness of the literally physical nature of God, and the fact that the dead are not so far away as normally thought. Others felt their knowledge of the faith, and of genealogy had increased, but some felt it was their faith rather than their rational mind that had been strengthened. Several noted how the temple was bathed in peace and gave a sense of place and an assurance of security in the future.

70. Max Weber's study of *The Protestant Ethic*, (1930), was an attempt at linking theological ideas with theories of action. I used something of a similar outlook in arguing that the Charismatic forms of religion which emerged in the 1960s and 1970s were related to values inherent in service-society. D. J. Davies in David Martin and Peter Mullen, 1984.

71. *Faith and Doctrines*. Church of Jesus Christ, Monongahela, Pa. 1969.

72. *The Gospel News* Vol.27 No.12. December 1971, p.6. This church also holds a belief in an American Indian Moses who is to appear. In the April 1986 edition the front page is devoted to the theme: 'The coming of an American Indian Moses in the near future is an essential message'.

73. Gwyn A. Williams, 1980:135.

74. The negro question is extensively explored in N. G. Bringhurst, 1981.

75. *This People*, December 1984, p.20ff.

76. Surveys of the theological debate may be found in, for example, Hans Conzelmann, 1969:307ff. and W. G. Kummel, 1966.

77. See note 43.

78. David Martin and Peter Mullen (eds), 1984.

79. See G. Obeyesekere, 1981.

80. I. M. Lewis, 1986.

81. See J. Talmage, 1968.

BIBLIOGRAPHY

Arbough, G. B. 1932. *Revelation in Mormonism*. Illinois: University of Chicago Press.

Ballard, F. 1922. *Why Not Mormonism?* London: Epworth Press.

Bateson, G. 1958. *Naven*. Stanford University Press.

Beckford, J. A. 1985. *Cult Controversies*. London: Tavistock.

Beecher, M. A. 1985. 'Entre Nous: An Intimate History of the Mormon History Association'. *Journal of Mormon History*, Vol.12.

Bellah, R. N. 1970. *Beyond Religion*. New York: Harper and Row.

Bennett, J. C. 1884. *Mormonism Exposed*. Boston: Leland and Whiting.

Bourdillon, M. C. F. and Meyer Fortes, (eds). 1980: *Sacrifice*. London: Academic Press.

Bringhurst, N. G. 1981. *Saints, Slaves and Blacks*. London: Greenwood Press.

Brunner, E. 1934. *The Mediator*. London: Unwin.

Bushman, R. L. 1984. *Joseph Smith and the Beginnings of Mormonism*. Chicago: University of Illinois Press.

Caudwell, J. 1865. (Publisher). *Mormonism, The Character of its Founder*. London.

Church History. See B. H. Roberts.

Clark, C. H. 1855. (Publisher). *Mormonism Unveiled*. London.

Clark, D. 1982. *Between Pulpit and Pew*. Cambridge University Press.

Clay, E. 1853. *The Doctrines and Practices of the Mormons and the Immoral Character of their Prophet Joseph Smith*. London: Wertheim and MacIntosh.

Conybeare, W. J. 1855. *Essays Ecclesiastical and Social*. Edinburgh Review. London: Longmans.

Conzelmann, H. 1969. *An Outline of the Theology of the New Testament*. London: S.C.M. Press.

Cross, W. R. 1950. *The Burned Over District*. New York: Cornel University Press.

Davies, D. J. 1972. *The Mormons of Merthyr Tydfil*. Unpublished Oxford B.Litt. Thesis.

—, 1973. "Aspects of Latter Day Saint Eschatology". *Sociological Yearbook of Religion in Britain.* ed. Michael Hill. London: S.C.M. Press.

—, 1984. *Meaning and Salvation in Religious Studies*. Leiden: Brill.

—, 1984. "The Charismatic Ethic and the Spirit of Post-Industrialism". *Strange Gifts.* (ed.) D. Martin and Peter Mullen.

—, 1985. "Symbolic Thought and Religious Knowledge". *British Journal of Religious Education.* Vol.7 No.2.

—, 1986. *Studies in Pastoral Theology and Social Anthropology*. Birmingham: University Institute for Worship.

Doctrine and Covenants. Utah: Church of Jesus Christ of Latter Day Saints.

Doctrine and Covenants. Independence, Missouri: Reorganized Church of Jesus Christ of Latter Day Saints.

Douglas, Mary 1966. *Purity and Danger*. London: Routledge and Kegan Paul.

—, 1970. (ed.) *Witchcraft Confessions and Accusations*. London: Tavistock.

—, 1975. *Implicit Meanings*. London: Routledge and Kegan Paul.

—, 1982. *In the Active Voice*. London: Routledge and Kegan Paul.

Durkheim, E. 1976. *The Elementary Forms of the Religious Life*. London: Allan Lane. (First French Edition published 1912).

Evans, R. L. 1984. *A Century of Mormonism in Great Britain*. Salt Lake City: Publishers Press. (First Edition 1937).

Festinger, L. and H. W. Riecken 1956. *When Prophecy Fails*. Minneapolis: University of Minnesota Press.

Francis, H. and D. Smith 1980. *The Fed. A History of the South Wales Miners in the Twentieth Century.* Cardiff: University of Wales Press.

Gaustad, E. S. 1984. "Historical Theology and Theological History: Mormon Possibilities". *Journal of Mormon History.* Vol.11.

Gennep, Arnold Van 1960. *The Rites of Passage.* London: Routledge and Kegan Paul.

Goody, J. 1982. *Cooking, Cuisine and Class.* Cambridge University Press.

Green, D. F. 1964. "Book of Mormon Archaeology: the myths and alternatives". *Dialogue* IV. 2. pp.71 ff.

Gutierrez, G. 1974. *Theology of Liberation.* London: S.C.M. Press.

Hansen, K. J. 1981. *Mormonism and the American Experience.* Chicago and London: University of Chicago Press.

Harrison, J. F. C. 1979. *The Second Coming: Popular Millenarianism 1780-1850.* London: Routledge.

Hayley, A. 1980. "A Commensal Relationship with God: the nature of the offering in Assamese Vaishnavism". In M. C. F. Bourdillon and Meyer Fortes 1980.

Haynes, J. 1853. *The Book of Mormon examined and its Claim to be a Revelation from God proved to be False.* London: Seeley and Co.

Hill, R. 1966. In Blain Porter (ed). *The Latter Day Saint Family.* Salt Lake City: Deseret Book Company.

Kasemann, E. 1964. Essays on New Testament Themes. *Studies in Biblical Theology 41.*

Kummel, W. G. 1966. *Introduction to the New Testament.* London: S.C.M.

Lanternari, V. 1963. *The Religions of the Oppressed.* New York: Knopf.

Leach, E. R. 1968. *Dialectic in Practical Religion.* Cambridge University Press.

Leeuw, G. van der 1967. *Religion in Essence and Manifestation.* Gloucester Mass: Peter Smith. (First Published in 1933).

Leone, M. P. 1979. *Roots of Modern Mormonism*. London: Harvard University Press.

Lewis, I. M. 1986. *Religion in Context, Cults and Charisma*. Cambridge University Press.

Lewis, T. H. 1956. *Y Mormoniaid Yng Nghymru*. Caerdydd: Gwasg Prifysgol Cymru.

Marett, R. R. 1933. *Sacraments of Simple Folk*. Oxford: Clarendon Press.

Martin, D. and P. Mullen 1984. *Strange Gifts*. Oxford: Blackwells.

Masters, J. 1857. (Publisher). *The Mormons, The Dream and the Reality*. London.

Mijuskovic, B. L. 1979. *Loneliness in Philosophy, Psychology and Literature*. Assen Netherlands: Van Gorcum.

Mol, Hans. 1976. *Identity and the Sacred*. Oxford: Blackwell.

Mulder, W. 1957. *Homeward to Zion*. Minneapolis: University of Minnesota Press.

Murray, R. 1975. *Symbols of Church and Kingdom a Study in Early Syriac Tradition*. Cambridge University Press.

M.W.W. See Richards Le Grand.

Navone, J. 1977. *Towards a Theology of Story*. Slough, Surrey: St. Paul Publications.

Needham, R. 1972. *Belief, Language and Experience*. Oxford: Blackwell.

—. 1973. (Ed). *Right and Left. Essays on Dual Symbolic Classification*. London: University of Chicago Press.

—. 1980. *Reconnaissances*. University of Toronto Press.

Obelkevich, J. 1976. *Religion and Ritual: South Lindsey 1825-1875*. Oxford: Clarendon Press.

Obeyesekere, G. 1981. *Medusa's Hair. An Essay on Personal Symbols and Religious Experience*. London: University of Chicago Press.

O'Dea, T. 1957. *The Mormons*. University of Chicago Press.

Richards, Le Grand 1958. *A Marvelous Work and a Wonder*. Utah: Deseret Books.

Riesman, D. 1950. *The Lonely Crowd*. New York: Yale University Press.

Riley, W. 1903. *The Founder of Mormonism*. London: Heinemann.

Roberts, B. H. 1957. *A Comprehensive History of the Church of Jesus Christ of Latter Day Saints*. Provo: Brigham Young University Press.

Rolston, H. 1985. *Religious Inquiry*. New York:Philosophical Library.

Shepperson, W. S. 1957. *British Emigration to North America*. Oxford: Blackwell for University of Minnesota Press.

Shipps, Jan 1985. *Mormonism*. Urbana and Chicago: University of Illinois Press.

Smith, W. C. 1963. *The Meaning and End of Religion*. New York: MacMillan.

Smith, W. R. 1894. *Religion of the Semites*. London: A & C Black.

Sperber, D. 1975. *Rethinking Symbolism*. Cambridge University Press.

Stroup, G. W. 1981. *The Promise of Narrative Theology*. London: S.C.M. Press.

Talmage, J. 1899. *Articles of Faith*. Salt Lake City. (Numerous editions and publications including 1952).

—, 1968. *The House of the Lord*. Salt Lake City: Deseret Press.

Tanner, J. and S. 1980. *The Changing World of Mormonism*. Chicago: Moody Press.

Tillich, P. 1953. *Systematic Theology*. London: Nesbit.

Towler, R. 1974. *Homo Religiosus*. London: Constable.

Towler, R. 1984. *The Need for Certainty*. London: Routledge and Kegan Paul.

Turner, V. 1975. *Revelation and Divination in Ndembu Ritual*. London: Cornell University Press.

Vrijhof, P. H. and J. Waardenburg, (eds.) 1979. *Official and Popular Religion*. The Hague: Mouton.

Weber, M. 1976. *The Protestant Ethic and the Spirit of Capitalism*. London: Allen and Unwin. (Second Edition).

Weiss, R. E. 1973. *Loneliness*. Massachusetts Institute Tech.Press.

Williams, G. A. 1979. *Madoc, The Making of a Myth*. London: Eyre Methuen.

—. 1980. *The Search for Beulah Land*. London: Croom Helm.

Willis, A. 1912. *Mormonism Whence is it?* London: S.P.C.K.

Wilson, B. R. (ed.) 1967. *Patterns of Sectarianism*. London: Heinemann.

—. 1970. *Religious Sects*. World University Library.

Winquist, C. E. 1980. *Practical Hermeneutics*. Ann Arbor: Scholars Press.

INDEX

A

Aaronic Priesthood. 11, 115, 158, 165.
Abberton, J. 117.
Aberamman. 28.
Abercanaid. 12.
Abercarn. 104, 106.
Aberdare. 9, 10, 26, 30, 128.
Abergavenny. 3.
Abergele. 27.
Abertillery. 76.
Aberystwyth. 47.
Achievement. 141, 149.
Activity. 88, 101, 154.
Adam. 16, 131.
Adam-God. 16, 50, 78, 143.
Adultery. 25.
Affleck, G. B. 105.
Alcohol. 6, 127, 148.
Allen, I. K. 125.
Alms-giving. 49.
American Civil War. 26.
American Constitution. 14.
American Indians. 89, 144 ff., 163, 167.
Anabaptists. 50.
Ancestors. 92.
Anderson, S. J. 40.
Angels. 34, 145

Anglesey. 22.
Anglicans. 12, 15, 27, 33, 77, 108, 129, 154.
Animal Magnetism. 51.
Anointing with oil. 9, 16, 67.
Anti-Mormon Groups. 26, 29, 43 ff., 77, 79, 104, 119.
Apostles. 11, 98.
Arrington, L. 4.
Articles of Faith. 91, 98.
Atonement. 21, 78, 83, 120.
Authority. 54.
Auxiliary Organizations. 109, 114.

B

Babylon. 4, 10, 20, 39, 80.
Baptism. 12, 54, 67, 126, 129, 130, 140.
Baptism for the dead. 34, 144.
Barry Island. 109, 128
Baseball. 140.
Basketball. 140.
Belfast. 139.
Belfast Telegraph. 139.
Bennett, F. R. 109.
Bennett, G. Q. 124, 126.
Bennett, Sir Thomas. 138.
Benson, E. T. 21, 148.
Bible. 19, 47, 50, 62, 88, 96, 112, 145, 155, 165.

Bickerton, M. 146.
Bickerton, W. 144.
Biggs, M. A. 106.
Biggs, T. 106.
Birmingham. 28, 41, 123.
Blackwood. 106, 130.
Blessings. 67, 77, 118, 135.
Blood-Atonement. 53, 83.
Bolitho, A. D. 46, 47, 52.
Book of Mormon. 6, 15, 19, 29, 50 ff., 67, 75, 78, 89, 91, 96, 139, 145, 146, 155, 160, 165.
Book of Moses. 74, 80.
Booth, R. H. 109.
Boston. 70.
Bourne, D. 140.
Brechfa. 22.
Brecon. 22, 40.
Brethren Church. 128.
Bridgend. 128, 129.
Brigham Young University. 164, 166.
Brighamites. 28, 96.
Bristol. 41, 46, 76, 93, 95, 123, 140.
Brough, S. R. 47.
Brown, H. B. 138.
Bureaucracy. 23, 125.
Burials. 122.
Burnham, J. 3.
Bushman, R. L. 61.

C

Cadman, W. H. 144.
Caernarvon. 22.
Caerphilly. 109.
Cambrian Association of Utah. 57.
Cannon, G. Q. 2.
Cardiff. 9, 26, 42, 45, 65, 76, 93, 95, 105, 106, 126, 128, 129.
Cardigan. 22, 47, 106.
Carmarthen. 22, 26, 47.
Carmarthen Weekly Reporter. 26.
Carthage. 7, 83.
Catholicism. 15, 17, 22, 83, 87, 96, 102, 129, 154.
Celestial Glory. 117.
Celestial Marriage. 99, 117, 144.
Centrifugal Religion. 17.
Centripetal Religion. 17.
Certificates of Membership. 12.
Change. 17.
Chapels. 87, 135, 138, 140, 141, 154.
Charisma. 30.
Charismatic Movement. 62, 154, 167.
Charles, P. J. 106.
Charlton, T. 140.
Cheltenham. 26, 93.
Cherry, A. 144.
Cheyenne City. 31.
Children. 78, 89, 93, 124.
Cholera. 9, 13, 16, 29.
Church of Jesus Christ Monongahela. 144.

Christadelphians. 46.
Christensen, S. F. 160.
Christian Science. 70.
Christiani, C. 105.
Christology. 86 ff.
Ciaranino, G. 144.
Civic Authorities. 109, 138, 139.
Civil Religion. 151.
Coffee. 6, 128.
Commitment. 27, 123 ff.
Coneybeare, W. J. 50.
Conferences. 155.
Congregational Church. 128.
Controversy. 29.
Conversion. 16, 21, 23, 36, 71, 131, 140.
Cornell, G. W. 148.
Cowdery, O. 29.
Crabtree, C. 140.
Crawshay Iron Works. 26.
Crawshay, R. 41.
Creation. 86, 144.
Crofts, J. W. 105, 106.
Cullom Bill. 32.
Custom. 17, 129.
Cwmbach. 9, 15, 31.

D

Dancing. 116.
Davies, A. C. 47.
Davies, D. 20.
Davies, J. T. 28.
Davies, T. B. 47, 48.
Davies, W. T. 126.
Day, W. 102.
Delusions. 71.
Denominations. 9, 81, 99.
Derry, C. 28, 143.
Descartes, R. 120.
Detroit. 146.
Dinas Mawddy. 22.
Dispensation. 77, 156.
Disestablishment. 77.
Dissonance (Cognitive). 66, 92, 162.
Divorce. 49, 80, 116, 124.
Doctrine. 17.
Doctrine and Covenants. 6, 75, 78, 99, 117, 127, 128, 137, 143, 144.
Domestic rites. 7.
Dougall, H. W. 85.
Douglas, M. 158, 165.
Dowlais. 7, 40, 107.
Dreams. 145, 146.
Dress. 93, 116.
Dual Purpose Rites. 120.
Dual Sovereignty. 118.
Dundee. 140.
Durkheim, E. 158.

E

Earthquake. 44.
Ebbw Vale. 33.
Edinburgh. 25, 79, 98, 139.

Edmunds-Tucker Act. 44.
Effort. 101.
Eisteddfod. 57, 98, 130.
Eldridge, H. 33.
Elect. 15, 23, 141.
Elijah. 9.
Ellis, M. S. 105.
Elohim. 99.
Emblems. 84.
Embodiment. 153, 154, 156.
Emigration. 4, 8, 9, 10, 13, 16, 18, 24, 26, 27, 29, 31, 33, 37, 46-50, 52, 63, 66, 69, 76, 77, 108, 126, 144.
Endowments. 92.
Endowment House. 45.
English Language. 19 ff.
Enoch. 74.
Ensign, The. 149.
Enthusiasm. 23, 43 ff., 69 ff.
Ephraim. 77.
Eschatology. 15, 32, 43, 50, 63, 149.
Eternity. 87 ff., 143, 153.
Ethics. 16.
Ethnicity. 56.
Evans, Abel. 29.
Evans, Arthur. 123.
Evans, Benjamin. 26.
Evans, J. E. 137.
Evans, L. M. 104.
Evans, R. C. 92.
Evans, R. L. 2, 7.

Evil. 55.
Evolution. 164.
Exaltation. 54, 117, 152, 153.
Exclusivism. 11, 40, 82, 108.
Excommunication. 11, 39.
Execution. 53.
Exodus. 19.
Experience (Religious). 84, 97, 132, 152, 153, 159, 166.

F

Faith. 59, 163, 166.
Fall, The. 120, 131.
Family. 93, 116, 118, 129, 130, 152.
Far West. 34.
Fasting. 20, 67, 145.
Ffestiniog. 22.
First Presidency. 114, 148, 166.
Flintshire. 27.
Folk-Religion. 61, 159.
Food laws. 127.
Foot-washing. 144.
Forscutt, M. H. 28.
Forward, I. 109.
Francis, H. 69.
Free Masonry. 119.
Funerals. 8, 122.
Furnier, T. S. 144.

G

Gaustad, E. S. 60.
Gender. 98, 99.
Genealogy. 2, 50, 85, 128, 135, 166.
Gentiles. 6, 15, 16, 34, 107, 120.
Germans. 45.
Gill, D. R. 48.
Glamorgan. 8, 76, 77.
Glasgow. 41, 139.
Glossolalia. 8, 30, 34, 35, 43, 44, 145, 146, 160, 111, 113, 117, 132, 135, 166.
God. 16, 23, 36, 54, 72, 73, 74 ff., 84, 86 ff.
Goold, J. G. 44.
Gospel News, The. 145, 146, 167.
Goytre. 76, 80.
Grace. 102.
Graham, W. 79.
Grant, H. J. 56, 116.
Grant, W. G. 165.
Green, A. S. 141.
Griffiths, E. M. 104.
Guidance. 115, 118.
Gwladfa. 64.

H

Hanks, M. D. 140.
Hansen, K. J. 160, 161.
Harlech. 27.
Harmon, Anne. 49.
Harmon, Edmund. 40.
Harmon, Mary. 49.
Harmon, Robert. 50.
Harris, C. D. 127.
Haverfordwest. 106.
Hawkes, W. T. 90 ff.
Haynes, J. 2.
Healings. 8, 12, 145, 153.
Health. 116.
Heaven. 17, 145.
Henshaw, W. 3.
Hereford. 10.
Heresy. 155, 156.
Herrick, J. 37.
Hierarchy. 49, 115.
High Council. 55.
Hiraeth. 20.
History. 1, 57 ff., 72, 96, 97, 131, 146, 154, 156, 160.
Holywell. 40.
Homo religiosus. 131, 162, 166.
Hosanna Shout. 123.
Howells, T. F. 39.
Hughes, T. 104.
Hull. 123.
Humility. 133 ff.
Humphries, M. 31.
Hyde, O. 5.
Hymnody. 11, 15, 17, 35, 81 ff., 159, 163.
Hypnotism. 51.

I

Iconography. 156 ff.

Identity. 15, 19, 27, 36, 38, 56, 59, 60, 63, 70, 82, 92, 104, 127, 134, 135, 166.

Ignorance. 49.

Immigration. 112.

Incarnation. 58.

Inclusivism. 40, 82, 108.

Independence, Missouri. 75, 80, 143.

Individual(ism). 121, 122.

Individual Emigration Fund. 26.

Industrialization. 69, 163.

Institutionalization. 123.

Interpretation of Tongues. 145.

Iowa. 12, 143.

Ipswich. 77.

Ireland. 39.

Iron Works. 39, 41.

Isle of Man. 3, 39.

J

Jackson County. 34, 38.

Jarvis, W. 25.

Jehovah. 78, 99, 124.

Jehovah's Witnesses. 124.

Jenkins, T. R. 128.

Jeremy, T. 26.

Jerusalem. 44, 80.

Jesus Christ. 12, 16, 34, 49, 54, 58, 59, 74, 78, 80, 83, 86 ff., 96, 99, 131, 145, 158.

Jews. 44.

John, D. 37.

John the Baptist. 158.

Jones, Captain Dan. 4, 7 ff., 11, 17, 39, 81, 139, 163.

Jones, Daniel. 37.

Jones, F. P. 101, 102.

Jones, J. G. 40.

Jones, Morgan. 95.

Jones, R. C. 105.

Josephites. 28.

Judaism. 152.

K

Kairos. 32, 160.

Käsemann, E. 72.

Kerr, C. 106.

Kidwelly. 37.

Kimball, H. J. 13, 117.

Kimball, P. C. 127.

Kingdom of God. 14, 16, 70, 74 ff., 111, 138, 149, 152.

Kinship. 99.

Kirtland. 34.

Kooyman, F. I. 84.

L

Labour Party. 105.

Lambert, A. C. 77.

Lampeter. 26.

Language. 12, 19, 56.

Latter Day Saint Student Association. 135, 166.

Lauder, Sir Harry. 98.
Laying on of hands. 54, 67.
Leach, Sir Edmund. 159.
Leeds. 41, 123, 144.
Leicester. 46.
Leigh, S. 33, 39.
Leone, M. P. 57, 149, 151.
Lewis, I. 154.
Lewis, S. 43.
Lewis, T. H. 163.
Lewis, W. J. 37.
Liberation Theology. 62, 63, 155.
Lienhardt, G. 47.
Literature. 15.
Liverpool. 37, 41, 77, 123, 140.
Llandyssil. 37.
Llanegwad. 47.
Llanelli. 9, 22, 26, 28, 31, 143.
Llansawel. 22.
Llwynypia. 105.
Lockyer, F. 95.
Loneliness. 120.
London. 41, 70, 123.
Lord's Supper. See Sacrament Service.
Lost Tribes of Israel. 44, 63.
Love. 93.
Luther, Martin. 55, 93, 120.
Lyman, A. 26.
Lyman, F. M. 88.

M

Machen. 104.
Machynlleth. 22, 47.
Madoc, Prince. 63, 146.
Manchester. 1, 8, 13, 41, 52, 109, 123.
Mantle, L. J. 46.
Marriage. 99, 109, 117.
Martell, T. C. 37.
Martin, J. 3.
Mason, F. W. 125.
Mass. 87.
Matter. 86 ff.
Matthews, A. M. 48.
Matthews, J. R. 44, 45.
McKay, D. O. 101, 104 ff., 130, 132, 137.
Melchizedek Priesthood. 34, 67, 80, 117, 158, 165.
Melling, P. 117.
Memorialism. 54, 84.
Merit. 106.
Merthyr Tydfil. 3, 9, 11, 13, 26, 30, 33, 37, 39, 47, 76, 95, 101, 104, 106, 109, 110, 123, 125, 129, 130, 137 ff., 150.
Mesmerism. 39.
Messiah. 29.
Methodists. 106, 155.
Michael, Angelic being. 78.
Michigan. 28.
Milford Haven. 109.
Military Service Act. 90, 125.

Millennium. 13, 14, 71, 77, 80, 92, 103, 111.

Millennial Chorus. 128.

Millennial Star. i, 1, 39, 40, 78, 99, 101, 112, 129, 149, 150, 158.

Miners. 27.

Miracles. 39, 43.

Miss America. 149.

Missionaries. 6, 7, 11, 48, 51, 56, 66, 105, 123, 125, 126, 134 ff., 166.

Missionary Society. 6.

Missouri. 75, 80.

Mol, Hans. 166.

Monmouthshire. 22, 47, 76, 77, 106.

Monogamy. 21.

Montanism. 50.

Mood. 69, 154.

Morgan, D. 43.

Morgan, F. R. 94, 95.

Morgan, M. 40.

Morgan, W. 40.

Mormon, name. 2, 116.

Mormon History Association. 61.

Mormon Tabernacle Choir. 81 ff., 151.

Morris, Ebenezer. 15.

Morris, Elias. 20, 31.

Mother Branch of Britain. 8, 76, 150.

Mother-God. 36, 77, 99, 117, 160.

Motherhood. 36, 137.

Mountain Ash. 106.

Murphy, R. 106.

Mutual Improvement Association. 65, 93, 109, 116, 123, 165.

Mysticism. 84.

N

Narberth. 47.

Narrative Theology. 62 ff., 153.

National Anthem. 130.

Natural Selection. 111, 164.

Nauvoo. 34, 75, 83.

Neath. 12, 124, 142.

Needham, Rodney. 118, 165.

Negro. 165, 167.

Nephite Disciples. 145, 146.

New Era. 149.

New Jerusalem. 11, 74, 80.

New Testament. 48, 74, 80.

New Tredegar. 28.

New York Evening Express. 44.

New York State. 69, 70.

Newcastle. 126.

Newcastle Emlyn. 37.

Newman, A. 124.

Newport. 10, 104.

Nielson, F. 140.

Noah. 47.

Nonconformists. 22.

North Wales. 12, 40, 125.

Norwich. 41, 79, 123.

Nottingham. 41, 43, 46, 123, 127, 140, 141.

Nottingham Guardian Journal. 140, 142.

O

O'Dea, Thomas. 99, 118, 151.
Office-holding. 115, 133.
Old Testament. 48, 53, 58, 77, 78, 83, 84, 104, 127, 154, 156, 160.
Oliphant, T. L. 125.
Openshaw, R. W. 105.
Opportunity. 86, 88, 92, 122.
Opposition. 34, 37, 83, 98, 104, 139.
Ordinances. 19, 82, 97.
Ordination. 3, 50, 148.
Organization. 77, 88, 96, 101 ff., 112, 137, 157.
Orgill, J. 102.
Osmonds, The. 148.
Oswestry. 3.
Otherworldliness. 16.
Overton. 3.
Owens, R. T. 47.
Oxford. 127.

P

Parents, Heavenly. 35.
Parker, T. 36.
Parousia. 72, 74, 75.
Parry, J. 29, 30.
Parry, Joseph. 57, 98.
Parry, N. E. 106.
Patriarchal Blessing. 77, 117 ff.
Pearl of Great Price. 15, 74, 78, 99.
Pembrokeshire. 46.

Penarth. 65.
Pencader. 22, 81.
Penllergaer. 29, 143, 144.
Penydarren. 28, 143.
People, The. Newspaper. 79.
Perpetual Emigration Fund. 12, 16, 17, 27.
Persecutions. 9.
Petting. 129.
Phelps, W. W. 83.
Phillips, W. S. 10, 13.
Plagues. 9, 39.
Politics. 14, 32, 36, 112.
Polygamous – Plural Marriage. 2, 3, 16, 17, 21, 32, 44, 52, 54, 57, 77, 96, 104, 143, 144.
Polytheism. 50.
Pontllanfraith. 106.
Pontypool. 76, 77, 93, 94, 95, 102, 106, 109, 116, 125, 126, 128, 129.
Pontypridd. 41, 48.
Pool of Potential Orientations. 14, 159.
Poor. 13, 33.
Popular music. 147.
Porth. 79.
Power. 97, 118, 163.
Pratt, Nephi. 30, 31, 33.
Pratt, Orson. 13, 41, 67, 93.
Pratt, Parley. 39.
Prayer. 20.
Predestination. 141.
Pre-existence. 83, 87, 150.

Prejudice. 106, 110.
Price, T. 109, 126.
Priesthood. 24, 83, 89, 99, 116, 118, 122, 148, 158.
Principles of the Gospel. 71.
Privacy. 119.
Progression. 24, 89.
Prophecies. 9, 30 ff., 44, 82.
Prophet. 11, 12, 82, 98, 115.
Protestant Ethic. 141, 167.
Protestantism. 15, 17, 82, 83, 88, 96, 104, 131, 141, 143, 149.
Provo. 67.
Public opinion. 108, 109.
Pulman, F. 109.
Pulman, R. 139.
Pulman, W. E. 126.

Q
Quorums. 55.

R
Rappaport, R. 151.
Reciprocity. 27
Records. 2, 12.
Recreation. 102.
Rees, D. M. 101.
Rees, J. D. 43.
Rees, T. W. 26.
Reese, W. G. 46.
Reformation, The. 24.
Relief Society. 95, 125.

Religious Language. 11.
Reorganized Church. 4, 28, 76, 79, 143 ff.
Repentance. 56, 121.
Responsibility. 101, 120.
Restoration. 14, 17, 21, 29, 35, 43, 55, 82, 86, 88, 89, 112, 143 ff., 155, 156.
Restorer, The. 28, 160.
Resurrection. 58, 67.
Revelation. 15, 19, 30, 50, 54, 70, 78, 143, 148.
Revivalism. 43, 65, 69 ff.
Reynolds, M. N. 76.
Rhodes Scholars. 127.
Rhondda Valley. 40, 79, 105, 106.
Rhymney. 7.
Rich. 13.
Richards, D. 12.
Richards, Le Grand. 127.
Richards, S. L. 111, 116.
Richards, W. 13, 14.
Rigdon, S. 29, 50, 144.
Rites of Passage. 63.
Ritual. 54, 56, 71, 88.
Roberts, B. H. 133.
Roberts, T. 79.
Root Metaphors. 38.
Rossiter, D. T. 101.
Royle, H. 3

S

Sacrament. 86 ff.

Sacrament Service. 54, 78, 84, 129, 151, 166.

Sacred, The. 119, 152, 158.

Sacred Space. 32, 34, 35.

Salt Lake City. 21, 31, 33, 65, 66, 97, 156.

Salt Lake Scottish Chorus. 98.

Salt Lake Valley. 12, 75.

Salvation. 18, 49, 89, 102, 112, 115, 117, 135, 137, 152, 157.

Salvation Army. 42, 43.

Salvation History. 56, 57 ff., 156.

Sankey and Moody Revivals. 70, 159.

Satan. 66.

Scandinavia. 45, 56.

Schreiner, A. 85.

Scotland. 39, 125.

Scottish Daily Mail. 139.

Sealing. 49, 99, 129, 153.

Second Coming. 10, 13, 30, 44, 53, 63, 65, 66, 71, 72, 137, 164.

Secrecy. 52.

Sectarianism. 21, 32, 38, 40, 71, 92.

Secular. 4, 108, 152.

Seventh Day Adventists. 127.

Seventy, The. 55, 149.

Sex. 98, 116.

Sheffield. 46, 102, 123.

Shepperd, L. L. 100.

Shipps, J. 151.

Simpson, G. 140.

Skeen, J. M. 105.

Skewen. 29, 143.

Smith, D. 69.

Smith, Joseph Jnr. 4, 5, 10, 19, 26, 28, 30, 34, 50 ff, 61, 67, 70, 75, 82, 83, 93, 128, 132, 133, 143, 155, 158.

Smith Joseph 3rd. 144.

Smith, J. F. 67, 119.

Smith, W. C. 163.

Smith, W. R. 158.

Smoot, R. 103, 112.

Snow, Eliza. 35.

Snow, Lorenzo. 55.

Social Change. 69.

Social Class. 49.

Soul, Spirit. 56, 98, 111.

Soup-kitchen. 33.

South Wales Argus. 104.

South Wales Daily News. 44.

South Wales Echo. 139.

Spalding, S. 29, 50.

Spanish Fork. 40.

Speaking in Tongues, see Glossolalia.

Speech. 133.

Spencer, Orson. 7.

Sperber, Dan. 159, 163.

Spirit of God, Holy Spirit. 30, 36, 54, 69, 71, 84, 118, 131, 133, 145, 146, 148.

Spiritualism. 70.

St. George Temple. 38.

Standard Works. 78, 155.
Stayner, C. W. 43.
Stephens, Evan. 81 ff.
Stockport. 144.
Story. 62
Strang, J. 28.
Strangites. 28.
Sunday Schools. 48, 77, 109, 125, 130.
Sunday Times. 52, 148.
Superstition. 49, 119.
Swansea. 19, 20, 21, 26, 33, 34, 39, 46.
Swiss, The. 45.
Symbolic Thought. 20, 159, 163.

T

Talmage, J. 98, 105, 106, 116.
Taylor, J. 11, 39, 45, 82, 83, 85.
Tea Parties. 6, 116.
Teetotalism. 6, 116, 128.
Temperance. 36.
Temple. 32, 33 ff., 66, 82, 86, 87 ff., 112, 134, 141, 152, 153, 154, 156, 165.
Temple, British. 130, 135, 137.
Temple Rites. 28, 67, 102, 117, 129, 137, 143.
Temple – work. 66.
Terry, V. L. 128.
Testimony. 48, 61, 123, 131 ff., 153, 155.
Theocracy. 19, 29, 44.
Theology. 1, 60, 62, 68, 86 ff., 143 ff., 154 ff.

Thomas, G. D. 94.
Thomas, H. R. 77.
Thomas, J. 47.
Thomas, R. A. 37.
Tillich, P. 160, 162.
Time. 32, 87, 143, 153.
Times, The. 45, 160.
Tithes. 26, 27 ff., 41, 47, 128.
Toronto. 39.
Torry and Alexander Mission. 71.
Tracts. 12, 45, 48, 53.
Transcendence. 152 ff., 159.
Tredegar. 28.
Tribes of Israel. 77.
Trinity, The Holy. 36, 143.
Turner, V. 161.
Twain, Mark. 51.
Twelve Apostles. 39.

U

Ugdorn Seion. 15.
Utah. 10, 14, 30, 31, 32, 37, 40, 48, 72, 79, 81, 96, 102, 111, 123.

V

Varteg. 100, 106, 125, 126.
Vegetarianism. 128.
Vicarious Ritual. 67, 92, 99, 135, 143, 165.
Virgin Birth. 15.
Visions. 145, 146.

W

Wait, E. E. 7.
Wallis, J. H. 117, 119.
Weber, Max. 30, 141, 167.
Wells, R. E. 149.
Welsh Conference. 5, 65, 70, 105, 106, 109, 123, 128.
Welsh Language. 7, 12, 20, 56, 138.
Welsh Red Indians. 63, 146.
Welsh Revivals. 43, 65, 71.
Western, J. A. 95, 100, 101.
Western Mail. 46, 100, 106.
Westmoreland. 11, 39.
Whitney, O. F. 111, 113.
Widmer, D. W. 128.
Widtsoe, J. A. 108, 112, 119.
Williams, G. A. 63.
Williams, R. 94.
Williams, W. 42.
Williams, W. B. 46.
Willis, D. 46.
Wilson, B. R. 164.
Winter Quarters. 9.
Women. 11, 41, 51, 93, 158.
Women's Suffrage. 45.
Woodruff Manifesto. 45, 54.
Woodruff, Wilford. 7, 45.
Word of Wisdom. 6, 31, 47, 116, 127, 166.
Working Classes. 51, 106.
Works of salvation. 102.
World Wars. 91, 123.
Worship. 49, 87, 123, 151, 153.

Y

Young, Brigham. 4, 12, 13, 28, 35, 38, 39, 78, 116.

Z

Zion. 6, 8, 10, 16, 17, 20, 26, 34, 38, 39, 43, 64, 66, 72, 74, 80, 81 ff., 130, 143, 156.
Zion, Call to. 30, 35, 47, 72, 125.
Zion, Language of. 11, 19 ff.
Zion, The Pure in Heart. 10, 13, 141.